T0369176

Oswald's Politics

Gary W. O'Brien

Order this book online at www.trafford.com
or email orders@trafford.com

Most Trafford titles are also available at major online book retailers.

© Copyright 2010 Gary W. O'Brien.
All rights reserved. No part of this publication may be reproduced, stored in a retrieval system, or
transmitted, in any form or by any means, electronic, mechanical, photocopying, recording, or
otherwise, without the written prior permission of the author.

Printed in Victoria, BC, Canada.

ISBN: 978-1-4269-2050-9

Library of Congress Control Number: 2009913679

*Our mission is to efficiently provide the world's finest, most comprehensive book publishing
service, enabling every author to experience success. To find out how to publish your
book, your way, and have it available worldwide, visit us online at www.trafford.com*

Trafford rev. 12/19/2009

 www.trafford.com

North America & international
toll-free: 1 888 232 4444 (USA & Canada)
phone: 250 383 6864 ✦ fax: 812 355 4082

"I am here because I believe in Marxist ideals. It is a matter of ideology. You don't understand."

Lee Harvey Oswald

Contents

PART ONE

INTERPRETATIVE ESSAY

1. Introduction

The study of Oswald's politics is not the favored choice of those who strive for an understanding of the assassination of President Kennedy. At first glance there seems to be much better evidence to get a clearer picture of the crime—for example, the wounds to the body, the ballistic and fingerprint evidence, or photographic and film analysis—for it is claimed that such evidence is less open to interpretation. The central problem of the Kennedy assassination is, however, that after decades of research, the physical evidence still does not lead us to definitive conclusions about what occurred in Dealey Plaza. So much contradictory data has accumulated that it seems no claim can be made with 100 per cent certainty one way or the other. Despite its inconclusiveness, the physical evidence has biased students of the assassination into deductive reasoning about the man accused of murdering the president. Most are conditioned to analyze Lee Harvey Oswald from the perspective of either his involvement or non-involvement in the crime. There has been little attempt to set the physical evidence aside and examine him from the historical perspective, that is, what we reasonably know about Oswald before November 22, 1963. Such analysis is integral to

any speculation about both his possible guilt or innocence and
the most important question of all, which the physical evidence
is unlikely ever to answer: why was JFK killed?

That Oswald was consumed by politics is beyond doubt. He
talked about them, wrote about them and became a political actor.
What drove his interest in politics predominantly stemmed from
the one simple defining characteristic of his life that researchers
do not dispute: Oswald was a reader. Oswald himself told Aline
Mosby in her interview with him in the Soviet Union at the time
of his defection that he was "a bookworm." His half-brother,
John Edward Pic, testified that while he attended elementary
school in Fort Worth, Oswald "always read a lot," and his full
brother, Robert, said that he "did like to read. He read quite
a bit."[1] His mother, Marguerite, told the Warren Commission
that her son "read history books, books too deep for a child his
age."[2] While at Youth House when he was thirteen years old it
was noted that "he appears content just to sit and read whatever
is available."[3] His home room teacher at Beauregard Junior High,
Myra Darouse, said that "she recalled that generally during the
school lunch period, Oswald would be by himself and quietly eat
his lunch, and after finishing his lunch would then begin to read
from various unrecalled books while the other students would
usually be engaged in conversation or other activity."[4]

Mrs. Edwin Enoces, who lived next door to Mrs. Oswald and
her son while they lived on Collingswood Street in Fort Worth,
stated in a sworn affidavit that "Lee Oswald was a lone wolf type
individual, just like his mother, Mrs. Marguerite Oswald. She
stated that Lee remained in the apartment practically all the time
and was constantly reading books...."[5] Daniel Patrick Powers
testified that while in the marines during the course of their
training Oswald "impressed me as an individual who was quite
intelligent and he would read quite a lot." While on their trip to
Japan for their first overseas posting Powers said Lee "used to read

quite a bit."[6] His commanding officer, John E. Donavon, felt that Oswald did not share a common interest with his fellow marines. He told the Commission, "For better or for worse, the average young American male in that age is interested in saving enough money to go buy another beer and get a date. This I don't believe would characterize him at all. He read a great deal."[7] Oswald told Max E. Clark that while he was in the marines "he had read a lot of Karl Marx and had studied considerably."[8] When living in the Soviet Union, he bought a newspaper everyday and "poured" through copies of *Time* magazine that began to arrive in bundles from his mother in Texas.[9]

Following his re-defection, his wife, Marina, testified that while they lived on Mercedes Street in Fort Worth "[h]e frequently went to the library. He read a great deal…they were books of a historical nature rather than fiction or literature."[10] Paul Roderick Gregory told the Commission that Oswald "was always going down to the library and coming back with all sorts of books…He read Lenin. I can't remember which book it was, but that is the only thing I have really seen him read. And then he always spoke about his, he said, this great love of history."[11] Gary E. Taylor testified that when he visited the Oswalds at their Elsbeth Street apartment in Dallas in November, 1962, he saw Lee's books, which were "primarily political philosophy."[12]

While in New Orleans in the summer of 1963, as we know from library records, Oswald took out a number of books on a wide range of subjects.[13] Marina stated, "I know that he read so much that when we lived in New Orleans he used to read sometimes all night long and in order not to disturb me he would be sitting in the bathroom for several hours reading."[14] Francis Martello of the New Orleans Police Department, who questioned Oswald in August 1963 told the Warren Commission that "from the way he spoke, it was quite obvious he had done a heck of a lot of reading in his lifetime, and his approach was academic, more or less theories but with no aggressiveness or emotional outbursts in any way shape or form."[15]

There have been quite different assessments of how much Oswald understood from his reading. He was never university trained and suffered from a spelling disability, which caused some to believe he suffered from dyslexia.[16] Many have been skeptical about his understanding of politics, claiming he had a "fevered" and "demented mind;" [17] "he was unable to understand Marx;"[18] "he was not very smart;"[19] he was a "semieducated hillbilly;"[20] and he was "rather confused, particularly, politically."[21] However, we have this assessment of Oswald by William Stuckey, the New Orleans radio-programme director: "...this was a man who was intelligent, who was aware that he was intelligent, and who would like to have an opportunity to express his intelligence— that was my impression."[22] Norman Mailer, who studied Oswald closely, observed that "his intelligence was there. He wasn't a great intellectual but was a very good one and for a non-educated intellectual he was damn bright. I heard him on radio shows and there he handled himself very well."[23]

Like many other young people of his generation, Oswald's engagement in politics was radical, anti-disciplinary and fauvistic, diverging from any established paradigm. He moved from being interested in the Socialist Party of America at the age of 16 to a seeming adherence to Stalinism by the age of 20. In 1959 he defected to the Soviet Union. In 1962 he re-defected, condemning the Soviet State as "totalitarian." Yet within weeks of returning to America, he subscribed to the *Worker*, the organ of the Stalinist Communist Party USA (CPUSA) and applied for membership in the Trotskyist Socialist Workers Party (SWP). Early in 1963 he posed as an urban guerilla in photographs taken by his wife and demonstrated his capacity for political terrorism by attempting to assassinate the right wing activist U.S. Army

General Edwin A. Walker. Yet throughout it all, he often made favorable comments about President Kennedy.

In the summer of 1963 he threw himself into the popular struggle, starting his own chapter of the Fair Play for Cuba Committee (FPCC) in New Orleans. Some months later it is alleged that he showed up in Clinton, Louisiana, in the company of the mysterious David Ferrie, among others. At the end of September in Dallas he was seen with two members of an underground anti-Castro Cuban exile group and allegedly made threatening remarks about JFK. A few days later he appeared in Mexico City, overtly embracing Stalinism once again. Trying to defect for a second time to Russia through Cuba, he was turned away. He went back to Dallas dispirited but with a continued interest in the American and Soviet Communist parties and in the FPCC. Yet on November 1, he seemed to abandon his radicalism altogether and applied for membership in the American Civil Liberties Union. Three weeks later, on November 22, 1963, he was arrested and later charged with the killing of a Dallas police officer and the assassination of the President of the United States.

Making sense of his politics is not easy and has understandably resulted in quite varied interpretations. In the aftermath of the assassination, the immediate reaction of many who knew or knew about him was that Oswald could never have shot the president for political reasons. Lyman Paine, Michael Paine's father, who himself had been active in Marxist politics, expressed great consternation on hearing news about Oswald's arrest and said, "No one, no member of the Friends of Cuba would want to assassinate the president. That was a crazy idea."[24] George de Mohrenschildt, who talked to Lee about politics more than anybody, wrote, "I did not know Lee to be a dangerous man, a man who would kill like a maniac without any reason..."[25] His wife, Jeanne, who also thought she understood Lee, said,

"Of course, he was opposed to segregation. He wanted complete equality of rights, because those people are just as American as everybody else, so it really is one of the worst problems we have... he is completely in accord with President Kennedy's policy on the subject. That is why it doesn't make exactly sense. He has no reason whatsoever, to our knowledge."[26] Michael Paine, who had four conversations with him, thought that although Lee was a "bitter person;" "he didn't seem to be dangerous."[27] The established Left immediately disowned Oswald, arguing, "the man accused of assassinating President Kennedy was not a true 'Marxist' despite his own assertions to that effect." As reported in the *New York Times* on November 23, 1963, the leaders of the Socialist Party of America, the Communist Party USA, the Socialist Workers Party, the Socialist Labor Party and the Progressive Labor Movement "all contended that true Marxists opposed violence against individuals. They cited Marx as having long battled terrorists such as Mikhail Bakunin, the Russian anarchist, who believed in destroying the state...Marx believed in class struggle with the individual counting for relatively little."[28] Because this act was so beyond the pale in traditional leftist thinking, other motivations that had nothing to do with politics were at work, or else they had the wrong guy.

The more official explanation of Oswald's politics put forward by the Warren Commission underplayed any serious ideological thinking. Its report subsumed Oswald's politics within a broader psychohistorical portrayal that saw him as a social misfit with serious psychological problems and alienated from the world around him. Yet within the report there exits the nagging feeling that political ideology as a motive could not be completely dismissed, as in the end "his commitment to Marxism and communism appears to have been a factor in his motivation."[29] However, the Commission dealt in stereotype labels of leftist dissent, giving the impression that Marxism was monolithic and exclusively Soviet oriented. In the end, the Warren Commission could not think outside the box in terms of radical politics and made no attempt to give a comprehensive analysis of his political essays or explain what precisely in either Marxist or other radical doctrines pointed to assassinating a world leader at the height of a Cold War. When it came down to essentials, Oswald was pegged as a lone nut—mentally, socially and politically.

The Commission's portrait of Oswald as a psychologically troubled person has been echoed may times since then, often by credible authors. William Manchester wrote, "Since childhood Oswald had been threatened by a specific mental disease, paranoia. In the end the paranoiac loses all sense of reality."[30] Jean Davison, while conceding that Oswald's "conscious motives were political," felt that his psychopathy better explained his politics than any environmental or intellectual influences.[31] Gerald Posner entitled his first chapter, "Which One Are You?—Oswald's Formative Years," implying Oswald had a hidden, schizophrenic personality. Posner hypothesized that understanding the mentally disturbed Oswald is "the key to finding what happened in Dallas on November 22, 1963."[32] John Loken speculated that Oswald's homicidal mind was set off from his watching two films prior to the assassination.[33] Diane Holloway wrote that if Oswald had been evaluated in the 1990s as an adult, psychiatrists would have placed him in the categories of paranoid personality disorder and antisocial personality disorder.[34] Vincent Bugliosi concluded that Oswald was "a deeply disturbed and frustrated individual… there's little question in my mind that to do what Oswald did, one would have to qualify him as a first-class 'nut'. His act could not have been more irrational."[35]

The House of Representative's Select Committee on Assassinations (HSCA) placed more importance on the ideological factor. In its 1979 report, the HSCA made references to "the depth of [Oswald]'s political commitment," "the importance of his political commitment" and "his devotion to his political beliefs," but admitted it could find "no one, specific ideological goal that Oswald might have hoped to achieve by the assassination of President Kennedy." However, it speculated that "Oswald was preoccupied with his political ideology and it was likely he acted in the assassination in light of that ideology." The Committee surmised that "Oswald could have seen Walker and Kennedy in the same ideological light."[36]

Others have also been confident that ideology was an important if not primary factor in the assassination. Albert H. Newman,[37] James W. Clarke,[38] and Max Holland[39] conclude that Oswald's support for the Cuban government drove him to kill JFK, whom he regarded as an avowed enemy of Castro. They anchor Oswald's political thinking to the Cuba question and place him clearly in the traditional Marxist camp. There are also those who saw Oswald as more than just a sympathizer of foreign leftist governments. Michael Eddowes,[40] Edward Jay Epstein[41] and Ion Mihai Pacepa[42] argued that Soviet government or the KGB may have used Oswald in the assassination of the president.

Oswald's politics have also been interpreted as being non-Marxist. Professor David Wrone viewed Oswald as more a follower of George Orwell, concluding: "the evidence shows he was an Orwellian in philosophy and anticommunist, antisocialist, and anti-Soviet in practice."[43] Norman Mailer, although he felt that Lee was a Marxist, believed "what Oswald offers seems more a libertarian pronouncement than a radical call to arms," and that "he was but five years ahead of his time—which is to say that by 1968 he would not have felt so prodigiously alone. By then, in Haight-Ashbury, many of his formulations would have seemed reasonable."[44]

The greatest controversy about Oswald's politics comes from those researchers who dismiss his politics as a cover for covert dealings with intelligence forces. They see him as a habitual liar whose politics were false and nothing but a front for "dirty hands" actions.[45] As has been often noted, the work of the Warren Commission was almost derailed before it got started when a rumor circulated from Texas Attorney General Waggoner Carr's office that Oswald was a paid FBI informer. FBI agent James Hosty's name was found in Oswald's address book along with his phone and license plate number. The address of 544 Camp Street, the location where Guy Bannister and the Cuban Revolutionary Council (CRC) had maintained their offices, was stamped on some of the leaflets Oswald distributed for the FPCC in New Orleans in 1963. John Newman speculated that while the evidence is circumstantial, Oswald may have served the local anti-Castro CRC recruiting program by flushing pro-Castro students out into the open where Bannister could identify them, and he may have been part of the CIA's penetration attempt to smear the FPCC.[46] Jim Garrison held that Oswald's Marxism was, to say the least, suspect. The New Orleans district attorney who in 1969 charged Clay Shaw with conspiracy in the murder of President Kennedy was convinced that Oswald worked for U.S intelligence forces and was an agent-provocateur.[47]

Despite the many mysteries of Oswald's alleged association with various people in Moscow, Minsk, New Orleans, Clinton, Dallas, Mexico City and elsewhere, the fact remains that there has never been probative evidence that Oswald's politics were carried out on behalf of state-security forces. The Assassination Records Review Board could not uncover any documentary evidence that suggested Oswald ever worked for the CIA in any capacity or that his activities served any intelligence purpose.[48] Although it is important that researching his associations and clandestine strategies continue, until contrary proven, we must put aside skepticism about the veracity of Oswald's politics and look seriously at what he wrote, what he said and how he acted politically.

This book will attempt to provide an explanation of Oswald's politics by analyzing his ideas and actions. It will present a compendium of all his political writings and other primary documents. It will begin by examining the unhistorical and misleading methodology used by the Warren Commission for studying his politics. It will then present an alternative explanatory model by examining possible environmental, historical and ideological influences which impacted on his political development. Section Four will review his political writings, that is, his fifty-page manuscript on life in the Soviet Union, his four political essays, his three auto-biographical essays, the political entries in his address book and some sixty letters in which he discussed political matters. Section Five will trace his most important political conversations. Section Six will conclude with a summary of his politics and hypothesize as to his possible involvement in the events of November 22, 1963, and motives.

2. Pyschohistory and the Lone Nut Theory

The bias against providing a serious analysis of Oswald's politics stems largely from the Warren investigation's conclusion that whatever politics he professed were merely a symptom of deeper psychological problems. If we are to get at what made Lee tick, the Commission put forward, it was his psychological profile that needed to be explored, not his political ideas.

The Lone Nut Theory has essentially two main tenets of thought. First, Lee Harvey Oswald was the assassin of President Kennedy and he acted alone. Second, and more important, the assassination was tragic and without reason. Not only was one of the most popular U.S. presidents killed at a crucial time in world affairs, but the crime was senseless. It was committed by a deranged person who acted irrationally. The theory laid down the template for concluding Oswald's motives can be seen only through a psychobiographical prism.

To understand where this theory may have been coming from, it is instructive to place the work of the Warren Commission in the context of its times. Psychohistory, which may be defined as the application of psychoanalysis to individuals on the basis of historical records, was a fairly new methodology in the late 1950s and early 1960s. Building on works by Sigmund Freud and Erich Fromm, psychohistory became a respected field of study with the appearance in 1958 of Erik Erikson's *Young Man Luther: A Study in Psychoanalysis and History.*[49] Erikson's work on Luther and the rise of Protestantism suggested that psychoanalysis could offer assistance in investigating facts and establishing historical

11

truth. *Young Man Luther* had great impact in academic circles and became the model of all later psychobiographies.

In the same year *Young Man Luther* was published, the president of the American Historical Association, Dr. William L. Langer, delivered his address entitled *The Next Assignment*. Langer "exhorted the membership of that organization to get on with the task of examining and analyzing the unconscious foundations of the social life of the past."[50] In 1964, another distinguished historian, H. Stuart Hughes, went so far as to advocate that individual psychoanalysis be made part of the professional training of serious historians.[51]

Psychohistory's surge in popularity in the 1960s was short lived. By the mid-1970s the methodology was regarded as questionable and highly controversial. One author claimed it was "bunk." Geoffrey Barraclough wrote: "For my part, I regard 'psychohistory' as a murky quagmire, unredeemed even by its core comical extravagances."[52] In 1980, David Stannard observed: "We have seen that, from the earliest endeavors to write psychohistory to those of the present, individual writings of would-be psychohistorians have consistently been characterized by a cavalier attitude toward fact, a contorted attitude toward logic, an irresponsible attitude toward theory validation, and a myopic attitude toward cultural difference and anachronism... Psychohistory, in a word, is ahistorical. That is its ultimate failing."[53]

Psychohistory usually focuses on childhood, the family and parenting practices in the belief that childhood history may uncover the "abuses" which will explain adult behaviour. Critics charge that its methodology relies heavily on post-mortem analysis, and as such its findings are unverifiable. Interpretations are too often based on imagined or flimsy evidence and gossip. As an explanatory theory, it is seen to have too many shortcomings.

For Professor Stannard, "psychohistory does not work and cannot work."[54]

It is not surprising that the Warren Commission was strongly influenced by the psychohistorical approach. Confronted with what looked like powerful evidence by the FBI that President Kennedy was assassinated by Lee Harvey Oswald and that he most likely acted alone, the Commission was eager to probe what it could about the Oswald's character and what might have prompted him to perform such a terrible act. Reaching out for a methodology, which in the early 1960s was "hot," was wrapped in academic legitimacy and claimed insight into deviant behaviour, and the motivations of historical individuals seemed logical and appealing.

Unquestionably, the Warren Commission was obligated to probe what it could about Oswald's psychological history. Newspaper stories appeared soon after the assassination that suggested Oswald was insane. On November 23, Dr. Renatus Hartogs, who was the psychiatrist who interviewed Oswald when he was remanded to Youth House in 1953, recalled that he told the press, "A person who would commit such an act has been very likely a mentally disturbed person, who has a personal grudge against persons in authority, and very likely is a person who in his search to overcome his own insignificance and helplessness will try to commit an act which will make others frightened, which will shatter the world, which will make other people insecure, as if he wanted to discharge his own insecurity through his own act...."[55]

On November 25, the day after Oswald was fatally wounded, the *New York Times* ran an article, "Doctors Question Oswald's Sanity—Leaving Clues for Pursuit a Psychopathic Trait."[56] The story cited a number of leading psychiatrists who said they suspected that Oswald "was paranoid or suffered from some other mental ailment." Their comments were based on such evidence like the Hidell identification card that made his capture easy and smiling in the photographs of himself following his capture. Such acts were typical of the psychopathic criminal. One nationally-known psychiatrist was reported to have said, "He believed that all assassins of presidents had been mentally ill."

Shortly after Oswald's death, a presiding judge of the Appellate Division, Justice Florence Kelley, instructed Oswald's record of his time at Youth House should be revealed because it was now pertinent to a matter of national interest.[57] Normally, psychiatric records are not divulged, because they are confidential. Law enforcement agencies as well as government institutions are not supposed to have access to psychiatric records unless it is absolutely necessary. In order to discover all there was to find about the assassination of the president, it was not unreasonable that the Oswald's records were ordered released. Justice Kelley is reported to have made the statement that Oswald's psychiatric report of his time at Youth House stated that he suffered from "incipient schizophrenia."[58]

A best selling book, *Four Days: The Historical Record of the Death of President Kennedy*, compiled by United Press International and *American Heritage* magazine and published within weeks of the assassination, implied he was a psychopath. The authors stated: "Lee Harvey Oswald—called innocent by his mother and his wife...and guilty by most others—denied everything. Oswald was born in 1939 in New Orleans, lived for a time in New York, where he was a chronic truant and, according to a school psychiatrist's report, a 'potentially dangerous' schizophrenic."[59]

The FBI made much of Oswald's apparent psychological problems. In its December 9, 1963, summary report of the assassination to the Warren Commission, as well as its January

13, 1964, supplemental report,[60] the FBI pounced all over the Youth House psychiatric findings. It summarized the report written by Dr. Hartogs as follows:

> The psychiatric report disclosed that Oswald displayed traits indicative of a greatly disturbed person. He was described as a seriously detached, withdrawn youngster and diagnosed as having a personality-pattern disturbance with schizoid features and passive-aggressive tendencies. He was said to be suffering the impact of existing emotional isolation and deprivation, lack of affection, absence of family life and rejection by a self-involved and conflicted mother.
>
> The report further indicated Oswald enjoyed a fantasy life revolving around his own omnipotence and power—a fantasy life through which he tried to compensate for his frustrations. He acknowledged fantasies about being powerful and sometimes hurting or killing people.
>
> The report also indicated that Oswald disliked everyone. He maintained a barrier between himself and others, exhibiting strongly resistive and negativistic features.[61]

The FBI summary report filled out its description of Oswald with biased terms such as "bitter,"[62] "a loner,"[63] "a seeming misfit,"[64] "cuckoo"[65] and "mental instability."[66] The FBI passed on to the Commission gossip such as the complaint by Oswald's Elsbeth Street neighbors that "Oswald drank to excess and beat his wife,"[67] as well as the incident reported by Mrs. John Pic, which Oswald's mother denied, that Oswald pointed a knife at her during a dispute over television.[68] Perhaps most important, the summary report planted with the Commission the hypothesis that Oswald's politics were not genuine but flowed from his psychological problems.

Not only the FBI but the Commission staff as well portrayed Oswald as someone who was "always confused in his own mind about all sorts of things." The undated memorandum to J. Lee Rankin, the Warren Commission's general counsel, from William T. Coleman Jr. and W. David Slawson on Oswald's foreign activities concluded that Oswald was "embittered" and "did not really understand all that he was saying."[69] Coleman and Slawson wrote: "The picture of Oswald that emerges from all of the evidence the staff has gathered is that of a man of average or possibly better than average intelligence, but with a mind that was confused, dogmatic and unused to the discipline of logical thought. For example, his political writings, when read closely are seen to be little more than a series of vague assertions that something or other "must" be done in this way or that way. The spelling and grammar are uniformaly bad...In sum, we believed that Oswald did not have any subtleness of mind, that he lacked a good understanding of human nature and that he had an unstable and neurotic character."[70]

At the request of Commission Chairman Earl Warren, who apparently wanted the report to have a historical as well as a legal perspective,[71] a professional historian, Alfred Goldberg from the Department of Defense, was brought on staff and started work at the end of February 1964. Goldberg had been at the London headquarters of the U.S. Strategic Air Forces in Europe during World War II. He did graduate study in history at John Hopkins University and received his Ph.D. in 1956. The following year he published *A History of the United States Air Force, 1907–1957*.[72] As a historian, undoubtedly he was aware of the psychohistorical approach. His primary responsibilities were to assist in writing the report and to prepare a "Speculation and Rumor" appendix.[73]

While there is no documentary proof that any of the senior staff actually read Erikson, *Young Man Luther* was "in the air," especially on university campuses, and it was from such campuses that many of the young Commission lawyers were recruited.[74] Wesley Liebeler, who headed the third major area of study, called "Lee Harvey Oswald's Background," may have been exposed to psychobiography when he was managing editor of the *University of Chicago Law Review*. He, along with Albert Jenner, interviewed Oswald's relatives and acquaintances in the hope of shedding light on motive. At some point it was agreed that a session with professional psychiatrists should be arranged to probe Oswald's state of mind more deeply. In July 1964 the Warren staff and the commissioners met with three psychiatrists to discuss the problem of the use of psychological terminology to describe Oswald's actions. The colloquium lasted an entire day. Liebeler wrote the first draft of the chapter on Oswald's possible motives, but both Rankin and Norman Redlich, another Commission counsel, found it "too psychological." Goldberg had to re-write it.[75]

Unquestionably, the six-paragraph Hartogs report was the key element of the Lone Nut Theory. In many ways, that document ranks in importance with the Backyard Photographs as evidence of Oswald's guilt. The stigma of having had a psychiatric assessment as a child, in which a professional concludes that the patient is suffering from a personality disorder, raised questions in many people's minds as to Oswald's sanity. It seemed to present a clear and simple motive for his actions on November 22, namely that Oswald was a nut. Although the psychiatrists at the July 1964 colloquium advised there was an insufficient basis for drawing psychological conclusions about him, the Warren Commission gave the impression that it accepted the Hartogs findings as fact.

In his report, Dr. Hartogs wrote:

...Lee is the product of a broken home as his father died before he was born. Two older brothers are presently in the United States Army while the mother supports herself and Lee as an insurance broker. This occupation makes it impossible for her to provide adequate supervision of Lee and to make him attend school regularly...Lee has a vivid fantasy life, turning around the topics of omnipotence and power, through which he tries to compensate for his present shortcomings and frustrations. He did not enjoy being together with other children and when asked whether he prefers the company of boys to the one of girls he answered "I dislike everybody...[Lee's mother] does not understand that Lee's withdrawal is a form of violent but silent protest against his neglect by her—and represents his reaction to a complete absence of any real family life... Lee has to be diagnosed as 'personality pattern disturbance with schizoid features and passive aggressive tendencies'. Lee has to be seen as an emotionally, quite disturbed youngster who suffers the impact of really existing emotional isolation and deprivation, lack of affection, absence of family life and rejection by his self-involved and conflicted mother....[76]

Hartogs belonged to the Freudian school of psychology, which explained deviant behaviour in terms of sexuality, parenting practices, the unconscious and the ego. He went on to co-author a book in 1965 about Oswald and Jack Ruby entitled *The Two Assassins,* which was written in the manner of Erikson's *Young Man Luther.* Although Hartogs had only interviewed Lee once for less than an hour, and had never met Ruby, *The Two Assassins* is filled with unverifiable speculation. It began with a section entitled "The Twisted World of Lee Harvey Oswald." He claimed that Oswald's motives arose from two levels of the mind: the conscious and the unconscious. Consciously, Oswald thought killing was important, as at sixteen years old he had allegedly said he would like to kill Eisenhower. Among the unconscious motives, there were likely many including the revenge of the South, the suppression of his sexual drive, which drove him into a period of destruction and to strike back at the father who had died before he was born.[77] Hartogs wrote: "Oswald, in fantasy, may have been killing the father he did not know as a child and for whom he undoubtedly felt deep feelings of love and hate… Oswald may have been telling the world of his anguish and rage by committing an act which left the whole country without a father as he had been left without a father. It may have been as though in his undying and dying hatred, he shrieked to the world, I have been deprived of a father, which is every man's birthright, who would have taken care of me and protected me from my wild impulses, and now I will deprive everyone else of a father, too."[78]

In his April 16, 1964, appearance before the Warren Commission, Hartogs said that he based his diagnosis of Oswald on his one interview with him, which lasted between 30 to 60 minutes, as well as other staff reports and an alleged 90 minute Monday afternoon "seminar" with other staff at which no notes were kept and that no one else could recall. He stuck by his diagnosis that Oswald was both schizoid and had a passive-aggressive personality disorder. When asked what made him conclude that Oswald had this severe disturbance, Hartogs replied it was his "extremely cold steely eyes," his "control of his emotions," his "cold, detached outer attitude" and "his suspiciousness against adults." Hartogs stated: "He talked about his situation, about himself, in a, what should I say, non-participating fashion. I mean there was nothing emotional about him and this impressed me." Hartogs was adamant that the cause of the symptoms Lee showed was not the result of conditioning. He felt they were "more deeper going. A personality pattern disturbance is a disturbance which has been existing since early childhood and has continued to exist through the individual's life." His view was the disturbance was caused by the lack of a father figure and his mother's neglect.[79]

Although Liebeler questioned whether it was really Lee Oswald who was the subject of the Monday afternoon staff seminar, counsel never pressed Hartogs as to the reliability of his diagnostic procedures. While Liebeler also called Oswald's caseworker, Evelyn Strickman Siegal, who "remembered absolutely nothing about him at all,"[80] as well as his parole officer, John Carro, no professional psychiatrist was asked to testify about Hartogs' procedures and conclusions. Given the importance placed on Lee's psychiatric assessment, it should have been incumbent upon the Commission to do so. At the very least, Hartogs could have been subjected to more vigorous cross-examination.

The Warren Report made no criticisms of Hartogs' findings and presented them as the professional psychiatric assessment of Oswald the troubled youth. Notwithstanding that chapter seven of the report begins with the disclaimer: "Since Oswald is dead, the Commission is not able to reach any definite conclusions as to whether or not he was 'sane' under prevailing legal standards"[81], the Commission went on to describe Oswald's character as having symptoms of someone suffering from a serious psychological dysfunction. While it said that it could not prove that Oswald was legally insane, it cleverly implied that he was.

The Commission concluded that the most important reasons for Oswald killing the president revolved principally around psychological problems. These were: "an overriding hostility to his environment;" an inability "to establish meaningful relations with people;" a perpetual discontent "with the world around him;" a "hatred for American society;" a "search for a perfect society doomed from the start;" a search "for himself for a place in history" and to be "a great man in advance of his time."[82]

Like all psychohistories, these conclusions were based on post hoc reasoning to establish connections to events. The Commission fell into the trap of trying to explain adult behaviour from earlier experiences. Typical of psychobiography, it focused on childhood, family and parenting practices. While the July 1964 colloquium with psychiatrists may have persuaded the Commission not to use explicit psychological theories and terminologies to describe Oswald, it hinted at the Freudian emphasis of sexuality in human nature. For example, the report stated: "It may also be significant that, as reported by John Pic, Lee 'slept with my mother until I joined the service in 1950. This would make him approximately 10, well, almost 11 years old."[83]

It is apparent that the portrait painted by the Commission of Oswald's character was one-sided and biased. It showed no understanding or sympathy for Oswald the dissident or that his anger with society might have been ideological. Other evidence that tended to go against many of the Commission's observations was not drawn out. For example, the premise that Lee was "hostile to his environment" and that he had "no meaningful relations" was certainly contradicted by the June—July 1960 entries in CE 24, his *Historic Diary*. There we catch glimpses of a young man who was very much connected to the physical beauty of the Soviet Union and its people and who at that point of his life seemed rather content.

Gary W. O'Brien

Other passages in the diary show Lee was not the angry person the Commission said he was. In October 1960 he wrote: "The coming of Fall, my dread of a new Russian winter, are mellowed in splendid golds and reds of fall in Belorussia. Plums, peaches, apricots and cherries abound for these last fall weeks. I am a healthy brown color and stuffed with fresh fruit (at other times of the year unobtainable)." In other entries, he wrote about the parties he attended, his long discussions with students at the university and his many love affairs.

To say that Oswald "does not appear to have been able to establish meaningful relationships with other people"[84] plays on words. What is meant by "meaningful relationships"? Was his marriage to Marina, despite its ups and downs, without any meaning? Notwithstanding the tensions and the beatings, which are not uncommon in families on the brink of poverty, there is much evidence that he loved his wife. No one denies that he adored his two daughters, June and Audrey. Priscilla Johnson McMillan felt that Lee "idolized his older brother Robert."[85] He had a favorite cousin, Marilyn Murret,[86] and responded warmly to Eugene Murret's invitation to give a lecture at his seminary on his experiences in Russia.[87] Growing up in New Orleans, he palled around with Palmer McBride and William Wulf. In the marines, he seemed to connect with at least two men, Nelson Delgado and Kerry Thornley, and played a good deal of chess with Richard Call.[88] Oswald appeared to enjoy his discussions with his commanding officer, Lieutenant Donovan, while they killed time during their four-hour radar watches. While in the Soviet Union, he was friends with Pavel Golovachev and Ernst Titovets.[89] Alexander Ziger, his boss at the radio factory, seems to have taken him under his wing and treated him like a son, inviting him to his house and on Sunday rides with his family into the country.[90] He must have established some sort of relationship with those factory workers in Minsk mentioned in CE 92 who

22

gave him personal information and talked frankly to him about their views of the Soviet State.

Upon his return to America, he became somewhat close to de Mohrenschildts as well as Gary Taylor. He had long talks with Paul Gregory, a student whom his wife, Marina, was giving Russian language lessons to. Lee seemed to open up to the young Gregory about many things in his life. While he worked at Jaggers-Chiles-Stovall in Dallas, he stuck a bit of a friendship with Dennis Ofstein, who seemed to like Lee and later wrote to him inviting him and his wife to visit his family socially.[91] While he had his moments with Ruth Paine, he appears to have enjoyed his talks with her estranged husband, Michael, and accepted his invitation to attend a meeting of the American Civil Liberties Union with him a month before the assassination.

The Warren Report repeated Marina's observation that "Oswald's interest in Marxism…may have been motivated by a desire to gain attention"[92] and stated that he "used his Marxist and associated activities as excuses for his difficulties in getting along in the world, which were usually caused by entirely different factors."[93] While it felt that his defection to the Soviet Union was in part a result of his commitment to Marxism, it appeared that "personal and psychological factors" were also involved.[94]

For the Commission, Oswald's political activism in New Orleans could be explained by his psychological difficulties. His FPCC organization was "a product of his imagination,"[95] simply an operation "in which one man single handedly created publicity for his cause or for himself."[96] His FPCC activities were "evidence of Oswald's reluctance to describe events accurately and of his need to present himself to others as well as to himself in a light more favorable than was justified by reality."[97]

The Commission felt there was doubt about how fully Oswald understood Marxism[98] but was confident that his "attachment to Marxism and Communist doctrine was probably, in some measure, an expression of his hostility to his environment."[99] His interest in the Cuban revolution was also interpreted through the mirror of psychological problems. It stated: "It should be noted that his interest in Cuba seems to have increased along with his sense of frustration in jobs, in his political activity and in his personal relationships. In retrospect his attempt to go to Cuba or return to the Soviet Union may well have been Oswald's last escape hatch, his last gambit to extricate himself from the mediocrity and defeat which plagued him throughout most of his life."[100]

Pyschohistory is not the only methodology to explain political development and behaviour, nor is it the standard one used in political science or history. Other methodologies were available to the Warren Commission at the time but were ignored. A more comprehensive approach was that described in *The Civic Culture*, published in 1963 by two Stanford University professors, Gabriel A. Almond and Sidney Verba.[101] The book has since become a classic university text for studying political behaviour.

Almond and Verba theorized that the "sources of political attitudes appear to be many. They include early socialization experiences and late socialization experiences during adolescence, as well as postsocialization experiences as an adult. They include both political and nonpolitical experiences, experiences that are intended by others to have an effect on political attitudes, and these experiences can come at a variety of times."[102] Their approach focused on the impact of political culture and political subcultures, the importance of social relations to civic competence and the influence of a variety of agents of political socialization.

Almond and Verba were quite critical of any methodology that emphasized pyschohistorical or psychocultural factors. The authors stated:

> The earlier psychocultural approach to the subject regarded political socialization as a rather simple process. Three assumptions were usually made: (1) the significant socialization experiences that will affect later political behaviour take place quite early in life: (2) these experiences are not manifestly political experiences, but they have latent political consequences...and (3) the socialization process is unidirectional: the more "basic" family experiences have a significant impact upon the secondary structures of politics but are not in turn affected by them...This approach to an explanation of political attitudes was too simple. One could not make unambiguous connections between early socialization experiences and politics; the gap between the two was so great that it could be closed only by the use of somewhat imprecise analogies and a rather selective approach to evidence.[103]

It does not appear that the Warren Commission or its staff consulted with the political science community with respect to advice about Oswald's political socialization or his political discourse. By explaining Lee's politics only through unverifiable psychological sources, the Warren Commission painted a one-sided and unhistorical picture of his political development. By focusing on speculative reasons for the source of Oswald's politics and not their substance, the Commission deflected all meaningful study of his possible ideological motives for assassinating the president. As will be shown, Oswald's politics were more than mere expressions of emotions.

3. The Political World of Lee Harvey Oswald

Any understanding of Oswald's ideas or political actions must make reference to America's political environment of the 1950s and the early 1960s and the historical events that characterized that period. Attention must also be paid to the intellectual influences he experienced in the course of his reading, as well as how Oswald came to be socialized into the political world. Four factors—political cultural traits, historical events, ideology and instruments of political socialization—are crucial to the analysis of Oswald's politics.

The political culture in which Oswald mostly grew up was that of the American South. According to historian Jeff Woods, the South's dominant characteristic during that period was a strong sense of nationalism defined by a "concern for personal and natural honor, a suspicion of centralized power and a belief in state's rights, a fundamentalist faith in Protestant Christianity, and a view of history shaped by the region's experiences of slavery, the Civil War and Reconstruction."[104]

Although his writings clearly demonstrate he was more an internationalist if not "state-less," Oswald never forgot he was a Southerner. In his 1959 interview with Aline Mosby in Moscow he called himself "a southern boy." He told Priscilla Johnson that "I was brought up like any Southern boy...."[105] He certainly did not enjoy living in the North, as his time in New York City was not a happy one. Neither did he like living in Belorussia. When he started making plans about where he and his new family would settle after returning to America, he told his brother

Robert he would "sort of like New Orleans."[106] While he cannot by any standard be described as a southern nationalist and never exhibited a regional siege mentality, there is evidence that he may have been influenced by the South's suspicion of centralized power and its fundamentalist Protestant faith.

Like most Southerners, Oswald opposed a centralized State. As he stated in one of his essays, he favoured "a loose confederation of communities at a national level without any centralized state whatsoever."[107] Such an arrangement admittedly went beyond the decentralized federalism historically preferred by many in the South, but it was still in keeping with the region's general sentiments. While his vision of governmental arrangements was probably more influenced by ideological factors, Oswald may have been pre-disposed to decentralized State systems by the South's political culture.

With the exception of the La Fontaines in *Oswald Talked*, who noted that "Oswald replaced God with Marxism,"[108] assassination authors have placed little importance on how religion may have affected him. For many Southerners during Oswald's impressionable years, religion was a powerful force. Marguerite's father was a Catholic, but her mother was Lutheran, and their children were baptized in the Lutheran religion and attended Lutheran Sunday School and the Lutheran Church.[109] Marguerite's older sister, Lillian Murret, became a Catholic through marriage and seems to have been religiously devout: one of her children, Eugene, became a Jesuit priest. Lee, who was also baptized a Lutheran, did not escape from being exposed to religious teachings. Oswald's mother told author Jean Stafford that in raising her family, "I have always done what I thought was right, and I always did it in a true Christian way."[110] When he was three years old, Lee spent 13 months in the Lutheran-run Bethlehem Orphanage in New Orleans with his brothers, as his mother claimed she could not afford to care for them. Robert described the orphanage as having a "Christian atmosphere."[111] When Lee and Marguerite moved to New York City in August 1952 Oswald attended a private Lutheran academy for two months.[112]

Oswald discussed religion with Billy Joe Lord on the SS *Marion Lykes* and told him, "Science had disproved the existence of God and there was only matter."[113] In subsequent conversations, he admitted he was an atheist,[114] showed bitterness towards religion,[115] and attacked religious sects for being part of the State's power structure.[116] Notwithstanding such statements, one can speculate that Oswald was not immune from the deeply felt religious fervor that gripped the American South during the 1940s and 50s. Oswald may have simply substituted his secular political ideology for spiritual commitment.

While serving in the marines, he once asked Kerry Thornley, "What do you think of communism?" After Thornley replied that he did not think too much of communism, Oswald said, "Well, I think the best religion is communism."[117] When asked by Lieutenant Martello while in jail in August 1963 what his religious beliefs were, Oswald said he should be classified as "a Marxist in his beliefs."[118] In his final police interview on Sunday, November 24, 1963, Secret Service Agent Kelly asked Oswald about his religion. Oswald replied "Karl Marx is my religion—I have no faith."[119]

While he may not have had religious faith, he showed many signs of being influenced by religious principles, particularly fundamentalist ones. Michael Paine said that Oswald had "quite a lot of very negative views of people in the world around him, very little charity in his view toward anybody."[120] Paine felt that Oswald was "extremely bitter and couldn't believe there was much good will in people. There was mostly evil, conniving or else stupidity—was the description—that was his opinion or would be his description of most people."[121] Oswald told George de Mohenschildt basically the same thing. In his manuscript de Mohrenschildt wrote:

> ...In our last meetings Lee often expressed his concern about this country—past and present. Its origins—according to him—by the hypocritical pilgrims, through Indian genocide, invasion of the continent by the greedy and hungry European masses, who, meeting racist attitudes of the Anglos, became even more racist themselves. Before busing confusion arose in this country, Lee was keenly sure of the racist cancer eating America's healthy tissues. "All people are sob's" he often said, "but the strongest and more ferocious always win, physically but not morally."[122]

Oswald's view of man may have had more in common with fundamentalist Christianity than the reductionist Marxist view that man's nature will be altered as his economic and social environment changes. Oswald was under no illusion about the working class being the world's salvation to lead the fight for a socialist revolution. His negative view of human nature may explain why he chose not to participate in labour activities in either the United States or Belorussia.

There were other indications that he viewed politics through quasi-religious lenses. Oswald's anger with the capitalist system was as much moral as economic. He called the capitalist exploitation of man by man "a moral sin."[123] Aline Mosby related the story about Oswald being first introduced to Marx's *Das Kapital*: "He was like a very religious man opening the Bible for the first time. His eyes shone like those of a religious enthusiast."[124] While lecturing Jesuit students in Mobile, Alabama, two priests thought that Oswald was not off the mark when he spoke out against stock speculation and the exploitation of the working class.[125]

A second political cultural trait of the American South which impacted on his political outlook was its anti-communist environment. While Lee was growing up, Louisiana, like other southern states, seemed pathologically dedicated to fighting communists. There was a Subversive Activities and Communist Control Law, a Communist Propaganda Control Act, and a Joint Legislative Committee on Un-American Activities, formally the Joint Committee on Segregation. State officials, such as those in the New Orleans Police Department's intelligence division, were on the lookout for communist conspiracies, particularly in the civil rights movement.[126] In New Orleans in March 1954, while Oswald was living there, Senator James Eastland, "the quintessential southern red- and black-baiter,"[127] undertook hearings of the Senate's Internal Security Subcommittee to investigate the Southern Conference Educational Fund. His investigation alleged that a number of prominent southern liberals were involved in a communist conspiracy.[128] The Marxist-oriented Oswald most probably knew about Eastland's crusade and was deeply offended by it.

In July 1956, when he was 16, Oswald and his mother moved to Texas. Only two years before the governor of Texas, Alan Shivers, announced that he would ask the legislature to make Communist Party membership illegal and punishable by death in the electric chair. He claimed that "Membership in the Communist Party is worse than murder. It is mass murder."[129] According to Don E. Carleton, "Shivers' recommendation threatened to transform the Red Scare in Texas into the ultimate stage of maximum terror."[130] The adolescent Oswald, intellectually curious about Marxism, could not have felt much affection for such a hostile environment or its State officials.

This Red-fearing culture, opposed to new ideas and a changing world, was in full form in the spring of 1963 when Oswald, as he described it, "stood for the first time in my life with a placard around my neck" passing out FPCC literature in Dallas.[131] A police officer, W. R. Finigan, recounted that when he first saw this "unidentified white male of medium height in a white shirt," he called his sergeant. Before the sergeant arrived, Finigan said, "U.S. Commissioner W. Maddon Hill came across the street and said 'Something should be done about that guy passing out literature.' Mr. Hill seemed to be very angry." When the sergeant arrived, the man ran away saying, "Oh hell, here come the cops."[132]

The mission to combat communist ideas had also been taken up nationally. McCarthyism, to America's shame, played out on the federal stage with congressional committees undertaking witch-hunting investigations of alleged disloyalty, subversion and treason. In 1949, 11 leaders of the Communist Party USA were charged and convicted under the Alien Registration Act. In 1954, Congress adopted the Communist Control Act, which outlawed the Communist Party and any "communist-infiltrated" organization. More convictions followed.[133]

Such illiberal actions by the State did not escape Lee. In the Mosby interview he said, "Of course, the conduct of America towards the Communists is harsh…that was to be expected. My sympathies are with them as the underdog. That's natural, too." Talking with Priscilla Johnson, he said he spent five years "observing the treatment of minorities in America: Communists, negroes and the workers especially." In an essay he wrote in 1962, he said, "Harassment of [the CPUS's] newspaper, their leaders, and advocates is treachery to our basic principles of freedom of speech and press."[134] Minority protection became a key component of his definition of democracy. In August 1963 he told Bill Stuckey: "And that is my definition of democracy, the right to be in a minority, and not to be oppressed."[135]

Oswald may have been pushed more earnestly into his radical views by the harassing, smearing and fear mongering of State institutions and police agencies, both in the South and nationally. The almost paranoid attitude Oswald displayed towards the FBI may have come not so much from his individual experiences with the Bureau but from the stories he heard and read about how other suspected communists and those who sympathized with them were treated. It is not unreasonable to assume that the red-baiting atmosphere he witnessed during his adolescent years impacted on Oswald's conception of the meaning of democracy and his view of the American State.

The segregated social environment of the South was also disturbing to Oswald. Living in New Orleans in the mid-1950s, he no doubt witnessed the Southern Right's massive resistance to the 1954 Supreme Court *Brown vs. the Board of Education* decision to desegregate public schools that included "quasi-legal tactics and outright terrorism."[136] Like many young people of his time, Lee was revolted by the deprivation of civil rights to blacks and often spoke out against it. He told Aline Mosby, "Being a southern boy, I've seen poor niggers. That was a lesson too. People hate because they're told to hate. Like school kids. In Little Rock they don't know the difference between a nigger and a white man but it was the fashion to hate niggers so they hated them. People in the United States are like that in everything." In CE 102, while pretending to speak before an audience, Oswald says, "As I look at this audience there is a sea of white faces. Where are the Negroes amongst you (are they hiding under the table). Surely if we are a democracy, let our fellow Negro citizens into this hall."

By far, the most important historical events of Oswald's lifetime stemmed from tensions of the Cold War. The world seemed on the verge of a nuclear holocaust with crises in Korea, Indo-China, Russia, Berlin and Cuba. The fear that the world would be blown to bits was very real and worried many. In 1947 the Doomsday Clock was created, and by the late 1950s "Ban the Bomb" protests had become a mass movement throughout Europe. Oswald too was frightfully concerned. As will be discussed in the next section, he developed a doomsday scenario which figured prominently in both his writings and political actions.

Another historical event that must be noted was the rise of the New Left, a widely diverse anti-capitalist and anti-imperialist movement that was also anti-generational. According to George Vickers, the origins of the term "New Left" can be traced to the United Kingdom during the late 1950s where a group of former Communist Party and other leftists disillusioned by Hungary and the revelations about Stalin began a journal called *The New Left Review*. The term carried over to America. Vickers notes that in a letter dated May 20, 1960, Michael Rossman, a political activist and one of the organizers of Berkeley's Free Speech Movement in 1964, perceptively wrote: "I see the rise of a New Left in this country, a Left of a nature that has not been seen within this century. It will be a Left unconnected with the past...."[137]

This new political formation included a wide range of intellectuals, including Paul Goodman, C. Wright Mills, Paul Baran and Paul Sweezy. Many were Marxist but not members of official, organized socialism.[138] In fact, most were steadfast in their opposition to the Communist Party USA which they saw as "old" and chained to the sectarian battles of past times. This "new" Left espoused "new" ideas such as government decentralization and wailed against the dehumanizing effects of technology and automation. It was especially critical of America's alienated environment, its conformism, consumer culture, passivity and bureaucratic education.[139] Centered primarily in the universities, it attracted scores of college students who wished to create a new kind of politics.

The movement most surely appealed to Oswald. Its intelligentsia were Marxist-oriented but not communist. Its spokesmen "exhibited great faith in the transforming potential of marches, meetings and mimeograph machines."[140] Although Lee's politics did not emerge from college campuses, Oswald saw himself as a student and identified with the radical sentiments of his generation.

There are numerous examples that show Oswald felt he was part of the student milieu. In the Supplement to College Application Form to Albert Schweitzer College in Switzerland under the heading "Occupation," Oswald wrote "Student."[141] Aboard the SS *Marion Lykes*, which brought him from New Orleans to Europe, he told Billy Joe Lord that he was "going to travel around Europe and possibly attend school in Switzerland if he had sufficient funds."[142] He told Mrs. George B. Church the same thing, that he was "going to attend a university in Switzerland."[143] When he arrived at the Hotel Berlin in Moscow, his *Historic Diary* notes he registered as a "student." When he went up to her hotel room for his interview, Priscilla Johnson wrote that Lee appeared "wearing a dark gray suit with a dark tie, and a sweater-vest of tan cashmere. He looked familiar to me, like a lot of college boys in the East during the 1950s."[144] Oswald told her that the Russians "have said they are investigating the possibilities of continuing my education at a Soviet institute."[145] Although the Russians sent him to work in a factory in Minsk instead, Oswald later applied to the Patrice Lumumba University of Friendship of Peoples in Moscow to study economics, philosophy and politics. His application was rejected.[146]

Paul Gregory told the Warren Commission: "I think he and I got along well because he considered me fairly smart because I was interested in the Soviet matters, and therefore our discussions were quite a bit about academic matters, and he pretended, or possibly was, fairly well educated. He seemed to read quite a bit. But he expected to go over there and get into a Russian university...and he was quite disenchanted when he was not accepted into this. That was his first idea, I believe, to go over there and go to school."[147] Gregory also related the story of how "one evening [Lee] went out to TCU and another time he went out to get the catalogue for Arlington State to try to get some night school or something, and evidently was a pure dream on his part, seeing he did not have the high school degree. And he always spoke that he wanted to go back to school and get a degree and study economics and history and philosophy and things like that."[148]

There was also the same middle-class appeal between Oswald and the New Left. Despite his claim when applying to the Supreme Soviet for citizenship in 1959 that he was "a working class person," Oswald's family status was lower middle class. His mother made investments in buying and selling homes and worked for a time in the insurance industry. While growing up, his two brothers spent three years at a military academy in Mississippi. Although the Oswalds experienced constant financial problems, they were not poor. His mother, Marguerite, made the following observation to Jean Stafford with respect to the Fort Worth cemetery where Lee was buried: "Like everything in life, this is divided up into classes. There is the section for the rich people, and some very fine people are buried there, and there the one for the poor people, and then there is one for the middle class. Lee Harvey Oswald is buried in the middle-class section, as it should be according to his station in life."[149]

Gary W. O'Brien

Despite being overseas for about 15 months, Oswald kept up with developments in America through his general reading. By the time he reached Moscow in November 1959 Oswald's thinking already reflected the social criticisms of this new movement. Lee told Aline Mosby that "'[t]he hysteria in America has gotten worse. If practice makes perfect, the U.S. is getting better,' he said sarcastically. 'You know, fashions, mode, clothes, food—and hating communists or niggers. You go along with the crowd. I am against conformism in such matters, such as fashionably hating minority groups.'" As will be discussed in later sections, Oswald's politics mirrored many of the same themes of the New Left and some of their strategic tactics.

With regard to his intellectual influences, it appears there were many. Above all, there was Karl Marx. One of his first surviving letters written on October 3, 1956, at the age of 16 was to the Socialist Party of America in which he told them that "I am a Marxist, and have been studying socialist principles for well over fifteen months."[150] He did not expound on what those principles were, but it is reasonable to assume they stemmed from the three socialist books he was familiar with: Marx and Engels' *The Communist Manifesto*, Marx's *Capital—Volume 1*, and Jack London's *The Iron Heel*.

On a very general level, the main themes of *The Communist Manifesto*[151] were: the importance of class struggle ("The history of all hitherto existing society is the history of class struggles"); the need for the "abolition of property in land"; the waning of nationalism ("National differences and antagonisms between peoples are daily more and more vanishing"); the theory that "working men have no country"; the need for a centralized State ("Centralization of credit in the hands of the State, by means of a national bank with State capital and an exclusive monopoly"); and the doctrine of revolution. ("The Communists...openly declare that their ends can be attained only by the forcible overthrow of all existing social conditions. Let the ruling classes tremble at a Communist revolution. The proletarians have nothing to lose but their chains. They have a world to win.")

As will be discussed, there were some ideas in *The Communist Manifesto* Lee agreed with and many he did not. What most interested Oswald was Marx's theory of bourgeois society. For this reason, Lee seemed more attracted to the first volume of Marx's *Capital*,[152] a much more complex document, than to the *Manifesto*.

According to George Lichtheim, "even the briefest outline of *Capital* would fill a volume."[153] Oswald most likely took away two major points. The first was the "capital-labour relationship," which involved the purchase of labour-power by the capitalist, and the concept of relative surplus-value. The second was Marx's methodology of how a social system must be analyzed. Marx explained his methodology for studying capitalism in the first paragraph: "The wealth of those societies in which the capitalist mode of production prevails, presents itself as 'an immense accumulation of commodities' its unit being a single commodity. Our investigation must therefore begin with the analysis of a commodity."[154]

The third socialist book that Oswald may have been influenced by was Jack London's *The Iron Heel*,[155] published in 1908. There is no doubt he knew about and liked London. In his December 22, 1958, application to the Albert Schweitzer College, under the heading "Extent and Nature of Private Reading," Lee listed first among other authors "Jack London."[156] He indirectly referred to reading London in his interview in Moscow with Priscilla Johnson when he said that as a teenager he "had read works by American Communists" in addition to reading Marx and Engels. He also referred to London in his manuscript on Russia, noting that Ernest Hemmingway, "unlike Jack London, was never a socialist."

There are many reasons to assume that London had an impact on Oswald. Lee may have wanted to join the Socialist Party's Youth League since London had also been an SP member. One can speculate that Oswald may have patterned himself after the main character of *The Iron Heel*, Ernest Everhard, who London portrayed as a stoic, a hero, a husband, someone who taught himself foreign languages, an independent socialist thinker and a futurist. As well as being a public, popular leader and spokesman for socialism, Everhard and his movement had a clandestine side as well. London describes "secret meetings" of leaders held in Everhard's house[157] and "the weeding out from our circles of secret agents of the Oligarchy…[and] the introduction of our own secret agents into every branch of the Oligarchy…."[158] Oswald's later clandestine tactics may have been inspired by London's novel.

Several parallels can be drawn between Oswald and London. In his childhood London moved constantly as did Lee. Carolyn Johnston in her biography of London describes him as a "voracious" reader who had "discovered the marvels of the Oakland Public Library."[159] Lee, as has been noted, was also an avid reader. In his essay "How I became a Socialist" London described his conversion in religious terms.[160] As previously noted, Aline Mosby wrote that when Lee first read *Das Kapital* he told her, "It was like a very religious man opening the Bible for the first time." Carolyn Johnson says that London "had an elementary understanding of Marxist principles," that he "was not an original thinker or brilliant theorist," and "his reach for exceeded his grasp."[161] Although Lee thought through and tried to adjust Marxist principles to his own thinking, Oswald could never be seen as a "brilliant theorist" by any standard. Oswald himself told Priscilla Johnson in Moscow that he didn't "claim to be an intellectual genius."

As did Oswald, London remained largely aloof from the factional struggles within the socialist movement and avoided direct participation in the labour movement.[162] London was a "futurist," as shown in his 1908 novel *Goliah*, where he presented his fullest image of a socialist utopia.[163] In CE 97, Oswald calls himself a "radical futurist," but his vision of the future was more dis-utopian, as he foresaw the two great superpowers shattered by nuclear war. Above all, "for London, the ultimate aim of socialism was democracy."[164] Lee described his ideal state as "democracy at a local level with no centralized state." Carolyn Johnson charges that with his admiration for the Wobblies, the anarcho-syndicalist International Workers of the World, London "accepted violence as an acceptable strategy."[165] The famous Backyard Photographs taken by Marina in the first part of 1963 were evidence that Lee also accepted violence as part of his political values.

Like many New Leftists, Oswald read and was influenced by non-Marxist writers. Within a year of enlisting in the marines, he was sent overseas to Japan. With regard to their trip on the *USS Bexor*, fellow-Marine Daniel Powers testified: "I'm not saying that [Oswald] read them, but the reason that I recall these titles is because I still have most of these paperbacks that I kept quite a few of these, and they were the *Age of Reason*, and *Age of Enlightenment*, and whether he read these or not, I'm not sure."[166] Power's testimony is evidence that Oswald was exposed to political philosophers other than Marx. In these books he was introduced to the ideas of Jean Bodin, Thomas Hobbes, John Locke and Jean-Jacques Rousseau, men who theorized, among other topics, about the modern political state including the best form of government and the search for stability during times of revolution and war. Of all these philosophers, Oswald may have paid the closest attention to Jean-Jacques Rousseau, who discussed the advantages of creating small city-states. Influenced by the example of Greek city states[167] and Geneva, Rousseau claimed that the best place to develop a common self was in a city of moderate size that focuses on public freedom. Rousseau dedicated his *Second Discourse* to the Republic of Geneva and imaged it as a model of harmony, perfection and democracy.[168] In the essay CE 98, in which Lee described his vision of ideal state-systems, Oswald seemed to embrace some of Rousseau's ideas.

Powers told the Warren Commission that another book Oswald had "for a period of time" was Walt Whitman's *Leaves of Grass*.[169] Whitman's collection of poems, originally published in 1855, is usually seen as extolling the virtues of democratic idealism and the contradictory values of the self and the community. Although not in any way a Marxist or a materialist, Whitman did speak from "a rebel's viewpoint" and described an America lost to industrialism. Hugh I'Anson Fausset in *Walt Whitman: Poet of Democracy*, wrote: "[I]t was with poor men, with working men and artisans that Whitman identified his democratic ideal as he identified himself."[170]

It has been observed that Whitman's real subject was the plight and destiny of self and that "the freer and more individual the individual is the more identity he will feel with the en-masse."[171] How much of the difficult *Leaves of Grass* Oswald actually read, let alone digested, is not known. Perhaps he only got past the first two lines:

"One's-self I sing, a simple separate person,

Yet I utter the word Democratic, the word En-Masse."[172]

This stanza may have been enough to introduce Oswald to the complicated question of estrangement and unity, which has been a perennial problem in political theory. As we shall see,

Oswald was taken with the issues of democracy and the form the modern State should have.

When Oswald returned to the United States from his overseas service, he was stationed at the USMC base in El Toro. There is clear evidence that while in California and before his defection to the Soviet Union in October 1959, Oswald read George Orwell.

Oswald may have been attracted to Orwell's works because it was popular reading at the time. Although speculative, Lee might also have been introduced to Orwell through reading Jack London. Orwell wrote the introduction to London's *Love of Life and Other Stories* in a 1946 re-issue of that book.[173] We know that Lee read at least two of Orwell's three most important political works. Nelson Delgado testified that Oswald had a book "about a farm, and about how all the animals take over and make the farmer work for them."[174] Even though the FBI agents who questioned Delgado about the book did not know its name, Wesley Liebeler, the Warren Commission's counsel, correctly identified it as Orwell's *Animal Farm*.[175] Kerry Thornely told the Commission that "at Oswald's advice"[176] he read Orwell's *1984*. It is not clear whether Lee also read Orwell's *Homage to Catalonia* regarding his experiences in the Spanish Civil War.

As noted earlier, David Wrone has called Oswald "an Orwellian in philosophy." Clearly, Orwell's ideas made their way into Oswald's political quiver. Stephen Ingle has noted that "as a young man, Orwell saw the world as being divided between exploiters and the exploited."[177] Orwell vigorously opposed imperialism— he had seen its negative impact on Indian and Burmese society where he had lived for five years. He was just not an armchair intellectual but an activist as well, going on his own to fight for the democratic republican side in Spain against the fascist forces of Franco. He was critical of newspapers, especially the British press, for repeating the lies of certain Spanish newspaper about the civil war. As shown in *Animal Farm,* he preferred Trotsky to Stalin. David Kubal in *Outside the Whale* has observed that Orwell was "temperamentally incapable of accepting [Soviet Marxism's] rigid discipline and suppression of the individual mind."[178] Orwell's rejection of Soviet-like totalitarianism in *1984* and his distrust of any leftist revolution made him a serious critic of the established Left. Oswald repeated many of the themes of Orwell, another non-Marxist, in his political essays.

In terms of agents of political socialization, two must be singled out. There is indirect evidence that an important influence was his one time step-father, Edwin A. Ekdahl. When Lee was four years old, his mother Marguerite married Ekdahl, an electrical engineer from Boston who is described as a "well-educated man with a Yankee accent."[179] For a time Ekdahl brought financial and social stability to the family. Vincent Bugliosi writes that Ekdahl got along well with Marguerite's boys "and they thought it a treat to have a stepfather who had a genuine interest in them, talked to them, took them out for ice cream and made every little excursion a special event."[180] The Warren Report noted that Lee "became quite attached" to Ekdahl.[181] It appears that Ekdahl liked Lee as well and spent time with him in these impressionable years. What is probably most significant for Lee's development was that Ekdahl had a college education. It may have been he who installed in Oswald a curiosity about the wider world and a desire to learn.

The important contribution of his fourth grade teacher Mrs. Clyde Livingston, must also be acknowledged. She told the FBI that that in September 1959 Lee "could not read and his spelling was poor." She spent a great deal of her spare time helping Lee who "did not mind the extra work and his attitude was good in learning to spell." During the course of his year in the fourth grade Lee "became a fairly good student."[182]

A seminal event in Lee's political socialization was his confined stay at New York's Youth House where he was sent on April 16, 1953, for psychiatric study because of his truancy from school. Youth House was a privately-financed institution for delinquent boys, and Oswald lived there for three weeks. According to his mother, Lee detested Youth House. When she first visited him there, he started to cry and said "Mother, I want to get out of here. There are children in here that have killed people, and smoke. I want to get out."[183] A Youth House staff member, Mr. Rainey, reported that "Lee has constituted a problem here of late. He is a non-participant in any activity on the floor. He has made no attempt at developing a relationship with any member of the group, and at the same time not given anyone an opportunity to become acquainted with him. He appears content just to sit and read whatever is available. He has reacted favorably to supervision; does what is asked of him without comment. There appears nothing on the floor of interest to him. Each evening at 8:00 PM he asks to be allowed to go to bed."[184] His social worker said that Lee "confided that the worse thing about Youth House was the fact that he had to be with other boys all the time, was disturbed about disrobing in front of them, taking showers with them etc."[185] His probation officer John Carro wrote: "PO inquired of Lee as to whether he would return home, whether he would attend school. The boy replied, 'I have a choice between going to school here between going to school or an institution. Does it matter? O.K. I go to school here. Lee stated that while he liked Youth House he miss[ed] the freedom of doing what he wanted. He did not miss his mother."[186]

Most studies about Oswald focus on how the staff of Youth House saw and felt about Lee. What is probably more important is how Lee reacted to them and Youth House generally. Carro is the only one who said that Lee "liked Youth House" but even that was qualified. It was obviously not a pleasant experience for him. Youth House has been described as "a dingy, jail-like building on Manhattan's Lower East Side, between First and Second Avenues, with barred windows looking out on tenements of the teeming city."[187] Marguerite called it "an old, old home in Brooklyn" whose conditions were "deplorable."[188] Claude Brown, who was sent there a few years before Oswald, wrote in his book *Manchild in the Promised Land*: "[Y]ou couldn't get out of the Youth House. The windows had iron gates on them, and the doors were always locked." Brown described it as a place where stealing, bullying and learning to "git by" were prevalent. He wrote: "[I]t was just like being out on the street, only better, because I could do everything I wanted to do—steal, fight, curse, play, and nobody could take me and put me anywhere."[189] In 1957, four years after Lee's confinement there, Youth House moved to more spacious facilities due to overcrowding.[190]

Oswald's first cognitive recognition of the political world is traditionally seen as having occurred after his release from Youth House in a New York subway station. Lee recalled in his interview with Aline Mosby that he became interested in Marxism about the age of 15 when "an old lady handed me a pamphlet about saving the Rosenbergs." Julius and Ethel Rosenberg, both active at one time in the Communist Party, were convicted in March 1951 of conspiracy to commit espionage by providing atomic secrets to the Soviet Union and had been sentenced to death. In May 1953 they were in jail waiting execution. To say that the formative event in Oswald's political development was the Rosenberg pamphlet is not the whole story. It can be surmised that there is a link between Lee's open receptivity of the Rosenberg pamphlet and his forced confinement at Youth House. That institution was Lee's first real experience with government, or better the State. In Lee's mind, Youth House represented the State, and his impression of it must have been strongly negative. The "Save the Rosenbergs" pamphlet most likely also said negative things about the American government. It may have been because of Youth House that Lee was receptive in taking and reading the pamphlet.

Lee's later political writings about the State must always be seen in the context of his Youth House ordeal.[191]

While Oswald never wrote about the Rosenberg case or their execution, like many on the American Left he must have had great sympathy for them as being victims of Cold War hysteria. For Lee, what was perhaps more important was that to the day of their execution they proclaimed they were innocent. In their book *Death House Letters* the Rosenbergs said they were "political prisoners incarcerated because they had been advocates of peace." However, as Ronald Radosh and Joyce Milton argued, from the Rosenberg's ideological perspective "the crimes of which they had been convicted were crimes only in the eyes of Cold War America: they were capitalist crimes. Considered from an objective Marxist viewpoint, there had been no crime at all."[192] The Rosenbergs felt they were simply helping the USSR contribute to the defeat of fascism and were aiding the cause of peace. While the case is still controversial, there is much evidence that at least Julius Rosenberg was guilty of spying.[193] To the end, the Rosenbergs remained loyal to what they considered to be their ideological truths. The lesson may not have been lost on Lee Oswald.

4. Political Writings

Most of Oswald's political writings were private. With the exception of CE 92 and CE 93, they were not shared with anyone and at one point almost destroyed. Marina said that shortly after the attempt on Walker's life, she told Lee that he must destroy any evidence of his involvement. Johnson McMillan wrote that Oswald burned the papers in his blue loose-leaf notebook in which he kept his typing lessons over the toilet: "He did this thoughtfully, with great reluctance, as if it were the funeral pyre of his ideas. But apparently he destroyed only the details of his plan. He did not burn his handwritten pages which contained his political philosophy and program."[194] Most of his writings were found in a suitcase in the Paine residence's garage when the house was searched for a second time by detectives at 1:40 PM the day after the assassination. According to police, within the suitcase was a "[b]rown envelope containing hand written manuscripts of Lee Oswald."[195] His essays have remained the least examined and overlooked items within the evidentiary base of the assassination.

The Warren Commission was dismissive of the writings, characterizing all the material he wrote after he left the Soviet Union as "more an expression of his own psychological condition than of a reasoned analysis."[196] This attitude that the essays were irrelevant to discovering any substantive motive for the assassination was apparent when his writings were entered into the record as exhibits. Clearly, the Commission's chief counsel, J. Lee Rankin, had not read them very closely. He first described CE 25, *Notes Written on Holland-American Line Stationery*, as "another diary". He then said he had possibly "misdescribed" it, adding "It may be more accurately described as a story of his experiences in the Soviet Union."[197] Being a theoretical essay which laid out key elements of Oswald's world vision, CE 25 was much more than "a story." CE 98, *A System Opposed to the Communist,* Rankin said "purports to be notes for a speech."[198] If he had studied it, he would have seen it was one of Lee's most important writings. There is nothing in the document to indicate that it was any kind of speech.

There was more confusion when Oswald's manuscript on Russia was introduced into the record. Rankin said that CE 92 "purports to be a book that Lee Harvey Oswald wrote about conditions in the Soviet Union." Chairman Warren asked, "The one that was dictated to the stenographer?" Rankin replied, "Yes, that is right." Norman Redlich added, "He had written notes, and she transcribed them."[199] Oswald never wrote a book; he only prepared a manuscript. CE 92 was not the one transcribed by Pauline Bates; she testified she only typed ten single spaced pages.[200] CE 92 is double-spaced and consists of fifty pages of typing done by the Commission staff.[201]

CE 95, which consists of thirty pages of his manuscript and was most likely typed by Oswald in Belorussia, was described by John Thorne, Marina's attorney, as "a photocopy of many pages of typewriting, typewritten words which are in English." Rankin explained the CE 95 was "also material concerning the book, regarding conditions in Russia."[202] How CE 95 related to CE 92 was not made clear to the commissioners. CE 95 begins shortly after sections 17—19, "Layout of the City of Minsk," and with the exception of text found on pages 362 to 364 of the handwritten CE 94, it goes to the end of the manuscript. By calling it only "material...regarding conditions in Russia," Rankin obviously did not grasp the political significance of the document in terms of Lee's anti-communist views. CE 97, *Notes*

Regarding the Communist Party of the United States, Oswald's last essay in which he further developed ideas laid out in CE 25, Rankin said "appears to be a critique on the Communist Party in the United States by Lee Oswald,"[203] revealing that he probably did not read it very far after the title.

The confusion continued when Albert E. Jenner Jr. questioned Pauline Bates about what exactly she typed for Oswald. In addition to wanting her to confirm that the document he showed her was in Lee's handwriting, he also wanted to know if she recognized the material. Jenner showed her pages that "are photostatic copies of what purport to be some manuscript notes." Some of the notes were on "lined paper with the ruled left-hand margin." He then read her extracts: "Resident of U.S.S.R." and "I lived in Moscow from October 16, 1959 to January 4, 1960 during which time I stayed at the Berlin and Metropole Hotel." What Jenner was obviously reading to her were parts of CE 93, *Notes on His Background,* which Lee wrote long after his re-defection and brought with him to Mexico City. It had nothing to do with his narrative on Russia.[204]

The Warren Report at least quoted citations from CE 92, 25, 97, 98 and 100.[205] The House Select Committee on Assassinations in its report did not even refer to the political essays. It was more interested in investigating his alleged clandestine activities than in exploring his political ideas.

In this section, Oswald's writings have been placed into four groups: (i) letters he wrote before he returned to America in June 1962, (ii) his political essays, (iii) letters he wrote after he re-defection, and (iv) his auto-biographical writings. All of these are found in the appendices to this book.

(i) His Letters Until June 1962

On October 3, 1956, at the age of 16 and a few months before the presidential election, Oswald wrote to the Socialist Party of America (SPA) asking about information of its Youth League and how he could join a branch in his area. Reference has been made previously that his curiosity about SPA may have been influenced by Jack London. How long Oswald's interest in the Socialist Party lasted is unknown. It may have ceased after the 1956 election when the SPA candidate polled fewer than 3,000 votes, causing the party to pursue a new strategy of no longer running independent candidates but to realign itself with the Democratic Party.[206] Certainly by the time of his interview with Aline Mosby, his view of the socialists had changed. As Mosby wrote, quoting Oswald: "'I don't want any socialist people to act for me', he said, his voice heavy with scorn. 'I dislike them as I know them in the United States. You don't just sit around and talk about it. You go out and do it. I just haven't got out of university and read about Marx. I've seen all the workers on the east side.'"

Oswald's planned defection to the Soviet Union was hinted about in his spring 1959 letter to his brother Robert when he wrote: "I'll be getting out of the corps and I know what I want to be and how I'm going to do it..." His letter to his mother postmarked September 19, 1959, the day before his departure for Europe, foretold his political desire to break with what he believed was a decadent and dying American society. With an attitude expressed by many young middle-class Americans, Oswald wrote: "Just remember above all else that my values are different from Robert's or yours."

His next letters all point to his conversion to Stalinism. The very day he arrived in Moscow from Helsinki, he wrote to the Supreme Soviet of the USSR asking to be granted citizenship to the

49

Soviet Union. Oswald later told both George de Mohresnshildt[207] and William Stuckey[208] that he had laid his plans about defecting the previous year in Japan. In his November 2, 1959, letter he told his brother Robert: "I have waited to do this for well over a year."

Oswald gave the Supreme Soviet the reasons for wanting citizenship as "I am a Communist and working class person. I have lived in a decadent capitalist society where workers are slaves. I am 20. I served in U.S. marines for three years. I served in occupation forces in Japan. I have seen American militarism in all of its forms." He repeated his self-description as "a Communist" (adding "and Marxist") in a paper found among his possessions in his hotel following his attempted suicide.

In an undated letter, he made a request to the U.S. Embassy that his citizenship in the U.S. be revoked and told them of his plan to apply for Soviet citizenship. He did not go into detail, saying only that "I take these steps for political reasons" to which he has given "the longest and most serious considerations." After his unsuccessful meeting with the American consul Richard E. Snyder, he wrote to the American Embassy on November 3 with a written request to renounce his citizenship. He noted he had appeared in person "for the purpose of signing the formal papers," but "this legal right I was refused at that time. I wish to protest against this action, and against the conduct of the official of the United States consular service who acted on my behalf of the United States government." As noted by Priscilla Johnson, Oswald displayed extreme bitterness towards the embassy.[209]

Oswald's first serious attempt at articulating his political beliefs was an eight-page letter to his brother Robert dated November 26, 1959. While the letter is usually seen as Lee's response to questions posed to him by Robert with respect to his reasons for defecting, it can also be regarded as an addendum to his interview with Aline Mosby, which Lee described as "distorted' and a "bad newspaper story." Lee asked Robert to do a favour and "give the contents of this letter (except that which is for your benefit) to some reporter, it will clarify my situation…"

How much of the November 26 letter or his other letters to Soviet officials reflected his actual political beliefs must be questioned. Oswald was no Orwellian when it came to always telling the truth in politics. He wanted to put his best foot forward for them at least until his request for asylum if not citizenship was approved and to make them believe he was a fellow traveler. He was no doubt aware that his November 26 letter would be opened by Soviet authorities. It was carefully hand written, which made it easier for both the Soviets and Robert to read.

Yet the November 26 letter has more wheat than chaff. Lee begins with a stereotype diatribe against liberal society and more particularly against its government (or the State) which came right out of the Marx's *Communist Manifesto* and London's *The Iron Heel.* The government supports an economic system which exploits all its workers. The system is extremely volatile as it is based on credit causing depression, inflation, speculation and war. Religion and education are tools of suppression by the State that keep the "population questioning their government's unfair economic system and plans for war." Art and culture are commercialized and science neglected. Such a society sanctions segregation, unemployment and automation and has no ideals.

What is most curious is how Lee discusses the idea of "freedom." Oswald seems to belittle this cardinal value of the American political heritage. He writes: "I will ask you a question Robert, what do you support the American government for? What is the Ideal you put forward? Do not say 'freedom' because freedom is a word used by all peoples through all of time. Ask me and I will tell you I fight for <u>communism</u>." As shown in CE 92,

CE 102 and CE 98, he would later change his mind about how important "freedom" and "democracy" were. He no doubt spent some time thinking about these political values while he stayed in Minsk, and they would form an important part of his critique of the modern State.

What Oswald said about the Soviet Union in the November 26 letter was not what he believed. As someone who had critically thought about Orwell's *Animal Farm* and *1984* he could not have been serious in his descriptions of Soviet society. Oswald wrote that under Soviet communism people are not slaves but live in peace and work only seven hours a day. There is social equality, medical care, and no unemployment. In what was a real whopper, Oswald said that people in the Soviet Union "believe in their Ideal and they support their government and country to the full limit." Even the KGB must have laughed at that when they opened his letter.

As for Robert's concern about how the defection affected him personally, Lee responded in a manner similar to the stoical hero of London's *The Iron Heel*, Ernest Everhard, who sacrificed everything, including his wife's personal comforts, to the revolutionary cause. Oswald wrote: "Happiness in not based on oneself, it does not consist of a small home, of taking and getting. Happiness is taking part in the struggle, where there is no borderline between one's own personal world, and the world in general."

Disturbingly, the letter also revealed his capacity for political violence. His claim that "[i]n the event of war, I would kill <u>any</u> American who put a uniform on in defense of the American government—any American," should have been a warning to the security forces in both the United States and Russia that violence was an important element of his political chemistry.

There is no other communication from Oswald left on the historical record for over a year following his December 17, 1959, letter to Robert. However, just twelve months later in December 1960 in what would be a life-altering decision, Oswald wrote to the American Embassy asking to come home. Although Oswald's disenchantment with the Soviet Union has been attributed to non-political factors, such as his failure to get his girlfriend, Ella German, to love him, all evidence points to a monumental change in his political thinking. In CE 92 Oswald wrote a biographical note about himself:

> Lee Harvey Oswald was born in Oct 1939 in New Orleans La. the son of an Insurance Salesman whose early death left a far mean streak of independence brought on by neglect. Entering the U.S. Marine Corps at 17 this streak of independence was strengthened by exotic journeys to Japan, the Philippines and the scores of odd islands in the Pacific. Immediately after serving out his 3 years in the USMC he abandoned his American life to seek a new life in the USSR. Full of optimism and hope he stood in Red Square in the fall of 1959 vowing to see his chosen course through. After, however, two years and a lot of growing up, I decided to return to the USA.

Lee did not elaborate on what "a lot of growing up" meant. It could be that during the course of 1960 Oswald began to formulate a political world vision not simply derivative from Marx. Oswald's action of December 1960 and his subsequent letter of February 1, 1961, requesting re-defection is usually interpreted in terms of Oswald wanting to flee the Soviet Union because he had grown tired of it. It may be just the opposite—that it wasn't Russia he was escaping from but America he was determined to return to. The real purpose in re-defecting was to begin a new life of political activism and achieve concrete political goals.[210]

Oswald used all his skills and poured all of his efforts into getting himself and his family out. In his letter to Secretary of the Navy John B. Connally on January 30, 1961, he described himself tongue in cheek as an ex-patriot like Ernest Hemingway, who had gone to live in Paris. He disowned the stories written about him that he was a Marxist and a Communist. He said that while he criticized "certain facets of American life," his story made him look like a turncoat and resulted in the navy giving him a dishonorable discharge that was not merited. He asked Connally to "take the necessary steps to repair the damage done to me and my family."

He was less than candid in his February 1, 1961, letter to the American Embassy asking for the return of his American passport. It was never demonstrated that Oswald ever felt any "responsibility...to America." As seen in subsequent letters, he only wished to make sure that there would be no legal proceedings against him if he returned.

His 1961 and 1962 letters trace his actions in getting his new wife, Marina Prusakaova, and his daughter June out of Russia and his frustrations with the State's bureaucratic process. He used his claim as an American citizen to ask United States Senator John Tower of Texas "to raise the question of holding by the Soviet Union of a citizen of the U.S. against his will and expressed desires." He drew upon the protection of the State for his own strategic purposes. His later letters reveal the reconciliation with his family—Marguerite and Robert—whom a year earlier Lee had said he wanted nothing more to do with. In many ways Lee, the prodigal son, was very fortunate they welcomed him so warmly back, and it appears that Lee was sincerely grateful, particularly to Robert.

(ii) The Political Essays

(a) CE 92 *(The Collective; Typed Narrative Concerning Russia)*

This essay was originally untitled. Pauline Bates said that it was going to be called "Inside Russia"[211] but Priscilla Johnson McMillan wrote that Oswald called it *The Collective*.[212] Albert Jenner in his questioning of George de Mohrenschildt about the manuscript described it as "a composition entitled 'The Collective' and 'Minsk, Russia.'"[213]

Johnson McMillan said that Marina first noticed Lee writing on a yellow pad following their return from Moscow after July 14, 1961. Oswald had photographs and a ground plan of the radio plant where he worked, but he would not let Marina see. He told her, "I'm writing my impressions of Russia...Maybe there are people in America who will want to read them. Maybe I'll publish them and maybe I'll keep them for myself."[214] In his March 27, 1963, letter to his mother, Lee made reference to his manuscript, saying, "As you say my trip here would make a good story about me. I've already thought about that for quite a while now, in fact, I've already made 50 pages of longhand notes on the subject."

Pauline Bates testified that Oswald told her that Marina "covered" for him when he wrote it and "muffle[d] the tone of the typewriter and everything so people wouldn't know that he was - what he was doing."[215] Bates said he had his notes in a large package and "they were on scraps of paper not even this big, some of them [indicating with finger], and some of them large pieces of paper, some of them typed, some of them handwritten in ink and pencil. And he said that he had to just do it when he could...And he smuggled them out of Russia. And he said that the whole time until they go over the border, they were scared to death they would be found out and [of] course, they would not be allowed to leave Russia."[216]

Lee's desire to write this narrative and his research on it commenced well before the Oswalds returned from Moscow. As we know from his *Historic Diary*, Oswald began to have unfavorable impressions of the Soviet State only a week after arriving in Minsk. On March 17, 1960, he met Pavel Golavachev, who became his closest friend, and most likely obtained from him much information about the wider reality of life in the Soviet Union. He discreetly queried his fellow workers at the radio factory about their views of the State. Johnson McMillan said the Lee "pelted Marina with questions: the retail prices of countless items, as well as details of Komsomol meetings she had been to."[217] He possibly soaked up what he could from what the students at the Foreign Language Dormitory told him as well as from Ernst Titovets. More serious research probably began following his decision to return to the U.S. in January 1961.

After arriving at Robert's house in Fort Worth on June 14, 1962, Oswald continued to work on the narrative. Although he considered it, he never had the manuscript published.[218] He lent the manuscript or parts thereof to three people: Robert Oswald, who said he read fifteen pages or twenty pages;[219] Gary Taylor, who claimed he read only one or two pages[220] and George de Mohrenschildt, who said he "just glanced through" it.[221]

While CE 92 is generally seen as being a statement of how much Oswald had turned against the "Great Soviet Union," it has a broader historical purpose as it provides insight into life in the USSR four years after Khrushchev's denunciation of Stalin in February 1956. In his speech before the Twentieth Congress of the CPUSSR, Khrushchev had painted a picture of the Stalinist regime as one of "suspicion, fear and terror," violent nationalism, anti-Semitism and assassination of political dissidents.[222]

Khrushchev clearly held out a promise of change. Although Oswald's purpose in writing it was to gain "the understanding [of] the character of the Russian people," CE 92 was also an attempt to examine how different the Soviet Union really was after the denunciation and the rhetoric of anti-Stalinism.

Oswald's ultimate finding was that very little had changed. As it was during the Stalinist period, Russian society had virtually no autonomy from the reach of the State. Life, Oswald wrote, "is the reflection of mass and organized political activity, deciding the actions of every individual and group, placing upon society a course, so strict, so disciplined, that any private deviation is interpreted as political deviation and the enforced course of action over the years has become the most comprehensible educational and moral training probably in the history of the world." "Spontaneous" demonstrations, newspaper and films were controlled by the Communist Party.

There was still no freedom of labour. Oswald noted: "Up until 1950 a person could not quit a job without police and state security permission. It was simply compulsory to work at the job one had been assigned to. Nowadays it is more common that foremen enforce a Soviet law making permissible the holding of any workers who cannot be replaced. In the event a worker does not choose to remain at his place of work or chooses to refuse a certain job, he can be tried by a People's Court and sent to a work camp or prison for terms ranging up to three years." There was still anti-Semitism. Oswald noted that on Soviet passports "a Jew is marked Jew, no matter where he was born."

The March 18, 1962, election that Oswald said he witnessed was a hoax. Oswald's view of Soviet elections were "when elections are initiated in the U.S.S.R., a whole huge, mechanical apparatus is started, not only to ensure victory, but to safeguard the State from any voice of dissent, either in absenteeism or opposition."

Khrushchev's favorite plan of placing young volunteers in virgin lands to get them working and improve the country according to Oswald "has been a spectacular failure." The pulling down of Stalin's statue in Minsk, which Oswald saw, was without real meaning. In a short essay called "A New Era" Oswald implies that Khrushchev knew this was only a symbolic ending of Stalinism. Lee wrote, "But Belorussia as in Stalin's native Georgia is still a stronghold of Stalinism and a revival of Stalinism is a very, very possible thing in those two republics."

Oswald's structure of the manuscript was significant. His analysis starts from the small and goes to the big: first the factory, then the city of Minsk, then to collective farms, then to Soviet society and then to the organization of the State (the Young Communist League, the Central Committee of the CPUSSR and Ministries, elections and the army). Oswald emphasizes again and again that the State is the master institution run by an oligarchy. It was almost as if Oswald had taken London's analysis of the "Iron Heel" in Oakland in 1912 and applied it to Minsk.

Oswald's concept of the "Kollective" is important. It was "the smallest unit of authority in any given factory, plant or enterprise" and "the controlling organ of all activities at any industrial level." As will be seen, it reflected his concern for the role of small organizations within larger political and economic systems and his dislike of encroachment on their sovereignty. It also showed Oswald was more familiar with political theory than he has been given credit for. He had read parts of *Das Kapital* attentively and picked up on the methodology Marx used, that in order to study a subject, it is necessary to break it down into its smallest unit and examine it in detail. For Marx in his study of capitalism, this smallest unit was the commodity, and he proceeded to analyze it in all its manifestations. For Oswald, to understand the Soviet State, one had to examine "the collective."

The intershop group (the Kollective) was the smallest unit within the Soviet system and its most important instrument. These groups were "the worlds in which the Russian workers live. All activities and conduct of members is dependent upon the will of the Kollective." It was controlled by the party secretary who in turn was controlled by the Communist Party which directed the State. The party's grip on the State was "total." Oswald believed he had presented empirical proof for his characterization of the Soviet Union as "a totalitarian State."

Oswald tried to explore the life of the Kollective "or rather inter-life" with the aim of getting to know the workers, "[H]ow they think, act, hope and have lived."[223] CE 92 shows a socially-orientated Oswald, quizzical about the people and world around him, not an alienated and angry deviant as the Warren Commission painted him. Although he followed Marx's methodology, the fifty-page essay is not a Marxist analysis: it is quite un-Marxist. For example, at one point Oswald writes like a true liberal when says that if the people so desired they could "beat the system" through the polling booth! CE 92 resembles more a sociologist's profile of working class life.

CE 92 is important for his description of Russian Marxism in the early 1960s as being little different from that practiced under Stalin with the party having absolute control over voting, the trade unions, the housing market, the collective farms, the military and people's mobility rights. CE 92 is also important for raising a theme Oswald would later repeat in other writings and his discourse: that large states with no boundary from civil society were insufferable, and that socialist states with nationalized industries and command economies were not democratic. CE 92 reveals that Lee was doing more in Minsk than "living high on the hog." The KGB's assessment of him that he "never seemed to do anything but go to work, walk around, and shop"[224] was quite inaccurate.

Gary W. O'Brien

(b) <u>CE 25 (*Notes Written on Holland-American Line Stationery*)</u>

This essay was probably transcribed aboard the *SS Maasdam* during the Oswalds return to the United States from June 1–13, 1962. Marina claimed she spent most of her time in the ship's cabin with baby June, but that she saw Lee taking several sheets of paper and then vanish upstairs to the ship's library and remain there for hours.[225] However Marina told the Warren Commission that with regard to CE 25, "I don't know when he wrote this, whether this was aboard the ship or after we came to the United States. I only know the paper itself and the handwriting."[226] In all, Oswald wrote approximately 1,800 words. Albert H. Newman describes them as "three fragments of what appears to be speeches before unspecified audiences. Oswald numbered them respectively 1-11, 1A-4A, and 1B-2B."[227]

The essay most likely took shape in 1960, the year U-2 pilot Francis Gary Powers was shot down over Sverdlovsk. That incident led to the cancelling of the Paris Peace Summit between President Eisenhower and Premier Khrushchev and the deteriorating of East-West tensions. The world seemed on the brink of nuclear war. The crisis was most probably responsible for shaping the world vision Oswald expressed in CE 25.

While not well structured or completely developed, the essay conveys a sense of how he saw history and a vague indication of the political programme he called for. It is not written with any coherent flow but appears to be a series of deeply held political thoughts that Oswald had committed to paper for the first time. Priscilla Johnson McMillan saw CE 25 as something of an achievement. She wrote:

> For an American who was only twenty-two, Oswald's experience was unique. He had, as he had written, lived in each of the opposing

camps, more or less as an ordinary citizen. Now, suspended between the two on the voyage home, he was looking at both, weighing both, trying to puzzle out a system that would combine the merits of each. And, as he had done so often in his life before, he was doing it, once again, alone. He had not been to college, nor had he been part of any political or intellectual milieu in the United States. In Russia, he had been cut off completely from such currents as might be stirring young people back home. Yet the political solution he reached, from his own experiences, from reading, and from talking to his friends in Minsk, was similar to the solution proposed by a generation of American activists in the later 1960s: participatory democracy at a community level. Oswald was a pioneer, if you will, or a lonely American anti-hero a few years ahead of his time.[228]

Johnson McMillan was partially right in her assessment that CE 25 must be seen in the context of New Left thinking. Oswald wrote that industrialization and mechanization have led to the loss of ideals that were "the democratic ideals of its overthrown predecessor, rural small enterprise." The fight for commercial markets with other imperialist powers has led to wars, crises and oppressive friction. The traditional ideological groups could provide no answers for leading America out of this mess since they defended the present world systems. The "communist, capitalist, fascist and anarchist elements in America" as movements "must surely lead to the bitter destruction of all and everything."

What is striking is how revisionist Oswald was for someone the Warren Commission described as committed "to Marxism and communism."[229] There is no attempt to provide a description of objective conditions. He does not use the concept of social class as the explanatory factor in social development. Instead he sees social class almost as a dependent variable. It is "industrialization and mechanization" which are history's locomotives, not the class struggle. Unlike Marx, Lee's teleological vision of history is not positive but negative. History has driven us into "a dark generation of tension and fear." In typical New Left vocabulary, Oswald wrote that industrialization and automation, while at first offering "a new, efficient and promising future," only brought "the greatest hardships upon the people," causing "a general decay of classes into shapeless socialites without real cultural foundations…"

Oswald's dislike of Soviet communism is clear. He criticized the contradiction between Marx's prediction that under communism the State will "wither away" as social classes disappear and the concrete reality of Soviet Union. Oswald stated: "[T]his is not the case and is better observed than contemplated. The state becomes more extensive in that while the powers of central ministries are delegated they are not reduced in the dividing of an organ of state powers into smaller units at lower levels."

Oswald criticizes Frederick Engels for belittling Eugen Duhring, the German philosopher whose writings were at one point influential within the German Social Democratic Party. Duhring, who is generally seen as advocating "ethical communism," favoured the establishment of social democracy at a local or community level whereas "Marx and Engels advocated a centralized state which would later 'wither away.'" For Lee, Duhring at least showed sympathy for non-oppressive governmental structures, while Engels provided cover to the Soviets for butchering the ideal that the State would disappear. Lee wrote: "As history has shown time again the state remains and grows whereas true democracy can be practiced only at the local level." Oswald then provides his definition of what a true State should be: "A loose confederation of communities at a national level without any centralized state whatsoever. In equal division, with safeguard against coalitions of communities there can be democracy, not in the centralized state delegating authority but in numerous equal communities practicing and developing democracy at the local level."

Oswald did not read Duhring directly as his writings had not yet been published in English. However, he must have read Engels' *Anti-Duhring (Herr Eugen Duhring's Revolution in Science)* in which Engels quotes enough of him for Oswald to have come to a good understanding of Duhring's ideal state-system. Engels observed that Duhring drew heavily from Jean Jacques Rousseau. Engels wrote that for Duhring "'the sovereignty of the individual' forms the base of the Duhringian state of the future; it is not to be suppressed by the rule of the majority, but to find its real culmination of it."[230] He says Duhring supposes agreements between each individual in all directions and the object of these agreements is mutual aid against unjust offences. Perhaps because it was out of his educational depth, Oswald did not get into any philosophical reasoning on how these equal communities were to come about.

Johnson McMillan was right in placing CE 25 in the context of New Left thinking but wrong about Lee being a pioneer "a few years ahead of his time." CE 25 was contemporary with New Left activism. In a strange coincidence, the very dates that Oswald was writing his *Essays Written on Holland-American Line Stationery* the Students for a Democratic Society (SDS) were gathering in Port Huron, Michigan for its first national convention. The purpose of the conference, held from June 11–15, 1962, was to develop a "statement of conviction and program for the young left in America." It resulted in the *Port Huron Statement* (PHS), which was called "an agenda for a generation."[231]

It is interesting to compare CE 25 with the PHS. Both saw similar problems and identified the same villains. The two statements expressed identical fears of nuclear war, the shortcomings of American ideals, the negative effects of automation, and the injustices of discrimination. Both rejected the heritage of the traditional Left—Oswald wrote that the communist movement in America "must surely lead to the bitter destruction of all" while the PHS charged that "the dreams of the older left were perverted by Stalinism and never recreated." Both called for a form of participatory democracy. Oswald desired a "real democracy" and favored a loose confederation of communities. The PHS stated: "As a social system, we seek the establishment of a democracy of individual participation, governed by two central aims: that the individual share in those social decisions determining the quality and direction of his life; that society be organized to encourage independence in men and provide the media for their common participation."

However, the liberal solutions outlined in the PHS were ones Oswald most probably would have disagreed with for not going far enough. The PHS called for disarmament, demilitarization, industrializing the world, providing more foreign aid through the United Nations, party reform and the rejection of violence. Lee most decidedly would have not agreed with the notion of enlarging the public sector and making the State stronger and would have seen party reform as wasted effort. More important, he would never have rejected violence as a political tactic.

Oswald, witnessing how close the world came to nuclear holocaust over the Powers U-2 incident and the Berlin Crisis, assumes there will be a devastating conflict between the two systems that will leave the country "without defense or foundation of governments." While he does not say so, he implies he is not unhappy with this development as it will destroy the state-systems in both the West and East. Oswald is determined that the old State not be reconstituted. He promises to put forward a programme of action that will be an alternative to all present systems and resolve a huge problem in political thought—the proper relationship between the individual, the State and its economic system. Beyond the notion that he favored a return to a confederation of communities, at this point we know little about his vision for a restructured State. Oswald may not have had time on the *Maasdam* to complete his thoughts or may have had only vague notions of what the ideal State would look like. Nine months later in his Neely Street essays Oswald would provide greater clarity to this issue.

He was not writing a political statement to be submitted for discussion and amendment by activists at an open convention as the SDS did. He is speaking what he believed. He talks modestly about rejecting any idea of a fee "to express his views." In the body of the *Notes* he asks, "Where can I turn?" At the conclusion he says, "I intend to put forward…an alternative" following the nuclear holocaust and reinforced the fact that "I have sought the answer." It is true that others will be necessary, but who they are is not stated, only "what is needed is a constructive and practical groups of persons who oppose revival of forces." But one thing is for certain: Lee "despise[s] the representatives of both systems whether they be socialist or Christian Democrats, whether they be Labor or Conservatives they are all products of the two systems." He implies then that the reform of liberalism and social democracy is impossible. CE 25 differs considerably with the following essay (CE 102) and reveals Oswald's ambiguity towards progressive liberalism.

(c) <u>CE 102 (*Speech Before*)</u>

This is another essay written aboard the *Maasdam*. It touches on four subjects: the potential of a right wing military coup in the United States carried out by the United States Marine Corps;

the immorality of segregation; the persecution of the American Communist Party; and the anti-communist actions of certain right wing groups. On this last point, Oswald says he knows what he is talking about as "there is possibly few other American born persons in the U.S., who know as many personal reasons to know and hate and mistrust communism."

Oswald is not writing here as a Marxist but more as a civil libertarian. He is concerned about the abuse of power and protecting the rights of minorities. It is consistent with his remarks in his interview with Bill Stuckey on "Latin Listening Post" on August 17, 1963, when he was asked about his definition of democracy. Oswald replied, "You know, when our forefathers drew up the constitution, they considered that democracy was creating an atmosphere of freedom of discussion, of argument, of finding the truth. The rights, well, the classic right of having life, liberty and the pursuit of happiness. In Latin America, they have none of those right[s], none of them at all. And that is my definition of democracy, the right to be in a minority, and not to be oppressed."

In *Speech Before* Oswald warns against unconstitutional actions by the military and says he agrees with President Truman that the Marine Corps should be abolished. He also points out the evils of segregation and the unconstitutional, anti-red persecution of communists. He offers his support for the coexistence of the two world systems, saying, "Our two countries have too much to offer to each other to be tearing at each other's truths in an endless cold war." He even grudgingly gives positive comments about America, saying, "Only in ours is the voice of dissent allowed an opportunity of expression," and admits he has "done a lot of criticizing of our system." He claims he prefers the U.S. over the USSR but with the caveat that the U.S. is "the lesser of two evils."

CE 102 was not a draft political manifesto but a speech. Who Oswald's audience was to be is not known. Perhaps it was "those constructive and practical groups of persons who oppose revival of forces" that Oswald referred to in CE 25. The writing is important as it forewarns Oswald's intention that upon his return to America he would be participating in public discourse and political action. *Speech Before*, however, was never delivered.

(d) CE 98 (*A System Opposed to the Communist*)

This essay and the following one, CE 97, could be called the Neely Street essays as they were both written in March 1963 when Lee lived at 214 West Neely Street in Dallas. Marina said that Lee, who was working full time at Jaggers-Chiles-Stovall, a graphic arts firm, would come home after work for supper and then retire to his "little closet," a nook and cranny space in the apartment where he had some privacy and where he would work until midnight or 1:00 AM.[232]

The Neely Street essays are often interpreted in the context of the daily events of Oswald's private life—his secretly taking photographs of General Walker's home on March 9 or 10, his ordering of a Mannlicher-Carcano rifle from Klein's Sporting Goods on March 12, and his picking up at his post office box both the rifle and a revolver on March 25. It is surmised that Oswald was hurrying and working hard on these essays so that in the event that he was captured for killing Walker, he would at least have left behind a justification for what he had done.[233] Such analysis misses the context of what was happening elsewhere among young people in America and overlooks what the essays say about the State and its relationship to the individual.

CE 98 is one of Oswald's most important theoretical writings. By providing in draft form visions of three different state-systems, he conceded that there can be more than one State-system, all seemingly acceptable to him. For example, there can be a reformed capitalist state which allows private property, small businesses and a free labour market, but with restrictions. Business or speculation can only be performed by a "single individual." Only single persons can exchange skills or knowledge for remuneration, presumably meaning that labour unions would not be permitted. Any "person may hire or otherwise remunerate any other single person for services rendered, so long as that service does not create surplus value." Any surplus value was not to be privately held. The central purpose of this State was to prevent economic exploitation of individuals.

Oswald was unwavering in his condemnation of economic exploitation and its sanction by the State. Although he broke with Marx on various points, he totally agreed with his moral critique of capitalism, and it was on this point, as well as the ideal of the "withering away of the State," that he considered himself a "Marxist." According to his childhood friend Palmer McBride, as early as age 16 Oswald "would say that the capitalists were exploiting the working class and his central theme seemed to be that the workers would one day rise up and throw off their chains."[234] Kerry Thornley testified that while in the USMC Lee would discuss how under capitalism "workers are exploited, that is some way they are robbed of their full reward for their work by means of entrepreneurs' profits...."[235] The theme of exploitation appeared in Oswald's November 26, 1959, letter to his brother Robert, as well as in the Johnson and Mosby Moscow interviews. De Mohrenschildt's manuscript *I am a Patsy! I am a Patsy!* quotes Oswald as saying that while stationed in Japan "I also learned there of other, Japanese, ways of exploitation of the poor by the rich. Semi-feudal, industrial giants which are paternalistically yet exploiting the workers - the proletarians. The wages in Japan are ridiculously low."[236] To Michael Paine, the theme of exploitation was Oswald's main political concern. Paine told the Warren

Commission about his first conversation with Lee which took place on April 2, 1963:

> One other thing happened in this first half hour, the most fruitful half hour I had ever had with him. He mentioned his employer. I probably asked him why did he leave this country to go to the Soviet Union, and his supreme theme in this regard is the exploitation of man by man, by which he means one man making a profit out of another man's labor, which is the normal employment situation in this country and to which he found- took, felt great resentment.
>
> He was aware that his employer made - he made more money for his employer than he was paid and specifically he mentioned how his employer of the engraving company goods and chattels that he had, that Oswald didn't have, and with some specific resentment toward this employer, and I thought privately to myself that this resentment must show through if he ever meets his employer, it must sort of show through and that his employer wouldn't find that man very attractive. So this was his guiding theme.
>
> The reason that it appears that this country, the system in this country had to go, had to be changed, was because of this supreme immoral way of managing affairs here, the exploitation of man by man which occurs in this country.
>
> We discussed about it occurring in the Soviet Union, the taxation of a man's labor, it occurs there also, and it appeared that only, he seemed

to agree or were talking about the specifics of
exploitation of many by man, he agreed that the
only difference was that in the Soviet Union it is
a choice which is impersonal.

The person who decides the man's wages and
labor does not stand to gain by it whereas in this
country the man who decides stands to gain by
it.[237]

A second state-system which Oswald believed was also
legitimate was a reformed communist state. All production,
distribution and manufacturing would be carried out on a
collective basis with restrictions. The State would not be involved
in these cooperative undertakings. Investments would be made
by its members in equal shares, presumably so no one member
would have a controlling interest. All investors would share in
the profits equally. They would also have to work personally in
the enterprise or perform some duties connected to it.

The third state-system which he called "The Atheian System"
was Oswald's ideal. Presumably it would be the one established
after the looming holocaust. In the other Neely Street essay CE
97, he described it as "pure communist." In that essay he wrote:
"The emplacement of a separate, democratic, pure communist
society is our goal, but one with union-communes, democratic
socializing of production and without regard to the twisting
apart of Marxist communism by other powers. The right of
private property, religious tolerance and freedom of travel (which
have all been violated under Russian 'Communist' rule) must be
strictly observed."

The Atheian System is really a statement of all Oswald
opposed in the two existing world state-systems. The American
state permitted fascism to grow and sanctioned racial segregation.

The Soviet state prevented free enterprise, would not allow religious institutions to properly function, nationalized industrial production and controlled most aspects of civil society. In Lee's ideal, fascism and all forms of discrimination must be abolished. Free enterprise would be guaranteed; religious institutions of any type could operate freely. There would be no monopoly practices and no nationalization. Individual and collective enterprise would be guaranteed, free compulsory education until age 18 would be considered a right, and no taxes would be levied against individuals. The taxes on surplus profit gains would "be used solely for the building or improvement of public projects." Most important, there would be "no centralized State." What government there was would be democratic and carried out at the local level. Presumably, its main functions would be preventative, such as abolishing fascism and discrimination, guaranteeing free and collective enterprise, stopping monopoly practices and forbidding "the dissemination of war propaganda…as well as the manufacturing of weapons of mass destruction." The State would, however, provide education to the age of 18 and collect taxes through "a single ministry subordinate to individual communities."

CE 98 shows once again how revisionist Oswald was. In the *Communist Manifesto* Marx and Engels had written that the State could be characterized as "a committee for managing the affairs of the whole bourgeoisie." It followed then that states existed to regulate class conflict. After the revolution, the State would be an instrument of class rule, this time on behalf of the workers.

Oswald, fundamentally breaking with Marx, did not see the State as having either a class or economic function. It was never to be an instrument of class rule and certainly not one for reorganizing society. The State's main role in both the reformed capitalist system and the reformed communist system was to prevent the exploitation of individuals, not classes. Economics would be left to individuals and cooperatives. In Oswald's Atheian System, the Marxian ideal had been achieved: the State had for all intents and purposes "withered away." There was no centralized state, only "democracy at a local level." Here, Oswald re-echoed the theme he had expressed in CE 25: "In equal division, with safeguards against coalition of communities there can be democracy, not in the centralized state delegating authority but in numerous equal communities practicing and developing democracy at the local level."

His theory, however, is not complete. Oswald does not discuss how after the holocaust these communities would come into being, how they would be legislatively or judicially organized or how the local democratic entities would interact with each other. Who would be responsible for health care? Would universities be left in private hands? How would defense and police functions be organized? More important, it never answered Whitman's predicament whereby, "One's self I sing, a separate person,/Yet utter the word Democratic, the word En-Masse."

(e) <u>CE 97 (*Notes Regarding the Communist Party of the United States*)</u>

This essay was hand-printed as opposed to written, indicating Lee may have attempted different drafts.[238] In an insightful analysis Priscilla Johnson McMillan hints at its possible relation to the assassination of President Kennedy but unfortunately she does not develop her reasons for saying this. Johnson McMillan wrote: "This is probably the most significant document Oswald wrote, revealing both his emotions and his political ideas...Politically, the author denounces both the U.S. and Soviet systems and the U.S. Communist Party; but his primary concern appears to be destruction of the capitalist system in the United States and its future replacement. Although written before the Walker attempt, the document looks forward to Oswald's own future. It gives a better idea than anything else he wrote of what appears to have been his conscious purpose in killing President Kennedy, and of the resigned, stoical, and yet exalted spirit in which he went about it."[239]

CE 97 is two essays in one. The first is a Trotskyist-like attack on the CPUS listing a number of reasons why it "has betrayed itself." The second is a statement of his political vision and call to action. The link between the two is the paragraph where he claimed no "future activist" could ever work through the Communist Party. As he said: "In order to free the hesitating and justifiable future activist for the work ahead, we must remove that obstacle which has so efficiently retarded him, namely the devotion of Communist Party U.S.A. to the Soviet Union, Soviet Government, and Soviet Communist International Movement."

In Oswald's view a new political movement needed to be launched, a "special party [that] could safeguard an independent course of action after the debacle." Lee returned to his earlier theme that there will be some cataclysmic event that will destroy the American state. He wrote: "It is readily foreseeable that a coming, economic, political or military crisis, internal or external, will bring about the final destruction of the capitalist system." He emphasized, however, that it is only a "hypothetical, but very probable crisis." When that happens, political action will be necessary to prevent the reconstruction of the old capitalist State. A new one is necessary, a "truly democratic system" based on the better qualities of the two modern world-states and "upon an American foundation, opposed to both world systems as they are now." He calls this new system "pure communist."

CE 97 is another expression of New Left thinking. By March 1963 the Students for a Democratic Society through its *Port Huron Statement* were beginning to attract attention on college campuses. The civil rights movement and protest over America's increasing involvement in Vietnam were gaining in popular support. A more participatory form of government was being called for. While there is no proof that Oswald ever read the PHS he wrote in the same spirit. He no longer uses the individual term "I" as did in CE 25 but rather the collective term "we," showing he wanted to be part of the popular struggle. The purpose of CE 97 was "to free the radical movement from its inertia."

Like the New Left, Oswald eschews violence but for a different reason. In the PHS the SDS concluded: "In social change or interchange, we find violence to be abhorrent because it requires generally the transformation of the target, be it a human being or a community of people, into a depersonalized object of hate. It is imperative that the means of violence be abolished and the institutions – local, national and international – that encourage nonviolence as a condition of conflict be developed." For Oswald the question of not using violence was only tactical. He foresaw "a coming, economic, political or military crisis, internal or external, will bring about the final destruction of the capitalist system." Given this event, there would be no need for violence: the State is going to fall on its own. Oswald wrote: "We have no interest in violently opposing the U.S. Government. Why should we manifest opposition when there are far greater forces at work to bring about the fall of the United States Government than we could ever possibly muster." The situation would be quite different after the crisis. Then Oswald says" "Armed defenses of our ideals must be an accepted doctrine just as refraining from any demonstrations of force must be our doctrine in the meantime."

As did the New Left, Oswald hoped to break from sectarian politics. He backed away from his earlier declaration made in CE 25 that he despised the representatives of both systems whoever they are. He borrows some of the ideas of the PHS that progressives be brought into this new political structure. He writes: "No party of this type can attract into its ranks more than a nominal number of fundamental radicals. It is not the nature of such an organization to attract such membership as, let's say, the Republicans or even the Socialist Party, but it is possible to enlist the aid of disenchanted members of the Socialist Party and even some from the more 'respected' (from a capitalist viewpoint) parties." The famous Backyard Photographs taken while he lived on Neely Street with Oswald holding copies of both the *Worker* and the *Militant* were visual symbols of how Oswald wanted sectarian radical politics to be put aside.

CE 97 marked a turning point for Oswald as he committed himself to collective political action for the first time in his life. "There can be no substitute for organization and procurement work," he wrote. "Work is the key to the future door..." His goal was rather modest however. It involved mainly communicating information in order to build a progressive party or movement. His "special party" was more a league than a political party. Oswald was not prepared to build a Bolshevik-style political machine. He respected individualism far too much to do such a thing. His new political organization had "no interest in directly assuming the head of Government in the event of such an all-finishing crisis. As dissident Americans we are merely interested in opposing foreign intervention." Oswald closes the essay by writing, "Membership in this organization implies adherence to the principle of simple distribution of information about this movement and acceptance of the idea of stoical readiness in regards to practical measures once instituted in the crisis."

The primary goal of this new activism was not the revolutionary one of overthrowing the capitalist state. Its objectives were to prevent the present state-system from being reconstructed after the looming holocaust and eventually to establish a "pure communist one." Two steps were necessary. The first was "to shut off opportunist forces from within" by confronting the Far Right and "probably Fascist groups." Clearly, CE 97 did foretell his attempt on April 10 to assassinate General Walker. The second was to begin building a broad movement of progressive individuals, one opposed to the present state and its policies. CE 97 also foretold his decision to enter the public arena.

(iii) The Post–Re-Defection Letters

Most of the letters following his return to America on June 13, 1962, until his death on November 24, 1963, demonstrated Oswald's zigzag through the ideological Left and his inability to attach himself to any one formation. He wrote three letters to the American Trotskyists (August 12, 1962, January 1 and September 1, 1963), five to the American Stalinists (June 10, August 13, August 28, August 31 and November 1, 1963), one to the Soviet Stalinists (November 9, 1963). six to the non-aligned Fair Play for Cuba Committee (April 19, May 26, undated and August 1, 1963), and one to the left-liberal American Civil Liberties Union (November 1, 1963).

He clothed himself in various political labels. On October 30, 1962, he applied for membership with the Trotskyist Socialist Workers Party but was rejected because there was no Dallas chapter. Before leaving on his trip to Mexico City on September 1, 1963, he wrote the SWP asking "how I can get into direct contact with SWP representatives in the Washington, D.C. – Baltimore area. I and my family are moving to the area in October…I am a long time subscriber to the Militant and other party literature which I am sure, you have a record."

Yet in contradiction to CE 97, he continued to show affection for the Stalinist CPUS. On August 31, 1963, Oswald applied for a job with its newspaper, *The Worker*, saying, "I am sure you realized that to a progressive person with knowledge of photography and printing the greatest desire imaginable is to work directly for the 'Worker.'" He once again embraced the

Russian Stalinists. In September 1963 he applied for a visa to return to live again in the Soviet Union and on November 9 sent a flattering letter to the Soviet Embassy in Washington saying his problems in Mexico City were not the Embassy's fault but that of the Cuban Consulate which was "guilty of a gross breach of regulations."

Despite his apparent contradictory allegiances, the letters hint at a consistent overall strategy outlined in CE 97. His political thinking had led him to one basic conclusion: it was now necessary to prepare for the aftermath of the looming crisis. In order to "shut off opportunistic forces from within" there was a need to attract support for a special party to chart an American course to reconstitute the State. The best way to do this would be seek out progressives through "the simple distribution of information of this movement to others." The most convenient instrument to be used in Oswald's opinion, at least in the summer of 1963, was the Fair Play for Cuba Committee. Such thinking is conveyed in his May 26, 1963, letter to V. T. Lee, the Secretary of the FPCC: "An office, literature and getting people to know you are the fundamentals of the F.P.C.C. as far as I can see…" and in his June 10 letter to the *Worker* where he said: "I have formed a 'Fair Play for Cuba Committee' here in New Orleans. I think it is the best way to attract the broad mass of people to a popular struggle."

The post–re-defection letters are important as they link his political ideas with his political activities. They also reveal his anti-disciplinary nature. V. T. Lee was clear in telling Oswald on May 29 that the national committee of the FPCC would not issue a charter to him at that time and would only do so when it was "reasonable" to expect that there was enough interest in New Orleans. The FPCC secretary also advised him against operating an office in public as "that would be easily identifiable to the lunatic fringe in your community."[240] Oswald ignored Lee's cautious, constitutional approach. In an undated letter, Oswald said, "I hope you won't be too disapproving at my innovations but I do think they are necessary for this area… Against your advice, I have decided to take an office from the very beginning. As you can see from the circular, I had jumped the gun on the charter business but I don't think it's too important. You may think the circular is too provocative but I want it to attract attention, even if it's the lunatic fringe." He unilaterally altered the fee structure to facilitate attracting members. As for the office, Oswald said that even if it stayed open "for only 1 month, more people will find out about the F.P.C.C. than if there had never been any office at all, don't you agree?" Oswald, like other young radicals of his era, lacked the patience to build a radical movement. He wanted his success to be immediate and could not tolerate any setbacks.

Much more serious was his note in Russian to Marina about what to do in the event "I am alive and taken prisoner," which she discovered on April 10, 1963, the night someone took a shot at General Walker but missed. Marina testified that Oswald admitted to her that he had tried to shoot Walker, that he had been planning it for two months, and that his motives were political. When she asked him who Walker was, Lee said he was a "fascist, that he was the leader of a fascist organization" and that "if someone had killed Hitler in time, it would have saved many lives."[241]

The post–re-defection letters also reveal Oswald's extreme, almost paranoid hatred for the FBI. Oswald detested state police forces and in his manuscript on Russia called the USSR a "police state." Not only did he have an ideological bias against these security forces, but a personal one as well. While he lived in Minsk, he was aware he was under surveillance by KGB. The same dislike Oswald had for the KGB he transferred to the FBI. Upon his return to the United States Oswald was interviewed twice by the FBI, on June 26, 1962, and on August 16, 1962.[242] In his November 9 letter to the Soviets he said that the FBI "is not now interested in my activity in the progressive organization Fair Play for Cuba Committee of which I was secretary in New Orleans (state Louisiana) since I no longer reside in that state. However, the FBI has visited us here in Dallas, Texas on November 1st. Agent James P. Hosty warned me that if I engaged in FPCC activities in Texas, the FBI will again take an 'interest' in me. The agent also 'suggested' to Marina Nichilayeva that she could remain in the United States under F.B.I. 'protection': that is she could defect from the Soviet Union, of course, I and my wife strongly protested those tactics by the notorious F.B.I...."

(iv) Auto-Biographical Writings

There writings include his unfinished CE 24 (*Historic Diary*) composed during his stay in the Soviet Union, CE 100 (*Self-Questionnaire*) written aboard the *Maasdam* upon his return to America, and CE 93 (*Notes by Oswald on His Background*) written in New Orleans somewhere around the end of August or beginning of September 1963. Also included under this rubric are the political entries in CE 18 (*Address Book*).

CE 24 is neatly printed by hand indicating the entries in another document had been re-copied. It is felt that it must have been written some time after the particular event had occurred and reconstructed from notes.[243] Edward Jay Epstein says that the diary may have been "fabricated" and that a "microscopic examination of Oswald's handwriting in this diary indicates that the entire manuscript was written in one or two sessions. The misdating of a number of events further shows that the writing took place at least one year after the events described. For example, in the October 31, 1959, entry Oswald discusses his visit to the United States Embassy in Moscow that day and notes in passing that John McVickar had replaced Richard Snyder as "head consul." This change he points to did not occur, however, until August 1961, twenty months later, when Snyder was recalled to Washington…Such anachronisms strongly suggest that the entire diary was prepared after the decision was made to repatriate Oswald to the United States."[244] Notwithstanding when it was written, CE 24 provides us with factual information about Oswald's time in the Soviet Union and leaves an important chronology.

CE 24 is a companion piece to CE 92. While it does not reflect Oswald's later political thinking, and his sincerity is often open to question, there are glimpses of his beliefs. For example, on his second day in Moscow his tourist guide asks him why he wants to apply for Russian citizenship. Oswald writes that "I explain I am a communist," which mimics the explanation he gave in his October 16, 1959, letter to the Supreme Soviet. There is, however, no mention of his time spent researching material for or writing *The Collective*. Perhaps this was done for the purpose of protecting his manuscript from the KGB in the event that the *Historic Diary* was discovered.

CE 100 is separated into two distinct sections. Version One is a description of Oswald's political thinking at the time of his re-defection and must be seen in relation to CE 25. It can also be compared to his November 26, 1959, letter to Robert Oswald written nearly three years earlier. Clearly, his emotional anger with the American State subsided during his stay in the Soviet Union, although he still uses the words "disgust," "discontent" and "horror." With regard to the fundamental question of why he defected, he says nothing about his being a communist or admiration for the "Great Soviet Union." As he did in the November 26, 1959, letter he acknowledges he went "as a mark of disgust and protest against American political policies in foreign countries, my personal sign of discontent and horror at the misguided line of reasoning of the U.S. government." He forthrightly admits that while in the Soviet Union he made statements against the United States, was guilty of breaking American law by taking their oath of allegiance and that the Mosby interview was "in barest essence" true. As to whether he was a communist, he provided his most truthful answer to date, which was, "Yes, basically although I hate the USSR and socialist system, I still think Marxism can work under different circumstances." Regarding the differences between the U.S. and Soviet States, Oswald wrote in very sweeping and shocking terms there were none "except in the US the living standard is a little higher, freedoms are about the same, medical aid and the educational system in the USSR is better than in the USA." Version One shows Oswald as unrepentant about his defection and still a believer in radical change.

Version Two was probably prepared in expectation of being interviewed by mainstream newspaper reporters who had read the 1959 Mosby and Johnson interviews. By anticipating their questions and drafting responses, Oswald hoped to be better prepared. Version Two is the misleading one, portraying Oswald only as a student who went to the Soviet Union "to see the land, the people and how their system works." He was coming home to build a new life and had to find a job to support his family. As he did when he arrived in Moscow, he could become a political chameleon. This time he described himself not as a believer in Soviet communism but as a progressive liberal who hoped "our peoples would live in peace and freedom." Not all of his answers were totally off the mark. Question 5 dealing with Oswald's complaint about inaccuracies in the Mosby interview can also be found in his November 26, 1959, letter to Robert. Also, although he was reluctant to admit it, deep down Oswald may have seen qualitative differences between the two world state-systems. When asked to compare the U.S. and Russia, Oswald praised America's freedom of speech, right to travel and freedom to believe in God.

CE 93 must be viewed as an addendum to his *Historic Diary*, adding details about Oswald's life while he lived in the Soviet Union and after his re-defection in America. As he did during his stay in the Soviet Union, he kept notes about his life events in America after his return. However, he chose only the details he wished to be made known. There is no mention of the non-Marxist political authors he had read and does not refer to his subscription to the *Militant* or his reading Leon Trotsky. The document could have been better edited. Some dates are not correct, he refers to "Latin Listening Post" as "Latin American Focus," and the description of his experiences on radio should have been placed under "Radio Speaker and Lecturer" and not under "Street Agitation." It was prepared in anticipation of his attempt to defect again to Russia, this time through Cuba. Although he self-identifies as a "Marxist," he wrote as if he were a Stalinist. Upon his return to America, he said he continued to receive "Soviet ideological and informative literature" and subscribed to the *Worker*. This time, however, the Soviets were not buying it. His attempt to defect a second time was unsuccessful.

CE 18 was found among his possessions by the Dallas Police when they searched his room at 1026 North Beckley in Oak Cliff.[245] Lee had purchased the address book in the Soviet Union, and it contained entries in both English and Russian. Many see it as providing possible clues to other individuals who may have been involved in the killing of President Kennedy. When Captain Fritz first confronted him with the *Address Book*, he wanted to know who those people listed in it were. The FBI conducted numerous interviews of those named in the book, attempting to discover the circumstances of how and why their names appeared.

Almost everybody who is suspected of being a conspirator in the assassination has some connection to CE 18. Jim Garrison attempted to link Clay Shaw and Jack Ruby with Oswald by claiming Shaw's address book and Lee's contained the same encoded phone number.[246] There are claims that the name of FBI Special Agent Warren DeBrueys is listed disguised as two Russian words and that Cuban exile Bernardo De Torres' name also appears. It is believed by some that the real name of Frank Sturgis, Frank Fiorini, comes up twice and that Gerry Patrick Hemming's name is there as well. Such observations are highly speculative.

CE 18 has also been used to diffuse associations. The name of Special Agent James P. Hosty appears on page 76 as well his telephone number and car license plate number. In a December 23, 1963, report on the *Address Book* to indicate evidentiary leads made by the FBI, the Hosty entry was deleted. The special agent who participated in preparing the report testified before the HSCA that the Hosty entry had not been included because it was not considered to be of significance as an investigative lead. Some, like Peter Dale Scott, believe that the appearance of Hosty's name in the book and its subsequent deletion by the FBI backs the allegation that Oswald was an FBI informant.[247] The HSCA saw it otherwise, concluding, "The committee, though it deemed the incident regrettable, found it to be trivial in the context of the entire investigation."[248]

The real significance of CE 18 is that it provides an empirical foundation for his political essays, testifying to the fact that his politics were not just a cover for some other hidden purpose. His interest in Far Right American political organizations is consistent with the appearance of General Walker's name on page 1 and the entry on page 55 of Lincoln Rockwell, the American Nazi Party leader and their newspaper, the *National Socialist Bulletin*. His claim in CE 93 that he tried to infiltrate an anti-Castro Cuban organization is supported in part by his entry on page 87 of the Cuban Student Directorate in New Orleans, the name of Carlos Bringuier, and the addresses of retail stores operated by Cuban exiles. There are entries for the *Worker*, the Communist Party of the United States, the Socialist Party, and Horace Twiford of the Socialist Labor Party who lived in Houston and whom Oswald tried to contact on September 25, 1963. CE 18 also provides evidence of Oswald's interest in reaching out to progressive organizations. On page 87 there appears an entry concerning the National/Progressive Youth Organization in New York and its youth organ, "Advance," which Oswald may have tried to contact. The entries on page 47 concerning various embassies, consulates and airlines in Mexico City supports other evidence that Oswald, and not some imposter, traveled to Mexico City in September 1963.

The document is not an exhaustive list of all of Oswald's contacts. There is no mention of the Socialist Workers Party, the Free Play for Cuba Committee, which individuals demonstrated with Oswald in front of the International Trade Mart in New Orleans on August 16, 1963 or the identities of "Leopoldo" or "Angelo". It only provides the names of people and addresses without explaining the reasons for the entries. There are still some notations that remain to be de-coded.

5. Political Speech

This section will trace what Oswald had to say about politics in the course of his conversations with a myriad of people. Such discourse fills out a large part of his political portrait and allows us to compare his speech to his writings.

Oswald's serious political development began at Beauregard High School following his return to New Orleans from New York City with his mother in January 1954. He started reading Marxist literature and openly discussed politics with at least two acquaintances, Palmer McBride and William E. Wulf. McBride was nearly two years older than Lee. They worked together as messengers for Pfisterer Dental Laboratories in early 1956. McBride gave the following statement to the Warren Commission:

> During his first visit to my home in late 1957 or early 1958 the discussion turned to politics and to the possibility of war. At this time I made a statement to the effect that President Dwight Eisenhower was doing a pretty good job for a man of his age and background, but that I did feel more emphasis should be placed on the space program in view of Russian successes. Oswald was very anti-Eisenhower and stated that President Eisenhower was exploiting the working people. He then made a statement to the effect that he would like to kill President Eisenhower because he was exploiting the working class. This

statement was not made in jest, and Oswald was in a serious frame of mind when this statement was made.

Lee Oswald was very serious about the virtues of Communism, and discussed these virtues at every opportunity. He would say that the capitalists were exploiting the working class and his central theme seemed to be that the workers in the world would one day rise up and throw off their chains. He praised Khrushchev's sincerity in improving the lot of the worker.[249]

Wulf was the same age as Lee. He first met Oswald in early 1956. He told the Commission:

...I think Oswald brought it up, because he was reading some of my books in my library, and he started expounding the Communist doctrine and saying that he was highly interested in communism, that communism was the only way of life for the worker, et cetera, and then came out with the statement that he was looking for a Communist cell in town to join but he couldn't find any. He was a little dismayed at this, and he said that he couldn't find any that would show any interest in him as a Communist, and subsequently, after this conversation, my father came in and we were kind of arguing back and forth about the situation, and my father came in the room, heard what we were arguing on communism, and that this boy was loud-mouthed, boisterous, and my father asked him to leave the house and politely put him out of the house, and that is the last I have seen or spoken with Oswald...All I can repeat is that we discussed communism in general and that Oswald showed himself to be a self-made, Communist. I don't think anybody got to him, if you want to put it that way. He just learned it on his own. At that time I knew very little about communism, and he was just—actually militant on the idea, and I can repeat he expressed his belief that he could be a good Communist, he could help the Communist Party out, if he could find the Communist Party to join it, and at that time he expressed that he couldn't....[250]

Oswald and his mother moved to Fort Worth in July 1956. On October 24, 1956, at the age of 17 he enlisted in the United States Marine Corps. Alan R. Felde first met Oswald while in the Infantry Training Regiment at Camp Pendelton near San Diego in October 1956. Felde's deposition to the Commission stated:

During his association with Oswald, Felde recalled Oswald continually discussed politics in which topic none of the other Marines had any interest. Oswald was an argumentative person and would frequently take the opposite side of an argument for the sake of debate...According to Felde, Oswald continually wrote to United States Senators about certain issues in which Oswald believed strongly but which were not know to Felde. One senator in particular who was in receipt of a number of Oswald's letters was Senator Thurmond [*sic*]. Felde remembered that Oswald expressed a dislike for people of wealth and that he championed the cause of the working man. On frequent occasions Oswald found fault with Eisenhower and Truman and had been against the United States participation in the Korean War since Oswald stated that one million men were killed in this war and nothing was accomplished. Oswald had condemned Eisenhower because of Eisenhower's poor tactics in the utilization of a tank unit at the time of the invasion of Europe. Felde had the impression at the time of his association with Oswald that Oswald was "left-winged."[251]

Nelson Delgado was a fellow radar operator at the Marine Corps Base at El Torro, California form late 1958 to September 1959. Their conversations took place following Lee's overseas service. Both were 19 years old. Delgado testified:

We had quite many discussions regarding Castro. At the time I was in favor of Castro, I wholeheartedly supported him, and made it known that I thought he was a pretty good fellow, and that was one of the main things Oswald and I always hit off so well, we were along the same lines of thought. Castro at the time showed all possibilities of being a freedom-loving man, a democratic sort of person, that was going to do away with all tyranny and finally give the Cuban people a break. But then he turned around and started to purge the Russian purge, started executing all these pro-Batistas or anybody associated with a pro-Batista, just word of mouth. I would say he is a Batista, and right away they would grab him, give him a kangaroo court and shoot him. He and I had discussed about that, and right and wrong way that he should have gone about doing it...We were going to become officers, you know, enlisted men. We are dreaming now, right? So we were going to become officers. So we had a head start, you see. We were getting honorable discharges, while Morgan--there was a fellow in Cuba at the time, he got a dishonorable discharge from, the Army, and he went to Castro and fought with Castro in the Escambres...And, let's see, what else? Oh, yes, then he kept on asking me about how about - how he could go about helping the Castro government. I didn't know what to tell him, so I told him the best thing that I know was to get in touch with a Cuban Embassy, you know. But at that time that I told him this we were on friendly terms with Cuba, you know, so this wasn't no subversive or malintent, you know. I didn't know what to answer him. I told him go see them. After a while he told me he was in contact with them.[252]

Kerry Thornley was also with Oswald at El Toro. He was an acting corporal and in a different squadron but shared a barrack next to him. In 1962, he wrote a novel entitled *The Idle Warrior* about a disgruntled marine who defects to the Soviet Union. He told the Warren Commission:

It became obvious to me after a while, in talking to him, that definitely he thought that communism was the best - that the Marxist morality was the most rational morality to follow that he knew of. And that communism was the best system in the world. I still certainly wouldn't - wouldn't have predicted, for example, his defection to the Soviet Union, because once again he seemed idle in his admiration for communism. He didn't seem to be an activist... [I]t seemed to be theoretical. It seemed strictly a dispassionate appraisal - I did know at the time that he was learning the Russian language. I knew he was subscribing to Pravda or a Russian newspaper of some kind from Moscow. All of this I took as a sign of his interest in the subject, and not as a sign of any active commitment to the Communist ends.[253]

John Donovan graduated from Georgetown University's School of Foreign Service in 1956 and commanded Oswald's radar squadron in the spring of 1959 at El Toro. Donavan testified:

His bond with me was that I was a recent graduate of the Foreign Service School, at least fairly well acquainted with situations throughout the world. And he would take great pride in his ability to mention not only the leader of a country, but five or six subordinates in that country who held positions of prominence. He took great pride in talking to a passing officer coming in or out of the radar center, and in a most interested of a given situation, listen to that officer's explanation, and say, "Thank you very much." As soon as we were alone again, he would say, "Do you agree with that?" In many cases it was obvious that the officer had no more idea about that than he did about the polo races - or polo matches in Australia. And Oswald would then say, "Now, if men like that are leading us, there is something wrong - when I obviously have more intelligence and more knowledge than that man." And I think his grave misunderstanding that I tried to help him with is that these men were Marine officers and supposed to be schooled in the field of warfare as the Marine Corps knows it, and not as international political analysts. And in some respects he was probably better informed than most people in the Marine Corps, namely, on international affairs…I know that Cuba interested him more than most other situations. He was fairly well informed about Mr. Batista. He referred to atrocities in general, not in particular. I think that we all know that there were injustices committed under the Batista administration. And he was against that. And he was against this sort of dictatorship. But I never heard him in any way, shape or form confess that he was a Communist, or that he ever thought about being a Communist.[254]

After an early discharge from the Marines, Oswald defected to the Soviet Union. Typical of this new generation of leftists, Oswald was curious to try out new experiences and see for himself how close to a Marxist paradise the Soviet Union really was. He also hoped he might be able to attend one of their universities. On October 15, 1959, the first day he arrived in Moscow, Oswald applied for Soviet citizenship. Five days later he was told his application was refused and that he would have to leave the country. In what was perhaps his first volunteerist political action, he tried to commit suicide but was unsuccessful. In his *Diary* he wrote: "My fondest dreams are shattered because of a petty official: because of bad planning. I planned too much! 7:00 P.M. I decide to end it."

Following his release from the hospital, he was told to stay at the Metropole Hotel in Moscow and to wait for an answer. During this waiting period, he had a thirty minute meeting with Chief Consul Richard Edward Snyder where he attempted to renounce his U.S. citizenship. Snyder told the Warren Commission that Oswald also stated "he would make available to the Soviet authorities or the Soviet Union what he had learned concerning his specialty – he was an electronics specialist of some sort, a radar technician – at any rate, he would make available to the Soviet Union such knowledge as he had acquired while the Marine Corps concerning his specialty. He volunteered this statement. It was rather peculiar."[255] Lee then returned to his hotel without his passport, which he had left behind in the Embassy, and more important without completing the procedure for renouncing his citizenship.

While still waiting a response from the Soviet authorities, he conducted lengthy interviews with two American journalists, Aline Mosby on November 13 and Priscilla Johnson on November 16, which were subsequently published in the American media. The recollections of both reporters of their interviews are found in Appendix Three. On January 4, 1960, he was told by the Soviet authorities that he would be sent to the city of Minsk in Belorussia.

He did not disclose any military secrets and made few public political statements while in Minsk. He was interviewed by Lev Setyayev, who claimed to be a reporter, but the interview it seems was never broadcast.[256] He discussed politics with one of the factory's engineers and department head, Alexander Ziger. He sought out the company of Cuban students studying in Minsk to discuss with them what was happening with the Castro revolution,[257] as well as students at the Foreign Language Institute.

In December 1960 he made his first request to return to the United States, which the KGB may have intercepted and was never received by the U.S. Embassy. He followed up with a further letter on February 13, 1961, which the Embassy did receive and was willing to consider. After numerous letters and frustrations with both the Soviet and American bureaucrats, he and his family were allowed to leave in June 1962.

Shortly after his return to America on June 13, 1962, he began pursuing his political interests. On June 18, only hours after settling temporarily with his new family at Robert's house in Fort Worth, he hired a typist to work on his manuscript, perhaps with hopes that it might be published. A few weeks later he began his zigzag through the Far Left. On August 5, he subscribed to the *Worker,* the newspaper published by the Stalinist Communist Party of the United States. On August 12, he wrote to the Trotskyist Socialist Workers Party asking them to "send me some information as to the nature of your party, its policies, etc. as I am very interested in finding out about your program." On October 30, he applied for membership in the SWP, but his application was rejected as there was no SWP organization in the Dallas-Fort Worth area. On December 15, he subscribed to the SWP's newspaper the *Militant.* He corresponded with the CPUS and offered to do photographic work for them.

During his stay in Fort Worth and Dallas from June 1962 until April 1963, he talked politics openly with many people. One of these was Paul Gregory, who was the son of Peter Paul Gregory, a Siberian-born petroleum engineer who taught classes in Russian at the Fort Worth Public Library. On June 19, 1962, Oswald went to his office seeking a letter to certify his proficiency in Russian. A week later, Gregory Sr. and Paul, a college student, visited the Oswalds at Robert's house and asked Marina to give Paul lessons in Russian over the summer of 1962.

Paul Gregory told the Commission that he and Lee talked about his impressions of the Soviet Union and that Oswald "said all the members of the Communist Party were always the ones that shouted the loudest and made the most noise and pretended to be the most patriotic, but he seemed to have quite a disgust for the members of the Communist Party. ...[H]e thought they were opportunists and it was my impression that he thought they were ruining the principles which the country should be based on. In other words, they were not true Communists. They were ruining the heaven on earth which it should be, in his opinion. That might have been a personal interpretation on my part."[258]

Gregory also said they discussed President Kennedy: "And while we were on Khrushchev, whenever he would speak about Khrushchev, Kennedy would naturally come into mind, and he expressed admiration of Kennedy. Both he and Marina would say, 'Nice young man.' I never heard him say anything derogatory about Kennedy. He seemed to admire the man, because I remember they had a copy of Life magazine which was always in their living room, and it had Kennedy's picture on it, or I believe Kennedy or someone else, and he always expressed what I would interpret as admiration for Kennedy...[A]s I can remember in their apartment that we did look at this picture of Kennedy, and Marina said, 'He looks like a nice young man.' And Lee said something, yes, he is a good leader, or something, as I remember, was a positive remark about Kennedy."[259]

By far his longest political conversations were with George de Mohrenschildt who was 28 years older. De Mohrenschildt was of Polish-Russian decent whose family had fled Minsk when he was a child. He had earned a doctorate in international commerce while living in Austria and had met the Oswalds through the Russian émigré community in September 1962. In 1976 De Mohenschildt prepared a manuscript entitled *I am a Patsy! I am a Patsy!* There he wrote about the many subjects he and Lee discussed, for example convicts in American jails, Oswald's life in the marines, his reading habits, the evils of segregation and JFK's efforts to end it. The main theme of their discourse was, however, Oswald's dislike of the modern State.

Alexandra de Mohenschildt, George's daughter, and her former husband, Gary Taylor, also witnessed his political speech. Oswald discussed with Alexandra his vision of an ideal State, which he later wrote about in CE 98. She told the Warren Commission: "Well, I'd say that his beliefs were more socialistic than anything else. I mean he believed in the perfect government, free of want and need, and free of taxation, free of discrimination, free of any police force, the right to be able to do exactly what he pleased, just total and complete freedom in everything…I think he believed in no government whatsoever, just a perfect place where people live happily all together and no religion, nothing of any sort, no ties and no hold to anything except himself…He resented any people in high places of any authority in government, or oh, in let's say the police force or anything like that…."[260]

Gary Taylor testified that "Lee, on various occasions, and I discussed the life he led in Russia, his experiences in Russia, and his general observations about it." They talked about family life, wages, housing, and travel restrictions in the Soviet Union. With respect to why he sought to return to the United States, Lee told Taylor "only that he was unhappy with both the way of life in Russia and – uh – the place that he had been given." With regard to his political philosophy, Taylor stated: "I would say that at the point of life which I knew him, he was somewhat confused about philosophy. He did not seem particularly happy with the form of government we have in this country or with government as it exists anywhere. I think he had been – and perhaps still was – a partisan of a Communist form of government but, as it is practiced in Russia, I don't think he liked it at all."[261]

Samuel B. Ballen was a self-employed financial consultant and officer for several corporations in Dallas. At George de Mohenschildt's urging, he interviewed Lee for possible employment in October 1962. Ballen told the Warren Commission: "I don't believe I can recall anything specific, but there were just during the entire course of this 2 hours, general observations, general smirks, general slurs that were significant to me that he was equally a critic of the United States and of the U.S.S.R., and that he was standing on his own mind as somewhat of a detached student and critic of both operations, and he was not going to be snowed under by either of the two operations, whether it be the press or official spokesmen." When questioned if Oswald ever demonstrated any particular hostility toward any official of the U.S. government, Ballen answered: "None whatsoever. My own subjective reaction is, that the sum total of these 2 hours I spent with him, I just can't see his having any venom towards President Kennedy."[262]

His most passionate political discussion was with Volkmar Schmidt, a young German geologist who had recently come to the United States to work in Dallas. He spoke with Oswald for over three hours at a dinner party given by the de Mohrenschildts' on February 13, 1963. Author Edward Epstein gives the following account of their conversation as it was related to him by Schmidt:

> Almost from the moment Oswald began talking about his experiences in the Soviet Union, Schmidt was impressed by his "burning dedication" to what he considered "political truth." In describing the reasons why he had become a Marxist, Oswald talked openly and candidly about the impoverished conditions under which he had been brought up and educated. In comparing social conditions in the United States and the Soviet Union, Oswald seemed remarkably articulate and objective. Even when Oswald talked about his own difficulties, he seemed emotionally detached from the experiences he was describing.
>
> When the conversation turned to the subject of the Kennedy administration, Schmidt expected

that Oswald would express the usual liberal sentiments about the president's attempting to bring about constructive reforms. Instead, Oswald launched into a violent attack on the president's foreign policy, citing both the Bay of Pigs invasion in April 1961 and the Cuban Missile Crisis of October 1962 as examples of "imperialism" and "interventions." He suggested that Kennedy's actions against Cuba had set the stage for a nuclear holocaust and further, that even after the Soviet missiles had been withdrawn from Cuba, American-sponsored acts of sabotage and "terrorism" against Cuba were continuing.

Schmidt changed the subject. He could see that Oswald had extreme and unyielding positions and realized it would do no good to argue with him. Instead, He tried to win his confidence by appearing to be in sympathy with his political views and making even more extreme statements.

In an intentionally melodramatic way Schmidt brought up the subject of General Edwin A. Walker, who had been forced to resign from the army because of his open support for the John Birch Society and other right-wing extremist causes. He suggested that Walker's hate-mongering activities at the University of Mississippi, which the federal government was then trying to desegregate, were directly responsible for the riots and blood-shed— including the death of two reporters—on that campus. He compared Walker with Hitler and said that both should be treated as murderers at large.

Oswald instantly seized on the analogy between Hitler and Walker to argue that America was moving towards fascism. As he spoke, he seemed to grow more and more excited about the subject.[263]

On June 26, 1963, less than two weeks after his return, Oswald was interviewed by the FBI. After the second interview, Oswald told Marina, "Now it's begun. Because I've been over there, they'll never let me live in peace."[264] Priscilla Johnson McMillan wrote that in the summer of 1962 Oswald showed signs that he thought about returning to the Soviet Union and that it was clear "that his return to the United States had had a contingent character in his mind from the outset, and that he was already contemplating a way out."[265]

In March or April 1963, while living on Neeley Street, Marina took photographs of Oswald in various positions dressed as an urban guerilla holding his rifle and his pistol as well as copies of Trotskyist and Stalinist newspapers, the *Militant* and the *Worker*. One of the photographs he sent to the *Militant*. The Backyard Photographs must be understood in the context of CE 97, which he had just finished writing and in which he stated "we have no interest in violently opposing the U.S. government" since "there are far greater forces at work to bring about the fall of the United States then we could ever muster." The "greater force" was the impending holocaust that would destroy the American state-system. The real fight would be after the world conflict with the armed groups who "represent hard core American capitalist supporters" who would seek "the revival of old forces." These groups had to be opposed. The photographs therefore represent Oswald's view of future tactics for the radical

Left, not contemporary ones. Their real meaning remains buried with Oswald as he never publicly explained their ideological setting.[266]

While the weapons, which he had mail-ordered, seem like harmless props in the photos, Oswald may have felt they could be put to a more deadly purpose. After some planning, on April 10, 1963, he attempted to shoot General Edwin Walker, a known racist evangelical Christian, a fierce opponent of communism and member of the right wing John Birch Society. The next day Lee, according to Marina, said that if someone had killed Hitler in time, many lives would have been saved.

The fear that fascism was strengthening in the United States was not unique to Oswald. It was a major theme of both the American Communist Party and the Socialist Workers Party. Oswald had read the *Daily Worker* regularly while he was in the Soviet Union[267] and subscribed to both the *Worker* and the *Militant* upon his return to the United States. These newspapers paid close attention to the activities of the ultra-right and warned of the danger of rising fascism in America. They were especially critical of radical right's drive for the resumption of nuclear testing, their smearing the campaign for civil rights and their attacks on organized labour and black leaders. In his writings Oswald referred to "fascist splinter groups" and the minutemen who "represent hard core American capitalist supporters." Like many, Oswald's hatred of the radical right was deeply felt, but in contrast to the political strategy of the traditional left he was not prepared to participate in the slower, democratic struggle to expose and defeat rising fascists. The Walker attempt is important in understanding a key element of Oswald's political chemistry, that he was a volunteerist, a militant who would take direct action by himself and who was blind to the consequences of his actions.

On April 24, 1963, Oswald moved to New Orleans, perhaps to leave the Walker shooting behind him, perhaps because New Orleans was where he had been born and had family, or perhaps it was good a place as any to start achieving his political objectives.

On May 26, 1963, he requested formal membership in the Fair Play for Cuba Committee and asked for a New Orleans FPCC charter. He later claimed to have rented an office at 544 Camp Street, a block away from where he worked at the Reilly coffee company. At his own expense and under the alias "Lee Osborne" (most certainly to keep the FBI off his track) he had copies printed of a "Hands Off Cuba!" handbill and application forms and memberships cards to the FPCC, New Orleans branch. The cards were signed off by "A.J. Hidell," another Oswald alias. On June 16 he picketed the USS *Wasp* by himself at the New Orleans Dumaine Street wharf, handing out FPCC leaflets.[268]

On July 27, at the invitation of his cousin Eugene Murret, he gave a thirty minute lecture on "Contemporary Russia and the Practice of Communism" to a group of Jesuit students at Spring Hill College in Mobile, Alabama. While he primarily discussed factory and village life in the Soviet Union, he also made the point, according to a summary of the lecture, "that he disliked capitalism because its foundation was the exploitation of the poor. He implied, but did not state directly, that he was disappointed in Russia because the full principles of Marxism were not lived up to and the gap between Marxist theory and the Russian practice disillusioned him with Russian communism. He said, 'Capitalism doesn't work, communism doesn't work. In the middle is socialism, and that doesn't work either.'" An account of his lecture at Spring Hill is found in Appendix Four.

Although presenting himself as a progressive interested in influencing U.S. policy to respect Cuba's sovereignty, Oswald was not beyond carrying out more clandestine actions. In CE 93 he claimed that "I infiltrated the Cuban Student directorate and harassed them with information I gained, including having the N.O. city attorney general call them and put a restraining order, pending a hearing, on some so-called bonds of invasion they were selling in the New Orleans area." His boast, however, was embellished. On August 5, 1963, he had paid a visit to the Casa Roca, a store owned by Carlos Bringuier, a prominent member of the Cuban Student Directorate (DRE). Two high school students, Philip Geraci III and Vance Blalock, were in the store at the time and they asked Oswald questions about guerilla warfare. Oswald told them he was an ex-marine and, in response to their questions, discussed what he had learned about blowing up bridges and derailing trains. He told Geraci that he had a military manual and that he would give it to him, Geraci. Geraci declined, saying, "That is all right. You don't have to. You can give it to Carlos."[269] Oswald returned the next day to give Bringuier his marine training manual.

Four days later, on August 9, he carried out another one-man FPCC demonstration, this time on Canal Street. If his express purpose was to "stage" a confrontation with DRE, it almost did not happen. After being told at his store that "in Canal Street there was a young man carrying a sign telling 'Viva Fidel,'" Bringuier and two of his buddies walked all of Canal to Rampart Street but could not find him. Bringuier then took a Canal streetcar and, still not locating him, returned to Casa Roca. He was then told one of the searchers had found him.

Bringuier went over to Canal Street. When Oswald saw him, according to Bringuier, "Immediately he smiled to me and offered the hand to shake hands with me. I became more angry and start to tell him that he don't have any face to do that, with what face he was doing that, because he had just come to me 4 days ago offering me his service and that he was a Castro agent, that he was pro-Communist..." The anti-Red Louisiana political culture then showed its head. According to Bringuier, "The people in the street became angry and they started to shout to him, "Traitor! Communist! Go to Cuba! Kill him! And some other phrases that I do not know if I could tell them in the record." Oswald remained placid throughout it all. When Bringuier took his glasses off and went near to hit him, Oswald crossed his arms in front of him and said "O.K. Carlos, if you want to me, hit me."[270] The police stepped in and took Oswald, Bringuier and his two friends to jail.

Lee spent the night in jail. He was questioned twice the next morning by New Orleans Police Lieutenant Francis Martello. The following is an excerpt from Martello's report:

> I then asked him if he was communist and he said he was not. I asked him if he was a socialist and he said 'guilty'. We then spoke at length concerning the philosophies of communism, socialism and America. He said he was in full accord with the book, Das Kapital, which book was written by KARL MARX. I know this book condemns the American way of government in entirety. I asked him if he thought that the communist way of life was better than the American way of life and he replied there was not true communism in Russia. He said that Marx was a socialist and although communism is attributed to MARX, that MARX was not a communist but a socialist. He stated this was the reason he did not consider himself to be a socialist. I asked him what his opinion was of the form of communism in Russia since he had lived there for two years and he replied 'It stunk'. He said they have 'fat stinking politicians over there just like we have over here' and that they

do not follow the real concepts of KARL MARX, that the leaders have everything and the people are still poor and depressed. I asked OSWALD why he would not allow members of his family to learn English as this would be required to educate his children and communicate with people. He stated the reason why he did this was because he hated America and he did not want them to become 'Americanized' and that his plans were to go back to Russia. He stated he had already applied to the State Department for a visa to go back by using the excuse that his wife was Russian. I asked him what he thought about President JOHN F. KENNEDY and NIKITA KHRUSHCHEV. He said he thought they got along very well together. I then asked him if he had to place allegiance or make a decision between Russia or America, which he would choose and he said 'I would place my allegiance at the foot of democracy'. I then asked him if he would consider himself a 'student of the world', explaining that I mean by this a person who attempts to find a Utopia on earth and that he said he could be classified as such an individual. I asked him if had any religious convictions and whether he believed in God since KARL MARX did not believe in God. I was trying to find out if he was an atheist. His answer to me was that he was christened as a Lutheran but that he has not followed any religion since youth. I asked him if he as an agnostic and he said he could be classified 'as a Marxist in his beliefs'. I then spoke to him about the Fair Play for Cuba Committee again and asked him if he knew that CASTRO had admitted that he was a Marxist-Leninist and he said he did. He was then asked if he truly believed CASTRO was really interested in the welfare of the Cuban people and he replied he was not going to discuss the merits of Cuba and that if this country would have good relations with the poor people of Cuba and quit worrying about CASTRO, that was his main concern; he stated this was the reason he was interested in the Fair Play for Cuba Committee.

OSWALD then returned to his cell block....[271]

Following his talk with Martello, Oswald requested to speak to an FBI agent. While the request may seem suspicious, it was not. Oswald knew the FBI was always close by and that sooner or later they would be calling him about his arrest. To avoid the suspense, and stop them from coming to a future employer and harassing him, he probably decided it would be better to have the interview right there in jail. Special Agent John Lester Quigley came down to the station and interviewed Oswald. Most of the discussion centered on his activities with the FPCC. Oswald seemed to control the interview presenting what Quigley thought were self-serving statements. Quigley in his testimony before the Warren Commission stated that Oswald explained "that he felt that the goal and theme of the Fair Play for Cuba Committee was that it was his patriotic duty to bring to the attention of as many people as he could, the fact that the United States should not attack Cuba at the time or interfere into their political affairs, and that by spreading what he considered the philosophy of the Fair Play for Cuba Committee, that the American people should be given an opportunity to go to Cuba and let them make their own mind as to what the situation was as of that time rather than just merely reading it in the newspaper...."[272]

On August 12, at his court hearing, in which Oswald sat in the seats normally reserved for Blacks, he pleaded guilty for disturbing the peace and fined $10. In typical anti-communist fashion, the judge dismissed the case against Bringuier and his two companions.

Lee continued to manifest publicly for the FPCC and like many New Leftists became media-wise. He alerted a TV station that on Friday, August 16, the FPCC would be demonstrating in front of the International Trade Mart. Oswald's demo lasted twenty minutes. He appeared with someone with an olive complexion as well as two students whom Oswald had hired. Following the demonstration he had a one hour conversation with Carlos Quiroga, an associate of Bringuier and a member of DRE, who had come to Oswald's house posing as a pro-Castro supporter to get information. During the conversation, according to Qurioga, "Oswald stated that if the United States should invade Cuba, he Oswald would fight on the side of the Castro government."[273]

Oswald's politics were starting to attract attention. On August 17, he was invited to appear on a New Orleans radio show called the "Latin Listening Post." His interview with the show's host, William Stuckey, lasted 37 minutes although only about 5 minutes of the interview was aired. A week later he was again invited by Stuckey to appear in a debate with Carlos Bringuier and Edward Butler, head of a Latin American anti-communist propaganda organization on another radio show, "Conversation Carte Blanche." During the debate, Oswald seemed unprepared and outmatched. Phone calls had earlier been made to Washington and the House Committee on Un-American Activities about Oswald's defection, and Lee had to spend more time talking about himself than about the FPCC.

After the broadcast he went for a beer with Stuckey at a local bar. The following are excerpts from the testimony Stuckey gave before the Warren Commission about their late night conversation:

> Oswald looked a little dejected, and I said, "Well, let's go out and have a beer," and he says, "All right." So we left the studio and went to a bar called Comeaux's Bar. It is about a half-block from the studio and this was the first time that his manner kind of changed from the quasi-legal position, and he relaxed a little bit. This was the first time I ever saw him relaxed and off of his guard. We had about an hour's conversation, 45 minutes to an hour, maybe a little more, maybe a little less... During that conversation he told me that he was reading at that time about Indonesian communism, and that he was reading everything he could get his hands on. He offered an opinion about Sukarno, that he was not really a Communist, that he was merely an opportunist who was using the Communists...I asked him at that time how he became interested in Marxism and he said that there are many books on the subject in any public library...

> ...He told me that he had begun to read Marx and Engels at the age of 15, but he said the conclusive thing that made him decide that Marxism was the answer was his service in Japan. He said living conditions over there convinced him something was wrong with the system, and that possibly Marxism was the answer. He said it was in Japan that he made up his mind to go to Russia and see for himself how a revolutionary society operates,

a Marxist society... [H]e wasn't very pleased apparently with some of the aspects of Russian political life. Particularly in the factories he said that a lot of the attitudes and this sort of thing was the same sort of attitude that you would find in an American factory. There was a lot of dead-heading, as we say in Louisiana...Nepotism, this sort of thing. Anybody with any authority at all would just use it to death to get everybody extra privileges that they could, and a lot of dishonesty, padding of production figures and this sort of thing. He said he wasn't very impressed...He said that nobody everybody seems to be almost alike in Russia because, after all, they had eliminated a lot of the dissenting elements in Russian society and had achieved fairly homogenous blend of population as a result...He did say this which was interesting, he said that they wouldn't allow any Fair Play for Cuba Committees in Russia... He didn't add anything other than what I have already said, but the implication was that we can do that here. "After all, you know here I have this organization and I am doing this. They probably would not let me do a similar thing in Russia," and this was his ton...He seemed like somebody that took very good care of himself, very prudent, temperate, that sort of person. It was my impression Oswald regarded himself as living in a world of intellectual inferiors...I base a lot of this on the conversation that we had in Comeaux's Bar. After all, I had paid some attention to Oswald, nobody else had particularly, and he seemed to enjoy talking with somebody he didn't regard as a stupid person, and it was my impression he thought that everybody else he had come in contact with was rather cloddish, and got the impression that he thought that he had - his philosophy, the way he felt about things, all this sort of thing, most people just could not understand this, and only an intelligent or educated person could. I don't mean to say that there was any arrogance in his manner. There was just - well, you can spot intelligence, or at least I can, I think, and this was a man who was intelligent, who was aware that he was intelligent, and who would like to have an opportunity to express his intelligence - that was my impression....[274]

Depressed about being publicly caught out about living in the Soviet Union, on August 28 Oswald wrote a letter to the Central Committee of the CPUS asking whether in their opinion "I can continue to fight, handicapped as it were, by my personal record..." His jump into collective politics he felt was a disaster since the anti-communist political culture of the South was going to swallow him. Like other inexperienced and undisciplined rebels of his generation, he could not suffer any setback.

There is compelling evidence that Oswald again zigzagged to more clandestine politics. The HSCA examined the allegations by six witnesses from Clinton, Louisiana, that Oswald appeared in their small town 130 miles from New Orleans in August-September 1963 when a voting-rights demonstration was in progress. Oswald allegedly first went to a nearby town seeking employment at East Louisiana State Hospital. Being told that his job would depend on becoming a registered voter, Oswald went to Clinton to register. More disturbingly, some of the witnesses said he was accompanied by David Ferrie, a known anti-communist and anti-Castroite, as well as Clay Shaw, the managing director of the International Trade Mart. The HSCA stated that "the Clinton witnesses were credible and significant...it was the judgment of the committee that they were telling the truth as they knew it." The HSCA concluded that the association between Ferrie, Shaw and Oswald three months before the assassination was "of an undetermined nature."[275]

He continued his clandestine activity, this time with the anti-Castro Latino community. In September 1963 he left New Orleans for Mexico City in the hopes of getting a visa to live again in the Soviet Union as well as an in-transit visa to stay for a while in Cuba. Before reaching Mexico City, he was credibly identified by Sylvia Odio and her sister Annie as being in Dallas in late September visiting her apartment with two men, either Cuban or Mexican. According to Sylvia, the names of Oswald's companions were "Leopoldo" and "Angelo" who said they were members of JURE, the Cuban Revolutionary Junta. They requested Odio's assistance in translating letters to raise money for JURE, whose political objective was to unite all opposition factions outside Cuba into an effective working organization. JURE called for free elections, restoration of human rights, a break with the Soviet bloc and release of political prisoners. It was fairly leftist, some calling it "Castroism without Castro."[276]

The circumstance of how Oswald came into contact with Leopoldo and Angelo is unknown. That there is clear evidence he was associated with at least one person from the Latino community while in New Orleans comes from the testimony of Evaristo Rodriguez. He told the Warren Commission that shortly before or after Oswald's confrontation with Carlos Bringuier on Canal Street on August 9, 1963, Lee had come into the Habana Bar late at night with a Latin man who spoke Spanish.[277] We also know that Oswald's companion at the Trade Mart demonstration on August 16 was a man with an olive complexion. His name is still unknown.

Oswald was introduced to Odio as "Leon Oswald" and one who was very interested in the Cuban cause. He did not say much, responding only to Sylvia's questions that he had never been to Cuba and yes as to whether he was interested in their movement. The next day Leopoldo called Odio and asked her what she thought of the American. Leopoldo told her their idea was to introduce him to the underground in Cuba. Leopoldo said Oswald "told us we don't have any guts, you Cubans, because President Kennedy should have been assassinated after the Bay of Pigs, and some Cubans should have done that, because he was the one that was holding the freedom of Cuba actually."[278]

It is entirely possible that Oswald was sympathetic to JURE from an ideological viewpoint. Given his commitment to democracy and opposition to imperialism, he most probably supported JURE's platform of free elections, restoration of human rights and independence from Russia. It is not inconceivable that he wanted to do some work for JURE in Cuba, if he managed to get in.

Oswald arrived in Mexico City on September 27, 1963, and stayed six days. Despite his discussions with officials at both the Cuban and Soviet embassies about his political views, he was unsuccessful in getting either his Russian or Cuban visas. CE 93 was obviously unconvincing and Oswald was devastated. A Soviet official, Valery Vladimirovich, who was with Oswald at the Soviet Embassy when his request for a travel visa was refused, gave this account of Oswald's visit:

> Continuing his conversation, Oswald repeated his desire to quickly obtain a visa to the USSR, where he wanted to clear up questions about his living there on a permanent basis. He said he was motivated by the fact that it was very difficult for him to live in the United States, that he was

constantly under surveillance, even persecuted, and that his personal life was being invaded and his wife and neighbors interrogated. He lost his job because the FBI had been around his place of employment asking questions. In recounting all this, he continually expressed concern for his life... Throughout his story, Oswald was extremely agitated and clearly nervous, especially whenever he mentioned the FBI, but he suddenly became hysterical, began to sob, and through his tears cried, 'I am afraid...they'll kill me, Let me in!' Repeating over and over that he was being persecuted and that he was being followed even here in Mexico, he stuck his right hand into the left pocket of his jacket and pulled out a revolver, saying "See? This is what I must now carry to protect my life."[279]

On October 3 he arrived in Dallas where his wife, Marina, was staying with Ruth Paine. On October 16, with Ruth's help, he got a job at the Texas School Book Depository. Oswald continued to discuss politics, especially with Michael Paine. They covered many topics including economic exploitation, religion, General Walker and the circumstances of his defecting to and re-defecting from the Soviet Union. One of their more important discussions centered around the American Civil Liberties Union, of which Paine was a member. Paine told the Commission that he invited Lee to attend their meeting on October 25, 1963, at Southern Methodist University. At the meeting a film was shown about a candidate in Washington State who, after winning the previous election, had lost the next one because of a smear campaign about his wife being once a Communist Party member. Following the film, a discussion was held in which someone said the John Birchers must not be considered anti-Semitic. According to Paine, "Lee at this point got up, speaking loud and clear and coherently, saying that, reporting that, he had been to this meeting of the right-wing group the night before or two nights before and he refuted this statement, saying names and saying how that people on the platform speaking for the Birch Society had said anti-Semitic things and also anti-Catholic statements or spoke against the Pope or something…That was good speaking. It was out of keeping with the mood of the meeting and nobody followed it up in a similar manner but I think it was accepted as - it made sense…."[280]

After the meeting on the way home, Oswald and Paine talked further about the ACLU. Paine said:

> So I was describing to him the purpose of the ACLU, and he said specifically, I can remember this, after I had described it and said that I was a member, that he couldn't join an organization like that, it wasn't political and he said something or responded in some manner, which indicated surprise that I could be concerned about joining an organization simply to defend, whose purpose it is, shall we say, to defend, free speech, free speech, per se, your freedom as well as mine. He was aware of enjoying his freedom to speak but he didn't seem to be aware of the more general principle of freedom to speak for everyone which has value in itself. And I think it took him by surprise that a person could be concerned about a value like that rather than political objective of some sort, and this was, struck me as a new idea and it struck me that he must never have met people who paid more than lip service, he wasn't familiar with the ways of expressing this value…I am sure I told him that it came to the defense of all people who didn't seem to be

receiving adequate help when it seemed to be an issue involving the Bill of Rights. I was then - that was a pang of sorrow that occurred after the assassination when I realized that he had then subsequently, a fortnight later, joined the ACLU, and still didn't quite seem to perceive its purpose, and then I realized - I had also perceived earlier that he was still a young fellow and I had been expecting rather a lot of him, when I first approached meeting him; this man had been to Russia and had been back and I had been - met some others who had been around the world like that and they are powerful people.[281]

On November 1, 1963, three weeks before the assassination, he filled out an application for membership in the ACLU, which would allow him to receive a one year subscription to their magazine *Civil Liberties*. He asked how he could contact ACLU groups in his area. He also rented a postal box and authorized both the FPCC and ACLU to receive mail there as well, signaling his possible plans for future activism.

The very same day FBI agent James P. Hosty Jr. visited the Paine residence and followed up with a second one four days later. News of these visits quite upset Oswald. At some point before the assassination, Oswald left a note at the FBI office in Dallas, the contents of which are unknown. On November 9, Lee wrote to the Soviet Embassy in Washington about his visit to the Cuban and Russian Embassies in Mexico City, saying that the FBI had warned him that if he engaged in FPCC activities in Texas, they would again take an "interest" in him. Oswald added that Agent Hosty told Marina that "she could remain in the United States under F.B.I. 'protection': that is she could defect from the Soviet Union, of course, I and my wife strongly protested those tactics by the notorious F.B.I...."

Less than two weeks later he was accused of assassinating the President of the United States and murdering a Dallas policeman. While in the Dallas jail, he discussed some of his political views with the head of the homicide division, Captain Will Fritz, and others. His interrogation, however, was not properly conducted. There was no tape recording of the conversations, the questioning was done in chaotic conditions, and no lawyer representing Oswald was present. On November 24, 1963, he was fatally wounded in the basement of the Dallas city jail by Jack Ruby.

6. Oswald's Politics: Summary and Speculation

This essay has traced the political development of the historical Oswald. That Oswald, although a very minor and isolated figure within the radical Left, was one of few dissident Americans who experienced living in the Soviet Union during a key period of the Cold War and then returned. Along the way he did some theoretical writing which, while not necessarily original, was not just derivative from Marx. He was also someone who was active in both the collective, public sphere of politics and the clandestine, underground one, with motives that were far from clear.

Oswald's politics can be better explained by social factors than attitudinal ones. The most important environmental influences were: (1) the political, social and religious conditions of the American South; (2) Cold War tensions; and (3) the rise of the New Left. With respect to those elements of Southern culture which impacted on his thinking, the following may be identified: the fundamentalist faith in Protestant Christianity that influenced Oswald's basically negative view of man and his zeal to change the world; suspicion of centralized power in a large, diversified State; and the "Red Scare" mentality that resulted in the unjust persecution and harassment of political minorities.

The influence of the Cold War—particularly the shooting down of Gary Power's U-2 spy plane in 1960 and the crisis over West Berlin in 1961—most likely caused Oswald to arrive at the apocalyptic thesis that the world faced a looming holocaust that would probably "bring about the final destruction of the capitalist system." This situation provided an unprecedented opportunity to restructure the State into one opposed to communism, socialism and capitalism where there would be "democracy at a local level with no centralized state." Oswald believed that with the aid of progressive thinkers this new ideologically designed phoenix could rise from the ashes of capitalism.

As for the New Left, there is no doubt he was in tune with its thinking and actions. Oswald's self-identification as a student, his middle-class roots, his anti-generational disposition, and his anti-capitalist, anti-imperialist biases made the New Left an attractive vehicle to him.

A number of agents of political socialization contributed to Lee's political development: for example, Edwin Ekdahl, who most likely sparked his intellectual curiosity; Mrs. Clyde Livingston, who helped him with his reading and spelling; those he was forced to associate with at Youth House, who left him with a negative view of the State; the lady in the New York subway station who handed him the pamphlet on saving the Rosenbergs; the students in the Foreign Language Institute in Minsk with whom he spent many hours talking; the Cuban students he met; Alexander Ziger, "the first voice of opposition" he heard in the Soviet Union, who advised him to return to the United States just six months after he arrived; the workers of the radio factory in Minsk who spoke to him about the control the Communist State had over their lives; George de Mohrenschildt, with whom he had many political conversations and with whom he shared many but not all his political ideas; and Michael Paine, who opened his eyes, perhaps too late, to the importance of a rights-based philosophy.

But it was his reading which drew him deeper into politics and focused his thinking. Lee searched for ideas from many sources. His reading was eclectic. While he drew from non-Marxist sources, without question he was heavily influenced by the major figures of the Russian Revolution. In his adult years, despite fundamental differences with him, his favorite author was still Karl Marx. In his last interview with the Dallas Police shortly before he died, he claimed that he was neither a Communist nor a Marxist-Leninist, but "a pure Marxist" who had read just about everything by or about Karl Marx.[282] He accepted Marx's moral critique of capitalism and his prioritizing internationalism over nationalism. However, he seriously disagreed with Marx in making class structure the basis for understanding politics and on the need for a centralized state. Oswald's proposed solution was a return to the earlier decentralized economies of small enterprise where "monopoly practices" would be considered capitalistic and democratic government would be structured "at a local level with no centralized State."

After Marx came Lenin. As demonstrated by his remark that "the biggest and key fault development of our era is of course the fight for markets between the imperialist powers themselves,"[283] Oswald was influenced by Lenin's classic work *Imperialism: The Highest Stage of Capitalism*.[284] However, he was in no way a Leninist. He rejected Lenin's methodology of studying class forces to discover class alliances and disagreed with him on the importance of a disciplined vanguard political party and the need for a centralized socialist state.

Albert H. Neman believed that of all other radical thinkers, Oswald was most attracted to Trotsky.[285] According to FBI agent Jim Hosty, Ruth Paine said that Oswald told her in early November 1963 that he "was a Trotskyite Communist."[286] There is much evidence to support this view. Trotsky, the "prophet," accused Stalin of betraying the Russian revolution. Oswald made the same accusation in one of his conversations with Paul Gregory, saying the Soviet leaders "were opportunists" and "ruining the principles which the country should be based on." Trotsky was a vigorous critic of Stalin's theory of socialism in one country and charged that he had turned all other communist parties belonging to the Third International into Russian puppets. Oswald echoed the same criticism in CE 97. Oswald once applied for membership in the Socialist Workers Party, requested from the SWP the book *The Teachings of Leon Trotsky*[287] and was a loyal reader of the *Militant*. The more libertarian vision of communism which Trotsky proposed may have influenced Oswald to appear in Dallas at the Odio apartment with two Latinos claiming they were part of JURE. Its leader, Manolo Ray, was a leftist who favored agrarian reform, greater human rights, social justice and free elections. Although it could never be claimed that Ray was a Trotskyist, Oswald probably was more sympathetic to Ray's vision for Cuba than he was to Castro's.

When judged as a whole, Oswald could never accurately be labeled a Trotskyist. He was far too much an individualist for any sort of Bolshevik approach to the revolution. His concept of socialism was broadly democratic and American, akin more to Jack London's ideas than to Russian Marxists. At most it could be said that like Trotsky, Lee was a critic of Stalinism.

Much has been written about Oswald's affinity with Castroism. The Warren Report devoted three pages to his interest in Cuba, observing that he wished to get to Cuba "where he had thought he might find his communist ideal."[288] The House Select Committee spent a considerable amount of time probing Oswald's relations with Cubans, both pro- and anti-Castro, and looked for evidence as to whether the Cuban government or Cuban exiles in the United States were involved in the assassination. Albert Newman believed the link between Oswald's assassination attempt on General Walker, his alleged desire to shoot Richard Nixon, and the assassination of President Kennedy was that all three were outspoken opponents of the revolutionary government of Cuba.[289] Jean Davison said that Castro's public warning in September 1963 that "United States leaders should think that if they are aiding terrorist plans to eliminate Cuban leaders, they themselves will not be safe" inspired Oswald to assassinate President Kennedy.[290]

Oswald was hardly alone in his attraction to Cuba or in his desire to want to go there. Some on the radical New Left, such as Eldridge Cleaver, lived there for a time. Others, like Jean-Paul Sartre and Simone de Beauvoir, only visited, and nearly all reportedly favorably on it. Intellectuals like I. F. Stone and Graham Greene were full of praise. Stone is reported to have said after his visit, "They live in a springtime of mankind," and singled out its full racial equality.[291] Graham Greene said that "Cubans have better lives than in the day of Batista" and "there is no religious prosecution and anyone can hear mass whenever he wishes."[292] A number of Canadians, whose country had not severed relations with Cuba, also went there.[293] Jack Scott of the *Vancouver Sun* wrote a favorable report entitled "The Revolution Brings Each Child a Quart of Milk a Day."[294]

For the radical Left, the key feature of Castroism was its stand against imperialism. The *Militant* in a December 1962 editorial heaped praise on the Castro regime as it marked its fourth anniversary of coming to power. It stated: "The revolution has made profound changes in the economic, social and political structure of Cuba by cutting the tentacles of imperialism and starting to build a planned economy. Moreover, it still stands! By mobilizing the masses behind the revolutionary program and by arming the workers and peasants, the Revolution has not only gone forward and deepened, but it has stood up to the world's most powerful imperialist power."[295]

What was vital to Oswald was not the Cuban revolution itself but its anti-imperialist struggle. Yet it was no more important to him than other anti-imperial conflicts he saw elsewhere in the world. In his "Latin Listening Post" conversation with Bill

Stuckey, Oswald stayed on message that what the FPCC was concerned with was the "principle" of non-intervention, as he said, "[I]n other words, keeping your hands off a foreign state." He told Stuckey, "We do not support the man. We do not support the individual. We support the idea of an independent revolution in the Western Hemisphere, free from American intervention. We do not support, as I say, the individual. If the Cuban people destroy Castro, or if he is otherwise proven to have betrayed his own revolution, that will not have any bearing upon this committee."

As has been noted, Oswald more clearly identified with New Left than any other ideological group. Like them, Oswald told the CPUS to get out of the way. He supported the New Left's ideas of more participatory democracy, less automation, less commercialism, no imperialism and more direct action. As they did, he took his intellectual inspiration from many sources. And also like them, he was ambivalent toward Kennedy. Paul Gregory's comments to the Warren Commission that Oswald expressed admiration for JFK have previously been noted. De Mohrenschildt's manuscript contains many passages where Oswald expressed favorable views about JFK.[296] Raymond Franklin Krystinik, who spoke with Oswald following the ACLU meeting, testified that Oswald told him, "Kennedy is doing a real fine job, a real good job," as far as civil rights were concerned.[297] Yet as we know he could be explosively negative about Kennedy, particularly with respect to the Bay of Pigs and the Cuban Missile Crisis. His dinner party conversation with Volkmar Schmidt and his alleged comment to "Leopoldo" that JFK should have been killed after the Bay of Pigs bear witness to this. A contradictory attitude towards liberalism and socialism was a distinguishing feature of both the New Left and Lee Harvey Oswald.

The divide between liberalism and socialism revolves around the perennial question of the relationship between the individual and the community and the more philosophical one between estrangement and unity.[298] As were Rousseau, Hegal and Marx, the New Left was cognizant of this problem. That Oswald had at least the intellectual capacity to recognize the question stemmed from his reading of Whitman, Orwell, Marx as well as, perhaps, Rousseau, who were preoccupied by the issue of self and the community. It is the major theme in Oswald's CE 98. He thought he had resolved it with his theoretical "Atheian System," which of course was much too simple as a philosophical model. It is unfortunate the essay was not developed in more detail. But its spirit and Oswald's desire to find "a system opposed to communism, socialism and capitalism" showed him dealing with a fundamental question in political theory.

The issue of estrangement and unity is one Oswald struggled with personally. Daniel Powers related to the Warren Commission that Oswald "was an individual who found it hard to come in close relationship to any one individual – it seems like about he was always striving for a relationship but whenever he did come, he would get into the group or something like that his – that this – just his general personality would alienate the group against him."[299] His marital relationship also reflected this. Although he loved his family, he was often separated from them and many times lived alone.

On the political level, this characteristic of Oswald—his estrangement from and unity with collectivist politics, his desire to protect his privacy and individualism while at the same time wanting to reach out to the world around him and change it—makes his political writings all the more important in understanding Oswald and his actions. As Norman Mailer has said, Oswald was a mystery but he was not necessarily an American one. He was an individual active in politics—a communal activity—but kept his true political thinking private. With the exception of *The Collective,* he did not let anyone read his political essays. McCarthyism, Red Scare politics and the actions of state police forces had left him wary about discussing heart-felt political ideas, especially if they were radical. Politics was therefore both a public and private affair for him. Although he at times openly demonstrated his leftist leanings while in the marines, he was relatively silent about his deeper thoughts and kept his planned defection a secret. He was under no illusion of the kind of society the Soviet Union was and therefore masked his real views when he applied for Soviet citizenship. Richard Snyder may have thought that his witticism "that as a Marxist he would be very lonesome in the Soviet Union"[300] went over his head but most likely it did not. Oswald, sensing that the Russians were listening to everything that was said in the embassy, was at a disadvantage. He had a far better understanding of socialism than Snyder would ever have, but he was forced to hold his tongue. While in Minsk, despite his genuine dislike of the American state-system, he made very few anti-American statements and didn't participate actively in Marxist reading circles at the factory. He never revealed his real reasons for wanting to return to America or his later decision to attempt to defect a second time. He felt he was forced to play the political chameleon. While he wanted a place on the established Left and strove to join forces with them, he sensed all their formations had shortcomings but was reluctant to reveal his dissent. Only in his private essays would his deep political convictions be articulated.

* * *

The Warren Commission, convinced of Lee's guilt and fixated upon psychobiography, chose the wrong methodology by which to study Oswald's politics. Focused on the triviality of Oswald's life experiences, it presented an ahistorical report which ignored the environmental factors that impacted upon his political development. It failed to identify the instruments of his political socialization. It missed his non-Marxian intellectual influences. It also missed the rise of the New Left even though by 1964 this new movement was becoming an important actor on the political stage.

The Commission dismissed the importance of his political writings, viewing them as irrelevant to what happened in Dealey Plaza. It was never particularly interested in the historical Oswald. It was only concerned about the life of the alleged assassin and what in his background might have motivated him to shoot JFK. The political essays were only "an expression of his own psychological condition." Whatever intellectual substance they contained could be ignored.

A key question then is how much evidentiary value are the essays? On the surface there seems to be contractions between them and his actions. Most of his essays point to his support for open, democratic politics. Yet, except for reference in CE 93 that as an organizer he infiltrated DRE, there is nothing in the essays about participating in clandestine activities and no direct discussion of the Walker shooting, the Clinton scenario or his visit to the Odios. With the exception of CE 92 and 93, there are no references to Cuba, although he seemed to enjoy the reputation of being a dedicated "Fidelista." As well, he never presented any theoretical defense for why he seemingly embraced Stalinism a second time, contradicting everything he said in CE 92 and 97.

Yet if examined closely, a great deal of his political activities are reflected in his writings. Many of the details of his defection appear in his *Historic Diary*. The political utopia he believed in and which he related to Alexandra de Mohrenschildt, that he "believed in the perfect government, free of want and need, and free of taxation, free of discrimination, free of any police force..." was described in *A System Opposed to the Communist*. His criticisms of the Soviet Union witnessed in his conversations with Paul Gregory, Francis Martello and others were ones he had made in *The Collective*. His actions in the New Orleans court house where he sat in the section reserved for Blacks reflected his opposition to segregation, which he talked about in *Speech Before*. If CE 97 can be interpreted somewhat broadly, even his actions on behalf of the Fair Play for Cuba Committee could be foretold when he discussed his intention to work hard and reach out to progressives.

What is often lost in the analysis of Lee's FPCC activities is his broader political vision, which held that after the "atomic catastrophe," there would be an opportunity to present an alternative to existing state-systems. In CE 25, Oswald claimed he alone would present this "alternative" with no help from anyone else. He said: "I despise the representatives of both systems whether they be socialist or Christian Democrats, whether they be Labor or Conservatives they are all products of the two systems." In CE 97 he moderated his views on political allies and started using the word "we." He talked now about the need for "a special party" and looked for support from "disenchanted members of the Socialist Party and even from more 'respected' (from a capitalist viewpoint) parties." This special party would be "steadfastly opposed to intervention by outside, relatively stable foreign powers, no matter where they come from." The goals of this "special party" at this stage were quite modest: "Membership in this organization implies adherence to the principle of simple distribution of information about this movement and acceptance of the idea of stoical readiness in regards to practical measures once instituted in the crisis." Written in March 1963, it preceded by a few weeks his first public support for the FPCC.

There appears to be a link between his FPCC activities and his nuclear holocaust theory. The FPCC was only a vehicle to attract progressive people into an anti-imperialist movement. His focus on Castro was only a means to what he considered a far more important end, that is: "the emplacement of a separate, democratic, pure communist society." Thoughts of assassinating the U.S. president for threats against the Cuban leader never factored into such a strategy and indeed would be counter-productive. Besides as evidenced by his November 9, 1963, letter to the Soviet Embassy and his visit to the Odio apartment with Leopoldo and Angelo, Oswald never personally held Castro or his government in high regard.

It not unreasonable to assume that the motives of Oswald, the accused assassin, lay in his political writings. The following is only interpretative. It does not offer "proof" that Oswald killed JFK—that can only be done conclusively through the physical evidence left in Dealey Plaza—nor does it prove what his motives may have been. On this we can only speculate, but hopefully in a more realistic way than was done by the Warren Commission. Nor does it show that Oswald was the only one to have a reason for murdering the president. Others may have had as well and may have been present in Dallas on November 22. What will be put forward is an ideological understanding of why Oswald may have wanted to shoot President Kennedy. Rather than being centered on deviant psychobehavioural factors, it is anchored to Lee's ideas and conclusions about the political world he lived in.

John F. Kennedy was the head of state for the United States and its most visible representative. As he rode by the Texas School Book Depository on that day in November in an open limousine, Kennedy was also its most vulnerable one. Based on the normative evidence of political ideas, the president was killed by Lee Harvey Oswald for four inter-dependent reasons: (1) as revealed in his political writings, Lee detested the modern State; (2) his political vision was being overtaken by world events; (3) he did not believe there was any way to either overthrow or reform the modern State; and (4) factions of the political formation in which he was ideologically aligned sanctioned such tactics.

Oswald's writings addressed a number of themes: civil rights, East-West relations, the danger of the rise of the ultra-right, the problems of capitalism, the de-humanizing effects of totalitarianism and the consequences of imperialism. But his one encompassing theme related to the modern State. By analyzing that theme, the clues as to his motives in wanting to kill JFK may be discovered.

CE 92 and CE 25, as well as the Neely Street essays, all focused on the State. Oswald was not necessarily interested in such issues as the definition of the State, or how States came into being. He was more interested in State forms. In CE 25 he discussed his reasons for opposing the form of the modern State and provided an alternative. In CE 98 Lee went into detail about his preferred State form calling it "The Atheian System," one which was opposed to communism, socialism and capitalism. Oswald never talked about reforming the State by altering its federal arrangements or decentralizing its functions through local structures. He adhered to the Marxist ideal of letting the State "wither away" as much as possible.

For Oswald, the modern State form included both the American and Soviet state-systems. From his perspective, he saw little difference between the two. In the first version of *Self-Questionnaire* Oswald asks, "What are the outstanding differences between the USSR and USA?" He answered, "None, except in the US the living standard is a little higher, freedoms are about the same, medical aid and the educational system in the USSR is better than in the USA." In CE 25 he wrote: "I have lived under both systems. I have sought the answers and although it would be very easy to dupe myself into believing one system is better than the other, I know they are not." In CE 102 Lee wrote: "In returning to the U.S. I have done nothing more or less than select the lesser of two evils." In CE 97 Oswald repeated that the Soviet and American States are basically the same: "No man, having known, having lived, under the Russian Communist and American capitalist systems, could possibly make a choice between them. There is no choice. One offers oppression, the other poverty. Both offer imperialistic injustice, tinted with two brands of slavery." Although at times he hinted there were qualitative differences—for example, in Version Two of CE 100, in CE 102, and in his beer conversation with Bill Stuckey—he continued to hold to his original hypothesis that there were no differences. At his arraignment for the murder of Officer Tippit at 7:10 PM Friday, November 22, Oswald shouted, "The way you are treating me, I'd might as well be in Russia."[301]

What linked the American and Soviet States for Oswald were four basic features: (1) lack of political and economic protection of the individual from the State; (2) imperialistic tendencies to search for markets and expand beyond their borders; (3) loss of tradition, ideals and social purpose; and (4) instability. Both were headed for a major clash and ultimate disaster. There was nothing about the modern State or its sub-systems worth saving. Certainly not its politicians, its ruling classes, its military or police organizations or its economic systems.

In Oswald's mind there were a myriad of reasons for detesting the State: for leading the world "into a dark generation of tension and fear," for the loss of America's "democratic ideals," for fighting for markets "which lead to the wars, crises and oppressive friction," for its imperialist action in the Far East and Cuba, for sanctioning racism and segregation, for its oppression of left wing radicals and other minorities, for championing capitalism and its exploitation of working people, and for letting America slip into "a general decay of classes…without real cultural foundations."

By assassinating the president, his motive was not to destroy the State as Bakunin and the Russian anarchists had advocated but to punish it and in doing so reveal its shallowness. Not tied to class analysis, Oswald allotted much more relative importance to the individual within the political system than traditional Marxist analysis allowed. Ideologically, the president was fair game. When Captain Fritz questioned him and said the president had been killed, Oswald, according to Fritz, replied, "people will forget that within a few days and there would be another president."[302] Oswald felt the State was so unfeeling that grief for its fallen leader would be short-lived. He could not have been more wrong. "A man so filled with life even Death was caught off guard,"[303] as the folk-singer Phil Ochs described JFK, and when he died, will never be forgotten.

A second possible reason for murdering the president was that not only was Oswald's personal world falling out from under him, so was his political world. He may have sensed the shortcomings of the New Left, that it had little sense of history, that it was reformist and undependable, and that it was naive to think that fundamental change would result from student activism. The central point of his political vision that there would be an atomic catastrophe or some internal crisis that would destroy the modern State was becoming more and more obsolete. Oswald was witness to the fact that while the crises in Laos, the Congo, West Berlin and Cuba were serious and scary, they did not produce the holocaust he expected. The world was slowly and steadily moving to peaceful coexistence. Historian Walter L. Hixson writes that the Cuban Missile Crisis "had the salutary effect of sobering both leaders about the real dangers of nuclear war, and it broke the impasse in the ongoing test-ban negotiations. In 1963 the two superpowers established a hot line for instant communication in the midst of any future crisis and signed the Limited Test Ban Treaty terminating above-ground nuclear tests. A new era of détente had begun...." [304] In his undelivered Trade Mart speech, JFK pledged that the United States ask "that we may be worthy of our power and responsibility, that we may exercise our strength with wisdom and restraint, and that we may achieve in our time and for all time the ancient vision of "peace on earth, good will toward men." Oswald may have been too adolescent and unbending to re-assess his fundamental political vision.

Yet there were many on the radical Left who also detested the modern State, but they had no intention of murdering its president. What distinguished Oswald from those militants was his lack of a theory of revolution.[305] He did not believe in revolution for two basic reasons. First it was unnecessary. As he said in CE 97: "We have no interest in violently opposing the U.S. Government. Why should we manifest opposition when there are far greater forces at work to bring about the fall of the United States Government than we could ever possible muster." The forthcoming holocaust would do the job nicely.

The second reason was that Oswald, like George Orwell, was skeptical about the success of any revolution. During his interview on "Latin Listening Post," he talked about the Cuban revolution, telling Bill Stuckey "[u]ndoubtedly, the overwhelming majority of people during last year, for instance, who have fled Cuba have been non-Batistaites, rather peasant class. You say the revolution is supposed to benefit these people. You know, it's very funny about revolutions. Revolutions require work, revolutions require sacrifice, revolutions and our own included, require a certain amount of sacrifice." The masses could not be relied upon to carry out revolutionary or even reformist goals. Stemming from his generally negative view of humanity, he doubted their desire or ability to do so. As he said in CE 97: "[A]ny organization cleverly manipulating words may sway the masses." To think that the New Left could build a broad-based radical coalition of Blacks, poor people and students who would bring real change to the State structure was living in a dream-world.

As for the State reforming itself, Oswald held out little hope. While he may have applauded Kennedy's efforts at civil rights reform, the modern State was too much of an "Iron Heel" to fundamentally alter. He did make a tentative step to try out the reform option as shown by his November 1 application to join the ACLU and his letter to Arnold Johnson. Yet that was scuttled by the visit of FBI Agent Hosty to the Paine residence the very same day. Hosty wanted to know where Lee worked, where he was living and about his political views and activities. Marina, knowing how the KGB operated, was frightened by Hosty's visit and felt he was there to embarrass or harass her. She begged Hosty not to interfere with Lee at his work.[306] When Oswald learned about the visit, Marina felt that Lee "was a changed man." He told Marina that the next time the FBI came she was to note the colour of their car, what model it was and to write down the license plate number.[307] Hosty had destroyed any notion Oswald may have entertained about reforming the State.

Four days later Hosty returned to the Paine residence, this time asking if Ruth "thought this was a mental problem, referring to Lee Oswald," implying that he might be mentally unstable.[308] Hosty's question revealed his sheer political ignorance about dissident politics and the radical left. As instructed by her husband, Marina got the information Lee had requested, which he later wrote down in his *Address Book*. In the November 5 interview, Ruth appealed to Hosty not to come again because "news of his first visit had upset Lee very badly."[309]

At some point after this second visit on November 5 and on or before November 12, Oswald went down to the FBI office and left Hosty a note. One of the enduring mysteries of the Kennedy assassination has been the note's contents. The letter can never appear as part of the historical record because Hosty destroyed it. Nannie Lee Fenner, the FBI receptionist to whom Oswald gave the note, said that when Oswald dropped it off he had a "wild look in his eye" and was "awfully fidgety." She said the note read in part, "I will either blow up the Dallas Police Department or the FBI office."[310] Hosty denied the note was threatening and claimed it said, in effect, "If you want to talk to me, you should talk to me to my face. Stop harassing my wife and stop trying to ask her about me. You have no right to harass her."[311] Hosty said he destroyed the note on orders of J. Gordon Shanklin, his superior. Shanklin denied this. The HSCA concluded: "Because the note had been destroyed, it was not possible to establish with confidence what its contents were."[312]

The Hosty note has usually been seen in the context of Oswald's relationship with the FBI; that is, whether he might have been an informant, or why Oswald did not want the FBI to talk to Marina. Whatever the contents were, the Hosty note was a key indicator of Oswald's relationship with the State itself. At a minimum, it was a sign that Oswald had abandoned any theory of reforming the State. If Fenner can be believed, it showed Lee was contemplating direct action.

While his ideas may have encouraged him to assassinate the president, they would have been without meaning if the tactics of 1960s radicalism forbade such acts. To understand the totality of his politics, it is incumbent to know where Lee Harvey Oswald really stood on the political continuum. As noted, it is clear that he can be defined as part of the New Left. But which part? Lacking any centralized structure or overall unity, the New Left was composed of various political views. An important component were those who subscribed to "volunteerism," the performance of individual radical actions with little regard to objective conditions. As Julie Stephens has shrewdly observed, the 1960s "marked a breakdown in the revolutionary model of political change."[313] In her book *Anti-Disciplinary Protest: Sixties Radicalism and Postmodernism*, Stephens notes that alongside the student-driven, liberal-oriented New Left, there also emerged a variant that she describes as anti-disciplinary politics. This radicalism "boasted no list of demands, no party, no aims and ideology and no leaders and no followers." In their desire "to make the revolution your own," these activists displayed little ideological coherence. This new political phenomenon, which included the likes of the Yippies and the Diggers, attempted "to forge a new politics uncontaminated by the perceived failures of vanguardist parties."[314]

Stephens analysis is very helpful. However, it must be realized that as the '60s dragged on and the Vietnam War became more controversial, this individual anti-disciplinary determination to just "do it" morphed into disciplined and more dangerous political formations like the Weatherman and the Red Army Faction who advocated armed struggle and the overthrow of established power. In their communiqués the Weatherman wanted to bring the war "back home." Some claimed they wished to create sufficient terror that would bring fascism. They hoped to deal not in abstract violence but "to show what violence is really like" and "to turn New York into Saigon."[315]

The New Left's progression from left liberalism to nihilism broke the heart of many "Old Leftists" who had given their lives in attempting to build a revolutionary community in a non-revolutionary situation. One such individual was Joseph R. Starobin, the former foreign editor of the CPUS's *Daily Worker*, who later became a professor at Glendon College, York University, in Toronto. In 1972 Starobin wrote critically of the New Left's penchant to "just do it." While praising the New Left for making radical ideas legitimate in America, "something older radicals never quite succeeded in doing," Starobin observed:

> Yet this same new left hardly recognizes where
> the "revolution" is. All the historic weaknesses
> are present in a fashion heartbreaking to anyone
> with a historical experience and perspective: the
> belief that change must be instant, the impatience

with concrete achievements, the attempt to demand more of any situation than it can give, the hallucinatory fascination with revolutions among less-developed peoples as though these can be imitated in more complex societies or hold any universal lessons, and thus the suicidal alienation from one's own society. This new left, when confronted by setback or the slowness in the diffusion of its message among the less swiftly moving mass, looks for the explanation within itself, as though the cure lies in self-purification and as though by some heroic voluntarism, some great act of will, the process of historical change can be forced forward. The result is a terrible factionalism, a self-destroying narcissism: have we not seen it all before? The new left's impatience with humble and ordinary people, engaged in the everyday work which sustains their lives and which they try to make satisfying and creative in contradictory circumstances becomes a form of elitism, because the new left believes that everything can be accomplished by self, by a heightened sensibility, and by a defiance of history. This elitism is all the more alienating because it speaks in the name of those humble and ordinary people.[316]

Starobin cried out against, in his words, "the impulse to 'do it,' that terrible slogan which [a Berkeley student] has now made into a career as well as a species of anarcho-syndicalist ideology...." Starobin concluded: "[T]his most corrupting variety of impotence that tries to hurdle the barriers it has erected by violent volunteerism – which had plagued the American left for generations – demonstrates its folly...What is the meaning of this collapse, this denial of those personal-political obligations, those ties of regard for parents, children, friends, students, colleagues which alone can be the foundation of a genuine radicalism – in the name of selfish, demonstrative, 'doing-it' wrapped in Guevarist, Fanonist, or Maoist robes? It is the repudiation of history. It is the terrible price of historical discontinuity."[317]

Lee Oswald was neither a Yippie nor a Weatherman but did belong to the "volunteerist" strain of New Left thinking so well described by Professor Starobin. In the end, he showed himself to be nothing more than a violent volunteerist who lost his sense of history which he once told Paul Gregory he loved so much, violated all tenets of democracy that philosophically he claimed to believe in, and broke his obligations to his children whom he cherished.

The hypothesis that Oswald's motive stemmed from a desire to punish is far from original. Many, including the Warren Commissioners, saw Oswald as basically misanthropic and that "he expressed his hatred for American society and acted in protest against it."[318] However, his actions on November 22, 1963, flowed not from a variety of psychological characteristics but those based on political ideology. If such an analysis is correct, the Kennedy assassination must be seen as an act of political terrorism.

Oswald was determined not to make the State's job any easier in investigating his crime and once again became a chameleon. He told Captain Fritz that he had no politics, that he did not shoot the president, that he did not shoot Officer Tippit, that he did not go to Mexico City, that he did not own a rifle, that he did not carry a long package into the Depository, that it was not his picture in the Backyard Photographs and that he had never lived on Neely Street. He also told Fritz that he did not want to talk about his Fair Play for Cuba card that was signed by A. Hidell. He is reported to have said, "You have the card. Now you know as much about it as I do."[319]

Norman Mailer was convinced that at his forthcoming trial, Oswald "would expound his ideas," that it "would be one of the greatest trials in American history if not the greatest" and "he would become famous and might have an effect on history even if he was executed."[320] This supposition is far from clear. Oswald, the public activist but private political thinker, the one unified with the revolutionary cause but estranged from the revolution, might well have vented about American policy toward Cuba and the evils of the capitalist system, but he most likely would not have explained the ideas behind his political writings. If properly cross-examined, they would have incriminated him. It is most probable that like the Rosenbergs, he would have maintained his ideological innocence to the very end.

We can also speculate about whether ideology was a factor in Oswald's alleged killing of Officer Tippit and Jack Ruby's very real murder of Oswald. We still don't know why Tippit stopped a man who resembled Oswald on Tenth Street in the Oak Cliff section of Dallas. The Warren Commission only guessed that "Tippit must have heard the description of the suspect wanted for the President's shooting" and it was for that reason "Tippit stopped a man walking east along the south side of Patterson."[321] It may be Tippit had other reasons for stopping the pedestrian. Oswald may have baited him. His dislike of the police as agents for the State was in keeping with his political views, and if his "volunteerism" had already reached the point that he was prepared to shoot the State's most powerful representative, he might not have hesitated to kill Tippit, one of its lesser representatives. That murder was carried out with a great deal of vengeance: Tippit was shot four times at very close range.

One can paint another picture of Jack Ruby besides that of a Kennedy sympathizer who shot Oswald so that the president's widow would not have to return to Dallas or one associated with the mob. Far from being apolitical as some have suggested,

Ruby was someone who was much in sympathy with right-wing extremism. We know that Ruby had contacts with Texas ultra-right militants, including Giles Miller, a Dallas businessman and an extreme right winger.[322] We know he had transcripts in his car of the far right anti-communist radio show "LIFE LINE" sponsored by the family of H. L. Hunt, the fanatically anti-communist oil billionaire,[323] when he went on Sunday morning to the Western Union Office to wire money to one of his dancers. The day before he had given a copy of a speech from "LIFE LINE" called "Heroism" to Russell Lee Moore (Knight) and according to Moore talked disapprovingly of radicals in Dallas.[324] H. L. Hunt disliked JFK intensively and had funded the dissemination of copies of a sermon by a Baptist minister in 1960 that said the "the election of a Catholic as president would mean the end of religious freedom in America."[325] Ruby's work as a courier to get mafia figures out of Castro prisons showed he had no love for the communists. That he was attuned to Oswald's left-wing activities was revealed by his correcting District Attorney Henry M. Wade at the Friday night press conference that the proper name for Oswald's New Orleans organization was not the "Free Cuba Committee" but the "Free Play for Cuba Committee." His description of Oswald immediately upon fatally shooting him as "you rat" and "the son of a bitch" may have stemmed from his hatred of communists. On the afternoon of the assassination, he visited his sister, Eva L. Grant, and as they both watched the television news about Oswald's arrest, Eva told Jack that Oswald was a "barbarian" and said, "That lousy Commie. Don't worry, the Commie, we will get him." Eva then heard Ruby say, "What a creep."[326] Many members of the Dallas Police Department most probably held little sympathy for "the communist" Oswald. Allegations have been made that one-half of the DPD members were also members of the Ku Klux Klan.[327] If any officers helped Ruby enter the basement of the Dallas Police Department that Sunday morning, their motive may well have been ideological.

This has only been an interpretative essay of Oswald's politics. Students of the Kennedy assassination can make their own analysis by reading his essays, letters and other documents, which appear in the Appendices. These are modified versions since Oswald, possibly suffering from dyslexia, was a notoriously poor speller and unstructured writer. As Norman Mailer did when publishing excerpts of *The Collective* in *Oswald's Tale: An American Mystery*, Oswald's writing has often been corrected since "[v]ery few people have patience to read a writer who spells badly."[328] Those wishing to view the writings of the historical record may do so by reading the exhibits published in the Warren Commission volumes.

PART TWO

APPENDICES

Appendix One - The Political Essays and Other Documents

1.1 Commission Exhibit 24 (*Historic Diary*, 16 H 94-105)

From October 16 1959 Arrival - Leaving

October 16 (1959). Arrive from Helsinki by train. Am met by Intourist Representative and in car to Hotel "Berlin." Register as "student." Five day luxury tourist ticket. Meet my Intourist guide Rima Sherikova. I explain to her I wish to apply for Russian citizenship. She is flabbergasted, but agrees to help. She checks with her boss, main office Intourist. Then helps me address a letter to Supreme Soviet asking for citizenship. Meanwhile boss telephones Passport and Visa Office and notifies them about me.

October17. Rima meets me for Intourist sightseeing. Says we must continue with this. Although I am too nervous, she is "sure" I'll have an answer soon. Asks me about myself and my reasons for doing this. I explain I am a communist, etc. She is politely sympathetic but uneasy now. She tries to be a friend to me. She feels sorry for me. I am something new.

Sunday October 18. My 20th birthday. We visit exhibit in the morning and in the afternoon the Lenin-Stalin tomb. She gives me a present, the book "Idiot" by Dostoevsky.

October 19. Tourism. Am anxious since my visa is good for five days only and still no word from authorities about my request.

October 20. Rima in the afternoon says Intourist was notified by the Passport and Visa Department that they want to see me. I am excited greatly by this news.

October 21 (morning). Meeting with single official. Balding stout, black suit fairly good English, asks what do I want? I say Soviet citizenship. He asks why? I give vague answers about "Great Soviet Union." He tells me "USSR only great in literature." Wants me to go back home. I am stunned; I reiterate. He says he shall check and let me know whether my visa will be extended (it expires today).

Evening 6.00. Receive word from police official. I must leave country tonight at 8.00 P.M. as visa expires. I am shocked!! My dreams! I retire to my room. I have $100 left. I have waited for two years to be accepted. My fondest dreams are shattered because of a petty official. Because of bad planning. I planned too much! 7.00 P.M. I decide to end it. Soak wrist in cold water to numb the pain. Then slash my left wrist. Then plug wrist into bathtub of hot water. I think "when Rima comes at 8 to find me dead, it will be a great shock." Somewhere, a violin plays, as I watch my life whirl away. I think to myself, "How easy to die" and a sweet death (to violins). About 8.00, Rima finds me unconscious (bathtub water a rich red color). She screams (I remember that) and runs for help. Ambulance comes, am taken to hospital where five stitches are put in my wrists. Poor Rima stays by my side as interpreter (my Russian is still very bad) far into the night. I tell her, "go home" (my mood is bad) but she stays. She is "my friend." She has a strong will. Only at this moment I notice she is pretty.

October 22. Hospital. I am in a small room with about twelve others (sick persons), two orderlies, and a nurse. The room is very drab as well as the breakfast. Only after prolonged (two hours) observation of the other patients do I realize I am in the Insanity Ward. This realization disquiets me. Later in afternoon, I am visited by Rima. She comes in with two doctors. As intern, she must ask me medical questions. "Did you know what you were doing?" Answer "yes." "Did you blackout?" "No," etc. I then complain about poor food. The doctors laugh. Apparently this is a good sign. Later they leave. I am alone with Rima (amongst the mentally ill). She encourages me and scolds me. She says she will help me get transferred to another section of hospital (not for insane) where food is good.

October 23. Transferred to ordinary ward, (airy, good food) but nurses suspicious of me. (They know). Afternoon. I am visited by Rosa Agafonova of the hotel tourist office, who asks me about my health. Very beautiful, excellent English, very merry and kind. She makes me very glad to be alive. Later Rima visits.

October 24. Hospital routine. Rima visits me in afternoon.

October 25. Hospital routine. Rima visits me in the afternoon.

October 26. An elderly American at the hospital grows suspicious about me for some reason. Because at Embassy I told him I had not registered as most tourists and I am, in general, evasive about my presence in Moscow and at hospital. Afternoon Rima visits.

October 27. Stitches are taken out by doctor with "dull" scissor.

Wednesday October 28. Morning. Leave hospital in Intourist car with Rima for Hotel "Berlin." Later I change hotels to "Metropole." All clothes packed, and money from my room (to the last kopeck) returned, as well as watch, ring. Ludmilla Dimitrova (Intourist Office Head) and Rosa invite me to come and sit and talk with them anytime. I get lonesome at new hotel. They feel sorry for me. Rima notifies me that Passport and Registration Office wishes to see me about my future. Later Rima and car pick me up and we enter the offices to find four officials waiting for me (all unknown to me). They ask how my arm is, I say O.K. They ask "Do you want to go to your homeland?" I say no I want Soviet citizenship. I say I want to reside in the Soviet Union. They say they will see about that. Than they ask me about the lone official with whom I spoke in the first place (apparently he did not pass along my request at all but thought to simply get rid of me by not extending my Soviet visa at the time I requested it). I describe him (they make notes). What papers do you have to show who and what you are? I give them my discharge papers from the Marine Corps. They say wait for our answer. I ask how long? Not soon. Later Rima comes to check on me. I feel insulted and insult her.

October 29. Hotel Room 214. Metropole Hotel. I wait. I worry. I eat once, stay next to phone, worry. I keep fully dressed.

October 30. Hotel Room. I have been in hotel three days. It seems like three years. I must have some sort of a showdown!

October 31. I make my decision. Getting passport at 12:00, I meet and talk with Rima for a few minutes. She says: stay in your room and eat well. I don't tell her about what I intend to do, since I know she would not approve. After she leaves, I wait a few minutes and than I catch a taxi. "American Embassy" I say.

At 12:30, I arrive at the American Embassy. I walk in and say to the receptionist, "I would like to see the Consular." She points at a large ledger and says, "If you are a tourist please register." I take out my American passport and lay it in the desk. "I have come to dissolve my American citizenship," I say matter-of-factly. She rises and enters the office of Richard Snyder, American Head Consular in Moscow at that time. He invites me to sit down. He finishes a letter he is typing and then asks what he can do for me. I tell him I have decided to take Soviet citizenship and would like to legally dissolve my U.S. citizenship. His assistant (now <u>Head</u> Consular) McVickar looks up from his work. Snyder takes down personal information, asks questions, warns me not to take any steps before the Soviets accept me. Says I am a "fool," and says the dissolution papers are a long time in preparing. (In other words refuses to allow me at that time to dissolve U.S. citizenship.) I state, "my mind is make up. From this day forward I consider myself no citizen of the U.S.A." I spend forty minutes at the Embassy before Snyder says, "Now unless you wish to expound on your Marxist beliefs, you can go." "I wish to dissolve U.S. citizenship." Not today, he says in effect. I leave Embassy, elated at this showdown. Returning to my hotel, I feel now my energies are not spent in vain. I'm sure Russians will accept me after this sign of my faith in them.

Portion of Historic Diary (CE 101, 16 H 440)

12:30. Arrive in "Bolga" type taxi. Two Russian policemen stand at the Embassy, one salutes as I approach one entrance of the Embassy and says "Passport." I smile and show my passport. He motions me to pass inside as I wish. There can be little doubt I'm sure in his mind that I'm an American. Light overcoat, no hat or scarf and non-Russian button down shirt and tie. Entering I find the office of "Consular" sign, opening the door I go in. A secretary busy typing looks up. "Yes?" she says "I'd like to see the Consular," I say. "Will you sign the tourist register please," she says dryly, going back to her typing. "Yes, but before I'll do that, I'd like to see the Consular," laying my passport on her desk, as she looks puzzled. "I'm here to dissolve my American citizenship." She rises and taking my passport goes into the open inner office, where she lays the passport on a man's desk, saying "there is a Mr. Oswald outside, who says he's here to dissolve his U.S. citizenship." "OK" the man says. "Thanks," he says to the girl without looking up from his typing. She, as she comes out, invites me into the inner office to sit down. I do so, selecting an armchair to the front left side of Snyder's desk (it was Snyder whom I talked to, Head Consular). I wait, crossing my legs and laying my gloves in my lap. He finishes typing, removes the letter from his typewriter and adjusting his glasses looks at me. "What can I do for you" he asks, leafing through my passport. "I'm here to dissolve my U.S. citizenship and would like to sign the legal papers to that effect." "Have you applied for Russian citizenship?" "Yes." He takes out a piece of paper and says "before we get to that I'd like some personal information." He asks name, personal information to which I answer, then "your reasons for coming." I say I have experienced life in the U.S., American military life, American imperialism. I am a Marxist, and I waited two years for this. I don't want to live in the U.S. or be burdened by American citizenship. He says OK. "That's all unless you want to propound your 'Marxist beliefs' you can go." I said "I've requested that I be allowed to sign legal papers divesting myself of U.S. citizenship. Do you refuse me that right?" He says: "Ugh, no but the papers will take some time to get ready. In the meantime where are you staying?" "Room 212 at the Metrople," I state, angry at being refused a right. I start to leave. "You'll tell us what the Russians do next." I turn very mad. "Of course" I say and leave.

2:00. A knock. A reporter by the name of Goldstein wants an interview. I'm flabbergasted. "How did you find out?" "The Embassy called us," he said. I send him away. I sit and realize this is one way to bring pressure on me. By notifying my relations in the U.S. through the newspapers. Although they would say "it's for the public record." A half hour later another reporter, Miss Mosby, comes. I answer a few quick questions after refusing an interview. I am surprised at the interest. I get phone call from "Time." At night, a phone call from the States. I refuse all calls without finding out who is it from. I feel non-depulsed because of the attention. 10:00 I retire.

November 1. More reporters. Three phone calls from brother and mother. Now I feel slightly exhilarated, not so lonely.

November 2-15. Days of utter loneliness. I refuse all reporters' phone calls. I remain in my room. I am racked with dysentery.

November 15. I decide to give an interview. I have Miss Mosby's card so I call her. She drives right over. I give my story, allow pictures. Later, story is distorted, sent without my permission, that is: before I ever saw and OK'd her story. Again I feel slightly better because of the attention.

Nov. 16. A Russian official comes to my room, asks how I am. Notifies me I can remain in USSR 'til some solution is found with what to do with me. It is comforting news for me.

Diary Addendum of Interview with Reporter Miss Mosby
(CE 24, Dallas Municipal Archives and Records Center; see also Holloway, *op. cit.*, pp. 27, 234)

Diary Interview November 14 with Miss Mosby. Miss Mosby enters. Greets me and sits down. I start by saying I wish it understood that I wish to see the story before it is sent. "All right" she says. It's all the same to me what you do in regards to your life. I'm just taking down your words." O.K. I say. First the reasons for my coming. She asks about military service.

I answer questions about my military service and then she asks why did you apply for Soviet citizenship? What are your reasons for coming here? I have waited for two years in order to dissolve my American citizenship. I have seen too much hate and injustice in the U.S. I had served in the occupation forces in Japan: an occupation of a country is imperialistic, what the Russians call "imperialism." I have chosen a Socialist country since there are two main systems in the world.

"Why the USSR?" she asks. "Why not Czechoslovakia where the housing problem is not bad?" "I have chosen the USSR since it is the leader of the Socialist camp and the symbolic champion of the cause of communism." "What other reasons led you to change your loyalty?" "In the U.S., as we know, there are many shortcomings. Racial segregation and the suppression of the under-dog, the U.S. Communist Party."

"How long have you been studying Marxism?" "I first started studying 'Marxism' when I was fifteen." I always had to dig for my books in the back, dusty shelves of libraries and old outdated books were the backbone of my reading. Books on philosophy, political economy, etc. "In my library in the most obvious places there are the prominent anti-communist books we know so well but as I say I always had to dig for my books."

"What were some impressions you got serving in the occupation forces?" "I saw the American military hauling cannons up a mountain side, the tools of war and opposition. I learned to hate the U.S. imperialistic military." Thank you she says. End.

November 17 - December 30. I have bought myself two self-teaching Russian language books. I force myself to study eight hours a day. I sit in my room and read and memorize words. All meals I take in my room. Rima arranged that. It is very cold on the streets, so I rarely go outside at all. For this month and a half, I see no one, speak to no one, except every now and then Rima, who calls the Ministry about me. Have they forgotten? During December I paid no money to the hotel, but Rima told hotel I was expecting a lot of money from USA. I have $28 left. This month I was called to the passport office and met three new officials who asked me the same questions I answered a month before. They appear not to know me at all.

December 31. New Years' Eve, I spend in the company of Rosa Agafonova at the Hotel Berlin. She has the duty. I sit with her until past midnight. She gives me a small "Boratin" clown for a New Years' present. She is very nice. I found out only recently she is married, has small son who was born crippled. That is why she is so strangely tender and compelling.

January 1 – 4 (1960). No change in routine.

January 4. I am called to passport office and finally given a Soviet document, not the Soviet citizenship as I so wanted, only a Residence document. Not even for foreigners but a paper called, "for those without citizenship." Still I am happy. The official says they are sending me to the city of "Minsk." I ask, "is that in Siberia?" He only laughs. He also tells me that they have arranged for me to receive some money through the Red Cross to pay my hotel bills and expenses. I thank the gentleman and leave later in the afternoon. I see Rima. She asks, "are you happy?" "Yes."

January 5. I go to Red Cross in Moscow for money with Interpreter (a new one). I receive 5,000 rubles, a huge sum!! Later in Minsk I am to earn seventy rubles a month at the factory.

January 7. I leave Moscow by train for Minsk, Belorussia. My hotel bill was 2,200 rubles and the train ticket to Minsk 150 rubles so I have a lot of money and hope. I wrote my brother and mother letters in which I said, "I do not wish to ever contact you again. I am beginning a new life and I don't want <u>any part</u> of the old."

January 7. <u>Diary Minsk.</u> Arrive in Minsk, met by two women Red Cross workers. We go to hotel "Minsk." I take room and meet Rosa and Stellina, two persons from Intourist in hotel who speak English. Stellina is in 40's, nice, married, young child. Rosa about 23, blond, attractive, unmarried, excellent English. We attract each other at once.

January 8. I meet the city mayor, Comrade Shrapof, who welcomes me to Minsk, promises a rent-free apartment "soon," and warns me about "uncultured persons" who sometimes insult foreigners. My interpreter: Roman Detkof, Head Foreign Technical Institute, next door.

January 10.The day to myself I walk through city. Very nice.

January 11. I visit Minsk radio factory where I shall work. There I meet Argentinian immigrant Alexander Ziger. Born a Polish Jew. Immigrated to Argentina in 1938 and back to Polish homeland (now part of Belorussia) in 1955.Speaks English with American accent. He worked for an American company in Argentina. He is the head of a Department, a qualified Engineeer, in late 40's, mild mannered, likable. He seems to want to tell me something. I show him my temporary documents and say soon I shall have Russian citizenship.

January 13 – 16. I work as a "checker" metal worker. Pay: 700 rubles a month. Work very easy. I am learning Russian quickly. Now, everyone is very friendly and kind. I meet many young

Russian workers my own age. They have varied personalities. All wish to know about me, even offer to hold a mass meeting so I can say. I refuse politely. At night I take Rosa to the theater, movie, or opera almost every day. I'm living big and am very satisfied. I receive a check from the Red Cross every fifth of the month "to help." The check is 700 rubles. Therefore, every month I make 1,400 rubles, about the same as the director of the factory! Ziger observes me during this time. I don't like picture of Lenin which watches from its place of honour and physical training at 11.-11.10 each morning (compulsary) for all (shades of H.G. Wells!!).

March 16. I receive a small flat, one-room kitchen-bath near the factory (eight minutes walk) with splendid view from two balconies of the river, almost rent free (60 rubles a month). It is a Russian's dream.

March 17 - April 31. Work. I have lost contact with Rosa after my house moving. I meet Pavel Golavacha, a young man my age, friendly, very intelligent, an excellent radio technician. His father is General Golovacha Commander of Northwestern Siberia, twice hero of USSR in W.W. II.

May 1 - May Day came as my first holiday. All factories, etc., closed. After spectacular military parade, all workers parade past reviewing stand, waving flags and pictures of Mr. K., etc. I follow the American custom of marking a holiday by sleeping in in the morning. At night I visit with the Zigers' daughters at a party thrown by them. About 40 people came, many of Argentinian origin. We dance and play around and drink until 2 A.M. when party breaks up. Leonara Ziger oldest daughter, 26, formally married, now divorced, a talented singer. Anita Ziger, 20, very gay, not so attractive but we hit it off. Her boyfriend, Alfred, is a Hungarian chap, silent, and brooding, not at all like Anita. Ziger advises me to go back to U.S.A. It's the first voice of opposition I have heard. I respect Ziger, he has seen the world. He says many things and relates many things I do not know about the U.S.S.R. I begin to feel uneasy inside, it's true!

June-July. Summer months of green beauty. Pine forest very deep. I enjoy many Sundays in the environments of Minsk with the Zigers who have a car, "Mosivich." Alfred always goes along with Anita. Leonara seems to have no permanent boyfriend but many admirers. She has a beautiful Spanish figure, long black hair, like Anita. I never pay much attention to her. She's too old for me. She seems to dislike my lack of attention for some reason. She is high strung. I have become habituated to a small cafe, which is where I dine in the evening. The food is generally poor and always exactly the same menu in any cafe, at any point in the city. The food is cheap and I don't really care about quality after three years in the U.S.M.C.

August-September. As my Russian improves, I become increasingly conscious of just what sort of a society I live in. Mass gymnastics, compulsary afterwork meeting. Usually political information meeting. Compulsary attendence at lectures and the sending of the entire shop collective (except me) to pick potatoes on a Sunday, at a State collective farm. A "patriotic duty" to bring in the harvest. The opinions of the workers (unvoiced) are that it's a great pain in the neck. They don't seem to be especially enthusiastic about any of the "collective" duties, a natural feeling. I am increasingly aware of the presence, in all things, of Lebizen, shop party secretary, fat, fortyish, and jovial on the outside. He is a no-nonsense party regular.

October. The coming of fall. My dread of a new Russian winter is mellowed in splendid golds and reds of fall in Belorussia. Plums, peaches, apricots, and cherries abound for these last fall weeks. I am a healthy brown color and stuffed with fresh fruit (at other times of the year unobtainable).

October 18. My 21st birthday sees Rosa, Pavel, Ella at a small party at my place. Ella, a very attractive Russian Jew I have been going walking with lately, works at the radio factory also. Rosa and Ella are jealous of each other. It brings a warm feeling to me. Both are at my place for the first time. Ella and Pavel both give ashtrays (I don't smoke). We have a laugh.

November. Finds the approach of winter now. A growing loneliness overtakes me in spite of my conquest of Ennatachina, a girl from Riga, studying at the music conservatory in Minsk. After an affair which lasts a few weeks, we part.

November 15. In November, I make the acquaintance of four girls rooming at the Foreign Language dormitory in room 212. Nell is very interesting, so is Tomka, Tomis and Alla. I usually go to the Institute dormitory with a friend of mine who speaks English very well. Erich Titovets is in the fourth year at the medical institute. Very bright fellow. At the dormitory we six sit and talk in English.

December 1. I am having a light affair with Nell Korobka.

January 1 (1961). New Years I spend at home of Ella German. I think I'm in love with her. She has refused my more dishonorable advances. We drink and eat in the presence of her family in a very hospitable atmosphere. Later I go home drunk and happy. Passing the river homeward, I decide to propose to Ella.

January 2. After a pleasant hand-in-hand walk to the local cinema, we come home, standing on the doorstep I propose. She hesitates, then refuses. My love is real but she has none for me. Her reason besides lack of love; I am American and someday might be arrested simply because of that. Example: Polish intervention in the 20s' led to the arrest of all people in the Soviet Union of Polish origin. "You understand the world situation. There is too much against you and you don't even know it." I am stunned. She snickers at my awkwardness. In turning to go (I am too stunned to think!) I realize she was never serious with me but only exploited my being an American in order to get the envy of the other girls who consider me different from the Russian boys. I am miserable!

January 3. I am miserable about Ella. I love her but what can I do? It is the state of fear which was always in the Soviet Union.

January 4. One year after I received the residence document I am called in to the passport office and asked if I want citizenship (Russian). I say no simply extend my residential passport to agree and my document is extended until January 4, 1962.

January 4-31. I am starting to reconsider my desire about staying. The work is drab, the money I get has nowhere to be spent. No nightclubs or bowling alleys, no places of recreation except the trade union dances. I have had enough.

February 1ˢᵗ. Make my first request to American Embassy, Moscow, for reconsidering my position. I stated, "I would like to go back to U.S."

February 28ᵗʰ. I receive letter from Embassy. Richard E. Snyder stated, "I could come in for an interview any time I wanted."

March 1-16. I now live in a state of expectation about going back to the U.S. I confided in Ziger. He supports my judgment but warns me not to tell any Russians about my desire to return. I understand now why.

March 17. I and Erich went to trade union dance. Boring, but at the last hour I am introduced to a girl with a French hair-do and red-dress with white slippers. I dance with her, then ask to show her home. I do, along with five other admirers. Her name is Marina. We like each other right away. She gives me her phone number and departs home with a not-so-new friend in a taxi. I walk home.

March 18-31. We walk. I talk a little about myself, she talks a lot about herself. Her name is Marina N. Prusakova.

Apr. 1st-30. We are going steady and I decide I must have her. She puts me off so on April 15, I propose. She accepts.

April 31. After a seven day delay at the marriage bureau because of my unusual passport, they allow us to register as man and wife. Two of Marina's girlfriends act as bridesmaids. We are married at her aunt's home. We have a dinner reception for about twenty friends and neighbors who wish us happiness (in spite of my origin and accent), which was in general disquieting to any Russian since foreigners are very rare in the Soviet Union, even tourist. After an evening of eating and drinking in which Uncle Wooser started a fight and the fuse blew on an overloaded circuit. We take our leave and walk the fifteen minutes to our home. We lived near each other. At midnight we were home.

May 1st. May Day 1961. Found us thinking about our future. In spite of fact I married Marina to hurt Ella, I found myself in love with Marina.

May. The transition of changing full love from Ella to Marina was very painful, especially as I saw Ella almost every day at the factory. But as the days and weeks went by, I adjusted more and more to my wife mentally. I still hadn't told my wife of my desire to return to US. She is madly in love with me from the very start. Boat rides on Lake Minsk, walks throughout the parks, evening at home, or Aunt Valia's place mark May.

June. A continuence of May, except that we draw closer and closer and I think very little now of Ella. In the last days of this month, I reveal my longing to return to America. My wife is slightly startled. But then encourages me to do what I wish to do.

July. I decided to take my two week vacation and travel to Moscow (without police permission) to the American Embassy to see about getting my U.S. passport back and make arrangements for my wife to enter the U.S. with me.

July 8. I fly by plane to Minsk on an iL-20. 2 hrs 20 minutes later, after taking a tearful and anxious parting from my wife, I arrive in Moscow. Departing by bus from the airfield, I arrive in the center of the city. Making my way through heavy traffic, I don't come in sight of the Embassy until 3:00 in the afternoon. It's Saturday, what if they are closed? Entering I find the offices empty but manage to contact Snyder on the phone (since all embassy personel live in the same building). He comes down to greet me. Shakes my hand. After interview he advises me to come in first thing Monday. (See - July 8 -13.)

July 8. Interview.

July 9. Receive passport. Call Marina to Moscow also.

July 14. I and Marina return to Minsk.

July 15. Marina at work. Is shocked to find out there every one knows she entered the U.S. Embassy. They were called at her place of work from some officials in Moscow. The bosses hold a meeting and give her a strong browbeating. The first of many indoctrinations.

July 15 - August 20. We have found out which blanks and certificates are necessary to apply for an exit visa. They number about twenty papers: birth certificates, affidavits, photos, etc. On Aug 20th, we give the papers out. They say it will be three and a half months before we know whether they'll let us go or not. In the meantime, Marina has had to stay for four different meetings at the place of work held by her bosses at the direction of «someone» by phone. The Young Communist League headquarters also called about her and she had to go see them for one and a half hours. The purpose (expressed) is to dissuade her from going to the U.S.A. Net effect: make her more stubborn about wanting to go. Marina is pregnant. We only hope that the visas come through soon.

August 21-September 1. I make expected trips to the Passport and Visa Office. Also to Ministry of Foreign Affairs in Minsk. Also Ministry of Internal affairs, all of which have a say in the granting of a visa. I extracted promises of quick attention to us.

September -October 18. No word from ministries (they'll call us). Marina leaves Minsk by train on vacation to the city of Khkov in the Urals to visit an aunt for four weeks. During this time I am lonely but I and Erich go to the dances and public places for entertainment. I haven't done this in quite a few months now. I spend my birthday alone at the opera watching my favorite, "Queen of Spades." I am 22 years old.

November 2. Marina arrives back, radiant, with several jars of preserves for me from her aunt in Khkov.

November-December. Now we are becoming annoyed about the delay. Marina is beginning to waver about going to the U.S. Probably from the strain and her being pregnant. Still we quarrel and so things are not too bright, especially, with the approach of the hard Russian winter.

December 25. Xmas Day, Tuesday. Marina is called to the Passport and Visa Office. She is told we have been granted Soviet exit visas. She fills out the completing blank and then comes home with the news. It's great (I think!). New Years we spend at the Zigers at a dinner party at midnight attended by six other persons.

January 4 (1962). I am called to the Passport Office since my residential passport expires today. Since I now have a U.S. passport in my possession I am given a totally new residential passport called, "Passport for Foreigners," and since they have given us permission to leave, and know we shall, good to July 5, 1962.

January 15.

February 15. Days of cold Russian winter. But we feel fine. Marina is supposed to have baby on March 1st.

February 15 - Dawn. Marina wakes me. It's her time. At 9:00 we arrive at the hospital. I leave her in care of nurses and leave to go to work. 10:00 Marina has a baby girl. When I visit the hospital at 5:00 after work I am given news. We both wanted a boy. Marina feels well, baby girl O.K.

February 23. Marina leaves hospital. I see June for first time.

February 28. I go to register (as proscribed by the law) the baby. I want her name to be June Marina Oswald but those bureaucrats say her middle name must be the same as my first. A Russian custom support by a law. I refuse to have her name written as "June Lee." They promise to call the city Ministry (City Hall) and find out in this case since I do have a U.S. passport.

February 29. I am told nobody knows what to do exactly, but everyone agrees "Go ahead and do it, "Po-Russki." Name: June Lee.

March. The last communiques are exchanged by myself and Embassy. Letters are always arriving from my mother and brother in the U.S. I have still not told Erich, who is my oldest existing acquaintance, that we are going to the States. He's O.K. but I'm afraid he is too good a Young Communist League member, so I'll wait 'til last minute.

March 24. Marina quits her job in the formal fashion.

March 26. I receive a letter from Immigration and Naturalization Service at San Antonio, Texas, that Marina has had her visa petition to the U.S. (approved!!) The last document. Now we only have to wait for the U.S. Embassy to receive their copy of the approval so they can officially give the go-ahead.

March 27. I receive a letter from a Mr. Phillips (an employer of my mother, pledging to support my wife in case of need).

April.

1.2 **Commission Exhibit 92** (*The Collective; Typed Narrative Concerning Russia*, 16 H 285-336; CE 94 16 H 347-387; CE 95 16 H 388-419; CE 96 16 H 421)

Forward

In the City of Minsk there are factories and plants and industrial enterprises. These enterprises employ over 250,000 people or fifty per cent of 539,000 people, the population of this city the fifth ranking in the USSR, after Moscow, Leningrad,

Gary W. O'Brien

Kiev and Riga. The capital of the Russian State Belorussia, it is an important industrial and statically located city.

In this story of the workers of this great city lies the key to understanding the character of the Russian people, the understanding of the aims and hopes of the biggest country in the world in land mass and the second greatest industrial power. I shall not in the course of this book refer to the agricultural and service classes.

In the course of reconstruction at the end of the Second World War under the reign of Stalin, major resources were utilized for the rebuilding of the Soviet State. All sacrifices were made, including the slighting of the light consumer industry, to rebuild the heavy industry, the steel mills and machine tool plants, the parts and locomotive works. This book is an attempt at presenting a picture of the people who work in the modern Russian working class.

Reference which I shall make and figures are taken from the book "USSR Statistics for 1960 put out by the Central Ministry of Books and Printing, Moscow" and figures taken from the text of the 22nd Congress of the KPSU, which form the still unpublished basis for the "USSR Statistics for 1962" book to be published in Moscow in early 1962.

This book is not however an economic analysis of the Soviet Union. It is a look into the lives of work-a-day average Russians.

About the Author

Lee Harvey Oswald was born in October 1939 in New Orleans, La. the son of an insurance salesman whose early death left a far mean streak of independence brought on by neglect. Entering the U.S. Marine Corps at seventeen, this streak of independence was strengthened by exotic journeys to Japan, the Philippines and the scores of odd islands in the Pacific. Immediately after serving out his three years in the USMC, he abandoned his American life to seek a new life in the USSR. Full of optimism and hope he stood in Red Square in the fall of 1959 vowing to see his chosen course through. After, however, two years and a lot of growing up, I decided to return to the USA.

This book is not a story about himself. He is only the narrator. He does think, however, that not too many people, at least Americans, had had the opportunity to look into an often incredible and sometimes terrifying world, but a world whose outward appearance is very like our own.

1-2. Description of Radio Factory

2-4. Quotas and Conditions

5-6. Description of T.V. Shop

7-9. Background of Shops

10-11. Individual Workers

12. Control of "Collectives"

13-15. Demonstrations and Meetings

15-16. Factory Make-Up and Peoples

17-19. Layout of the City of Minsk

20. Tourist permits and "tourist"

21-22. Passports

23. Collective farms and schools

24. Vacations

25. Student Quarters and Institute

26. Population fig. and textbooks

27. Figures for books and foreign books

PART 1 – THE COLLECTIVE

1-2. Description of Radio Factory

The lives of Russian workers are governed, first and foremost, by the "collective," the smallest unit of authority in any given factory, plant, or enterprise. Sectional and shop cells form a highly organized and well supported political organization. These shop committees are in turn governed by the shop and section party chiefs who are directed by the factory or plant party secretary. This post carries officially the same amount of authority as the production director or president of the plant, but in reality it is the controlling organ of all activities at any industrial enterprise, whether political, industrial, or otherwise personal relations. The Party Secretary is responsible for political indoctrination of the workers, the discipline of members of the Communist Party working at the plant, and the general conduct and appearance of all members.

The Minsk Radio and Television plant is known throughout the Union as a major producer of electronics parts and sets. In this vast enterprise created in the early 50s, the party secretary is a 6'4" man in his early forties and has a long history of service to the party. He controls the activities of the 1,000 Communist Party members here and otherwise supervises the activities of the other 5,000 people employed at this major enterprise in Minsk, the capital of the third ranking republic Belorussia.

This factory manufactures 87,000 large and powerful radio and 60,000 television sets in various sizes and ranges, excluding pocket radios, which are not mass produced anywhere in the U.S.S.R. It is this plant which manufactured several console model combination radio-phonograph television sets which were shown as mass produced items of commerce before several hundreds of thousands of Americans at the Soviet Exposition in New York in 1959. After the Exhibition these sets were duly shipped back to Minsk and are now stored in a special storage room on the first floor of the Administrative Building - at this factory, ready for the next international Exhibit.

I worked for twenty-three months at this plant, a fine example of average and even slightly better than average working conditions. The plant covers an area of twenty-five acres in a district one block north of the main thoroughfare and only two miles from the center of the city with all facilities and systems for the mass production of radios and televisions. It employees 5,000 full time and three hundred part time workers, fifty-eight per cent women and girls. This factory employs 2,000 soldiers in three of the five main shops. Mostly these shops are fitted with conveyor belts in long rows, on either side of which sit the long line of bustling women.

Five hundred people, during the day shift, are employed on the huge stamp and pressing machines. Here sheet metal is turned into metal frames and cabinets for televisions and radios.

Another five hundred people are employed in an adjoining building for the cutting and finishing of rough wood into fine polished cabinets. A laborer's process, mostly done by hand, the cutting, trimming, and the processes right up to hand polishing are carried out here at the same plant. The plant also has its own stamp making plant, employing one hundred and fifty people at or assisting at eighty heavy machine lathes and grinders. The noise in this shop is almost deafening as metal grinds against metal and steel saws cut through iron ingots at the rate of an inch a minute. The floor is covered with oil used to drain the heat of metal being worked so one has to watch one's footing. Here the workers' hands are as black as the floor and seem to be eternally. The foreman here looks like the Russian version of "John Henry," tall and as strong as an ox. He isn't frilly, but he gets the work out.

The plant has its electric shop, where those who have finished long courses in electronics work over generators, television tubes, testing experiment of all kinds. The green work tables are filled high here. Electric gadgets are not too reliable, mostly due to the poor quality of wires, which keep burning out under the impact of the usual 220V. In the U.S. it is 110V.

The plastics department is next. Here forty-seven women and three physically disabled persons keep the red hot liquid plastic flowing into a store of odd presses, turning out their quota of knobs, handles, non-conducting tube bases, and so forth. These workers suffer the worst condition of work in the plant, an otherwise model factory for the Soviet Union, due to bad fumes and the hotness of the materials. These workers are awarded thirty days vacation a year, the maximum for workers.

2-4. Quotas and Conditions

Automation is now employed at a fairly large number of factories, especially the war industry. However, for civilian use, their number is still small.

At this plant at least one worker is employed in the often crude task of turning out finished, acceptable items. Often, one worker must finish the task of taking the edge of metal off plastic and shaving them on a foot driver lathe. There is only so much potentiality in presses and stamps, no matter what their size.

The lack of unemployment in the Soviet Union may be explained by one of two things: lack of automation and a bureaucratic corps of sixteen workers in any given factory. These people are occupied with the tons of paperwork which flow in and out of any factory. Also the number of direct foremen is not small to the ratio of workers: in some case one to ten; in others one to five, depending on the importance of the work.

These people are also backed by a small array of examiners, committees and supply checkers and the quality control board. These people number (without foremen) almost three hundred people, total working force 5,000 – three to fifty without foremen.

To delve deep into the lives of the workers, we shall visit most of the shops one after another and get to know the people. The largest shop employs five hundred people. Eighty-five per cent are women and girls. Females make up sixty per cent of the work force at this plant.

Here girls solder and screw the chassis to the frame attaching, transistors, tubes and so forth. They each have quotas depending upon what kind of work they are engaged in. One girl may solder five transistors in four minutes while the next girl solders fifteen wire leads in thirteen minutes. The pay scales here vary but slightly with average pay at eighty rubles without deductions. Deductions include seven rubles, general tax, two and a half rubles for bachelors and unmarried girls and any deductions for poor or careless work the inspectors may care to make further down the line. They start teams of two, mostly boys of seventeen or eighteen, turning the televisions on the conveyor belts right side up from where there has been soldering to a position where they place picture tubes onto the supports. These boys receive for a thirty-nine hour week, sixty-five to seventy rubles, not counting deductions. Further on, others are filling tubes and parts around the picture tube itself. All along the line there are testing apparatus with operators hurriedly affixing shape type testing currents, withdrawing the snaps that fit out a testers card, and passing the equipment back on the conveyor. Speed here is essential.

5-6. Description of T.V. Shop

The Communist Party Secretary here, as in most shops, has promised to increase production by two per cent in honor of the coming end of the third year of the current seven year plan. Now the televisions are carried around the conveyor to go back down the line where others sit to complete the process. The smoke from the careful soldering doesn't keep the girls from chattering away and that, coupled with the boys at the end of the line, testing the loudspeakers, makes for a noisy but lively place, with the laughter of girls mixing with music and occasional jazz programs, which the testers favor for purely personal reasons until the foreman looks his way.

As we go out we see crates of the finished product with the well known, "made in Belorussia," stamp.

One of the most interesting things in observing Russian life and conventions is the personal relationship to each other. There exists a disciplined comradeship springing from the knowledge that in Soviet society the fundamental group is the "Kollective" or intershop group. These groups, with the shop or section party chiefs and foremen, are the worlds in which the Russian workers live. All activities and conduct of members is dependent upon the will of the "Kollective."

In the shop where I worked, the experimental shop of the Minsk Radio and Television factory, there were fifty-eight workers, including the Party Shop Secretary, who is a Communist worker assigned into the shop by the factory Party Secretary, and the Master Foreman, assigned by the shop production head who is assigned in turn by the director of the factory.

7-9. Background of Shops

The key person in the shop, as every one appreciates, is Comrade Lebizen, forty-five years old, the Party Secretary. His background is that after serving his allotted time in the Young Communist League before the war, he became a member in good standing of the Communist Party of the Soviet Union, CPSU. During the war, he was for a short time a tankest, but his talents seemed to have been too good for that job so he was made a military policeman, after the war, starting at this newly built factory. He was appointed by the factory Communist Party chief as Shop Secretary, responsible for shop discipline, party meetings, distribution of propaganda, and any other odd "jobs" that might come up, including seeing to it that there always enough red and white signs and slogans hanging on the walls. Lebizen holds the title (besides Communist) of "Shock worker of Communist Labor." This movement was started under Stalin a decade ago in order to get the most out of the extreme patriotism driven into Soviet children at an early age. Indeed, Lebizen is a skilled mechanic and metal worker and for his work he receives one hundred thirty to one hundred forty rubles per month minus deductions. This Shop Party Secretary, together with the section party chief, usually selects workers for the title "shock worker of Communist Labor." These people are not necessarily Communist Party members, although it helps in the same way Party membership helps in any facet of life in the U.S.S.R.

Factory meetings of the "Kollectives" are so numerous as to be staggering.

Take for instance during one month the following meetings and lectures are scheduled: one professional union, which discusses the work of the professional union in collecting dues, paying out receipts on vacations orders, etc.; four political information every Tuesday on the lunch hour; two Young Communist meetings on the sixth and twenty-first of every month; one production committee made up of workers discussing ways of improving work; two Communist party meetings a month called by the section Communist Party Secretary; four School of Communist Labor meetings (compulsory) every Wednesday; and one sport meeting per month (non-compulsory) - a total of fifteen meetings a month, fourteen of which are compulsory for Communist Party members and twelve compulsory for all others. These meetings are always held after work or on the lunch hour. They are never held on working time. Absenteeism is by no means allowed. After long years of hard discipline, especially under the Stalin regime, no worker will invite the sure disciplinary action of the Party men and inevitably the factory Party Committee because of trying to slip out of the way or giving too little attention to what is being said.

A strange sight indeed is the picture of the local Party man delivering a political sermon to a group of usually robust, simple working men who through some strange process have been turned to stone. Turned to stone all except the hard faced Communists with roving eyes looking for any bonus-making catch of inattentiveness on the part of any worker. A sad sight to anyone not used to it, but the Russians are philosophical. "Who likes the lecture?" "Nobody, but it's compulsory." Compulsory attendance at factory meetings isn't the only way to form spontaneous demonstrations and meetings. The "Great October Revolution" demonstrations, the May Day demonstrations are all formed in the same way, as well as spontaneous meetings for distinguished guests. The well organized Party men mark off the names of hundreds of workers approved to arrive at a certain place at a given time. No choice, however small, is left to the discretion of the individual.

Part II - The Experimental Shop

10-11. Individual Workers

For a good cross section of the Russian working class, I suggest we examine the lives of some of the fifty-eight workers and five foremen working in the experimental shop of the Minsk radio plant. This place is located in the midst of the great thriving plant which produces some of the best known radios and TVs in the Soviet Union.

The shop itself is located in a two story building with no particular noticeable mark on its red brick face. At 8:00 sharp, all the workers have arrived and at the sound of a bell sounded by the duty orderly, who is a worker whose duty it is to see to it that the workers do not slip out for too many smokes, they file upstairs, except for ten turners and lath operators whose machines are located on the first floor. Work here is given out in the form of blueprints and drawings by the foreman Zemof and junior foreman Joreman Lavcook to workers whose various reliability and skills call for them, since each worker has with time acquired differing skills and knowledge. Work is given strictly according to so-called "pay levels:" the levels being numbered one to five and the highest level "master." For level one a worker receives approximately 68 rubles for work, level two a worker receives 79.50, for three, 90 rubles, for four, 105 rubles, for five, 125 rubles, and for masters about 150. These levels of pay vary slightly because workers receive a basic pay of, for first level, 45 rubles and bonuses, bringing the total to 68 rubles, including reductions for taxes. The basic pay of a master is 90 rubles. Except in instances for poor quality work, bonuses are always the same, giving use to a more or less definite pay scale. A worker may demand to be tested for a higher pay level at any time. Only skill is "a barrier" to higher pay. The foreman and shop head all receive about 120 rubles basic pay, but much higher bonuses are awarded to the best shops by the Factory Committee for good production standards.

Our shop head Shephen Tarasavich Velchok is a stout, open faced, and well skilled metal worker who, although he hasn't got a higher education which is now a prime requisition for even a foreman's job. He managed to finish a four year night school specialty course and, through the help of the director of the factory, Mr. Ukayvich, became shop head in an important segment of this large plant, employing 5,000 people. Shephen has an almost bald head except for a line of hair on the left side of his head, which he is forever combing across his shiny top. Aged forty-five, he is married with two children aged eight and ten. It may be explained that the Russians seem to marry much older than their American counterparts. Perhaps that can be explained by the fact that in order to receive an apartment, people often must wait for five or six years and since security is so unstable, until a commonly desired goal is reached, that is an apartment for oneself, most Russians do not choose to start families until later in life. Shephen is responsible to the Factory Committee and director for the filling of quotas and production quantity. His foreman Zemof is thirty-eight years old, has a wife and fifteen month old baby, and not too long ago moved out of his one room flat without kitchen or private toilet into a newly built apartment house and flat of two small rooms, kitchen and bath, a luxury not felt by most Russians. A tall thin man with dark creases in his face, his manner, nervous, spontaneous and direct, betrays his calling. His job: keep the work on the premises going as quickly and efficiently as possible. His assistant, junior foreman Lavcook, is much younger, ten year younger, enigmatic, handsome, and quick. He climbed to his post through a night school degree and a sort of rough charm, which he instinctively uses in the presence of superiors. The shop's mainstay is composed of seventeen so-called "Shock workers" whose pictures hang on a wall near the stairs so that all might strive to imitate them. Usually of the fifth level or master class of workers, they are experienced at work and politics.

Most shock workers are men of the older aged groups, forty to fifty, not always members of the Communist Party. They carry the production load and most of the responsibility of the interlife of the "Kollective".

The remaining forty-one workers are divided about half into eighteen to twenty-two year olds, now metal workers, trying to fulfill their obligatory two years at a factory, before going on to full time day studies at a local university, or one of the specialized institutes, and older workers who have been working at the plant for four to six years and occupy the middle number worker levels three to four. These workers are aged about twenty-four to thirty and form the mass of laborers at the factory. Seventy per cent have families, apartments are few. Most occupy rooms belonging to relatives or rooms let to rent by holders of two or three room apartments, often for as high as twenty rubles a month, although rent in the Soviet Union is paid by the square meter and three fifteen meter rooms with kitchen and bath cost about 32 rubles a month. The housing shortage is so critical that people count themselves lucky to even find a person willing to let his room. Room renting also is the most common form of speculation in the USSR. Often it reaches heights all out of proportion with reality, such as the man who derived 60 rubles a month from letting his room in the summer while he himself was living in a summer house, or "Dacha," in the country. Such speculation is forbidden and carries penalties, including deportation to other economic areas of the USSR for terms of up to six months. Still these are the most common instances. Most workers in Minsk come from peasant stock, which repopulated the city at the end of the Second World War. Like most Russians they are warm hearted and simple but also stubborn and untrustworthy.

12. Control of Collectives

The life of the "Kollective" or rather inter-life, since it often touches upon more than just the work, is the most reflective side of the complex working of the Communist Party of the USSR. It is the reflection of mass and organized political activity, deciding the actions of every individual and group, placing upon society a course, so strict, so disciplined, that any private deviation is interpreted as political deviation and the enforced course of action over the years has become the most comprehensible educational and moral training probably in the history of the world.

To understand the work and workings of the "Kollective" one must first ask who controls, who leads the "Kollective?" The answer to that is a long one. All plants and factories in the Soviet

Union have party committees, headed by one graduate of higher party schools whose function is to control discipline members of the Communist Party and who, working in conjunction with the directors of the factory, control all factors pertaining to the work, alterations, and production of any given line. It must be noted that officially the party men occupy a position exactly equal to the head of any factory. However the facts point out that he has, due to the fact that Communist hold the leading positions in plants, considerable more sway over the activities of the workers than anyone else. No suggestion of the Party man is ever turned down by the directors of our factory -that would be precedent to treason. The Party man is appointed by the headquarters of the Central Committee of the Communist Party and in turn the Party man designates who shall be Shop and Section Party Secretaries, posts well coveted by employed Communists. These Communists in reality control every move of "Kollectives." They are responsible for the carrying out of directives pertaining to meetings, lectures, and party activities in the local cells.

These meetings or "Sabranias" are almost always held at the lunch hour or after working hours. The number of meetings of a strictly political nature is not small, considering that on an average eight meetings are held a week and of these you have "Young Communist, Party Communist meeting," "political information" and the "School of Communist Labor." These are every week and are compulsory for all workers. Also, monthly meetings include "Production Meeting," "General Trade Union," "Shop Committee," and "Sport Meeting," none of these are compulsory. The numbers of meetings held a month average twenty. Fifty per cent of these are political or bi-political meetings. Meetings last anywhere from ten minutes to two hours. Usually the length of "political information meetings" held every Tuesday is fifteen minutes. An amazing thing in watching these political lectures is that there is taken on by the listeners, a most phenomenal nature, one impervious to outside interference or sounds. After long years of hard fisted discipline, no worker allows himself to be trapped and called out for inattentiveness by the ever present and watchful Party Secretary and members of the Communist Party. This is mostly seen in political information of Central Committee Party directive readings. At these times it is best to curb one's natural boisterous and lively nature. Under the 6' by 6' picture of Lenin, founder of the Soviet State, the Party Section Secretary stands. In our section is a middle aged pocked man by the name of Sobakin, an average looking man wearing glasses, his wrinkled face and twinkling eyes give one the impression that any moment he's going to tell a racy story or funny joke, but he never does. Behind this man stands twenty-five years of Party life. His high post, relatively speaking for him, is witness to his efficiency. He stands expounding from notes in front of him, the week's "Information," with all the lack of enthusiasm and gusto of someone who knows that he has no worries about an audience or about someone getting up and going away.

Part III –Demonstrations

13-15. Demonstrations and Meetings

In the same way, May Day and other "demonstrations" are arranged, as well as spontaneous receptions for distinguished guests. I remember when I was in Moscow in 1959, I was just passing in front of the Metropole restaurant when out of the side streets came a ten-man police unit which stopped all people on the street from passing in front of the entrance, surrounding the crowd, and keeping them hemmed in (not detouring the flow of traffic as would be expected) for three minutes, until right on schedule, an obviously distinguished foreign lady was driven up to the restaurant where a meeting in her honor had been arranged. She was taken through the "spontaneous" welcoming crowd, after which the police were withdrawn, allowing the passers by to continue.

Another instance of this was in 1961 when a Chinese delegation arrived in Minsk and was driven from the railway station to a house on the outskirts of the city. Even though it was 10:30 at night all along the way members of the MVD (security) forces ran into apartment buildings and student dormitories ordering people out on to the streets to welcome the arriving guests.

Although there was no prior notice of any delegation, another "spontaneous" welcoming committee met the cavalcade of black limousines and dutifully waved back at the darkened cars with the slightly protruding yellowish waving hands.

I myself was visiting friends in the Foreign Language Dormitory when we were called out for this purpose by a security agent. I went right along with all the others into the crowd and I know this story to be not only true but standard operating procedure.

At the Minsk radio factory, holiday demonstrations (there are two a year), May Day and Revolution Day, are arranged in the following manner. Directives are passed down the Communist Party line until they reach the factory shop and mill "Kollectives." Here they are implemented by the Communist Party Secretary who issues instructions as to what time the demonstrators are to arrive. At the arrival point, names are taken well in advance of the march so that late comers and absentees may be duly noted: neither one is allowed. At the collection point, signs, drums, and flags are distributed and marchers formed in ranks. In the City of Minsk on such days, all roads are closed to driving trucks across them, except the prescribed route. This, as well as meticulous attention to attendance, insures a ninety per cent turnout of the entire population. Stragglers or late risers walking through the streets may be yanked into the steady stream of workers by the police or voluntary red armed "people's militia." Anyone who argues may be subject to close investigation later on, the one thing to be avoided in any police state.

In roughly the same way, a ninety-eight per cent majority of the voting population is always funneled into voting for the one candidate for the one post, one party system in the Soviet Union. Before State, Republic, or City elections, an "agitator" calls at the residence of each and every person in the city. He inquires regarding the number of eligible voters (voting age throughout the USSR is sixteen years), age, sex, place of work, etc. He insures that all eligible voters know when, where, and how to vote. He can explain who are the candidates, although he is forbidden by law to campaign for one or the other and insures the prospective voter that his name will be on the voting register, located at the poll, which he must sign before voting by secret ballot. At the voting poll, after signing the register, a person receives a voting list with the names of all candidates for different posts. He may either place an X next to his choice or strike out any name he doesn't like or write in any name he wishes. Names written into the ballot are counted but no one can be elected to any post or office in this manner. It may, however, mean that this person will be a candidate for a chosen post sometime in the future elections. All candidates are approved by the Central Committee of the Communist Party, although a candidate does not necessarily have to be a Communist Party member (he may be non-party). The system in the USSR insures that no person rises to any heights at all without being approved by the Party, even if he has made an application for the Party. At the 22nd Congress KPCU Khrushchev revealed that out of a population of 216 million, five and one half million are members of the Communist Party. That is less than ten per cent of the total population, actually engaged in production, not counting children and pensioners, etc.

15-16. Factory Makeup and Peoples

But in order to get to know the workers, how they think, act, hope, and have lived, I will take an example from the lower and middle and upper age groups, starting with the lower.

Usha Shklieavich, born in what is now south western Belorussian territory, is twenty-four years old, makes ninety rubles a month, without deductions. He is married and has a young baby. He and his wife live in a small room in a house, the property of his in-laws. He is on the waiting list for a small flat, "hopes" to receive it in "four or five years," hopes to enter the university night course next year so that he can become a radio engineer. He went to school during and after the war in the East where his family took him during the evacuation. Moved still further East after an all out attempt at a drive by the Nazis in which his mother was killed. After finishing his schooling at the age of nineteen, like most Russian boys, he was drafted into the Army, served in Hungary when the Counter Revolution broke out as a jeep driver. When I asked him who started the war there, he says "American Imperialists" and "spies." When asked who he killed he says "he didn't kill anyone." When asked who was killed during the Revolution, he says "Hungarians." Asked what he thinks of that Revolution, he says, "It was a glorious victory by our forces." Shklieavich also tells a story about how he was "newly arrived with the occupation forces, was walking down the street when he came upon a group of young Hungarian citizens. One of them was a girl he says, and she looked at me so hard I thought she must of known me. One of the younger people came forward and asked for a match. Just then a Hungarian 'People's Policeman' came around the corner." This is probably what saved Shklieavich's life. The policeman shouted just as one of the younger people came up behind him and hit him on the head. When he awoke, "there were two of the group dead and the others ran away." Surely a revolution of spies and imperialists I jibed.

A picture of a different sort is that cut by Askonavich. Mild mannered, he served his army service a long time ago, on the Leningrad front during the war. Married for ten years, he has three children, aged forty-four. He has a hawk like nose, bushy eyebrows, and profuse straw colored hair. He makes 115 rubles a month, lives fairly well, owns a television, radio and refrigerator in his two room flat with neighbors who share kitchen and bath: a very good arrangement for the Soviet Union. He pays fifteen rubles a month rent, has a middle school education, had finished a metal workers course at night school, at the night school facility of the university in 1958. He has been working at this plant for five years. A skilled tradesman, he is respected and is a member of the shop production committee. Non-Communist, he believes in the policies of the Party as do almost all Russians. His hobby is fishing on the banks of the little creek near his home during the summer. Every morning he spends twenty minutes on a bus coming to work. This is the most inconvenient aspect of his otherwise simple and average life. Does he have money, personal belongings? "No money, but I have an apartment." That is the most important thing in life. People have been known to do odd, even unlawful things to get even a little higher on the housing waiting list such as faking the ownership of a baby or two to get special rating. The opening of apartment houses is always done with a great deal of gusto and preparation. Indeed, for the lucky ones, receiving their orders on rooms and flats, it is a big moment, a moment culminating years of waiting and often years of manipulation. The lucky few get the word to move out of their old quarters, usually one room in oblong buildings, built after the war, which are mostly to be later torn down. As soon as a newly built house is ready, enough to support the rush of happy home owners, it is opened even though there may not be light fixtures or toilet seats just yet. What does that matter! In 1960 there were 2,978,000 living places built in the USSR - USA: 1,300,000 including Hawaii and Alaska.

One man whose family received a flat not long ago is Orisses. At our shop a master, a shock worker and a Communist for many years, he is almost sixty years old. Now with dark but graying hair, long nose and protruding cheek bones, set under very old and weighted eyes, contesting to his long years as a laborer, a laborer with his hands. During the war Orisses, too old to be taken into the Army in the first draft, remained in Minsk with his wife when the Germans arrived. He lived here for eight months, until things got too hot for him, as it did for most of the remaining population who didn't support the Germans outright. He fled into the deep pine forest with his wife where he served with the famed guerilla fighters. As it is well known, these people held most of the territory of Belorussia during the entire four years of occupation by the Germans of Minsk and other points in Belorussia. One day Orisses, in talking about the war rolled up his sleeve and showed me two unmistakable scars - bullet holes. When talking about Minsk during German occupation, one feels a trickle running along the neck. There was a chimney in Minsk, he says, next to the crematorium. The smoke from that chimney was as black as death day and night, night and day, the smoke of that belching chimney never stopped rising over the ruined skeleton of Minsk, ninety per cent razed to the ground during the war with only three major buildings still standing after the war: the opera house, the government house, and a church. These buildings, all except the church, which is now closed, are still in use.

PART IV

17-19. Layout of the City of Minsk

The reconstruction of Minsk is an interesting story reflecting the courage of its builders. In a totalitarian system, great forces can be brought into play under rigid controls and support. The success of the Russian "sabootniks" is testimony to that. So also is the result of the reconstruction of Minsk and other cities of the USSR. This reconstruction is still, in part, going on but the design and structure of the city already gives no idea of the condition of the capital of the Belorussian State in 1945, only sixteen short years ago. The architectural planning may be anything but modern but it is in the manner of almost all Russian cities.

With the airport serving as its eastern boundary we find a large spread-out township in appearance, one city only. The skyline pierced with factory booms and chimneys betrays its industrial background township. I say in appearance because the tallest building here is the nine story black apparatus house flanking the main street Prospect Stalin, which is over two miles long and the only such boulevard. In the republics, all other streets are narrow rock laid streets, curving the city like rivers of stone branching off the main street ending out at the other end by extensive marks. The design and content of this Prospect is very reflective of the life of this city, from north to south of this straight as an arrow vain of the city. It includes in the first two miles the center district of the city, Hotel Minsk, and the Main Post Office. The hotel was built in 1950 on the direct orders of Khrushchev who was grieved at the fact that only one, old, dilapidated hotel existed at that time when he paid an official visit to this the capital of Belorussia. The hotel was built in three months, a record for the entire Soviet Union, and has over five hundred rooms, a modern, well serviced and built hotel. Box shaped, it serves many tourists traveling from Germany and Poland through Minsk to Moscow.

The post office handles all mail coming in and out of the city. Built in 1955, it has four columns at its entrance in the Greek style.

Next down the Prospect are a clothing store and children's store. The central movie house, the best one in Minsk, seats four hundred people in a small unventilated hall. Next to it stands a shoe store, and across from it, the central beauty shop, the main drug store, a gasranon (Russian food store) and a furniture store. Next is the Ministry of Internal Affairs, whose boss is tough military Colonel Nickoley Arsnof, of the "People's Militia." He holds the title Minister of Internal Affairs. Around the corner is his subsidiary, the KGB Committee for Internal Security, (Intelligence and Secret Police). Across from the Ministry is the ever crowded prospect book shop. Across from this is the even more crowded restaurant, one of five in the city where for two rubles a person can buy fried toung or plates of chicken with potatoes and fried cabbage, instead of just the "Kotlets" (bread and ground meat patties) or schnitzel with a little more meat and less bread and beef stake pure (ground beef patties served with potatoes and cabbage and sometimes macaroni. These are always served in workers' dining rooms and stand-up cafes for they open at night). And sometimes sweet rolls, coffee and fall fruits, salads and tomatoes can also be bought.

Down from this cafe called "Springtime," is the bakery shop. Here for thirteen kopecks a person can buy unwrapped bread (white), for seven kopecks, sweet rolls of different kinds, twenty kopecks, and black bread (the black bread loaf is twice as large as the white is, therefore cheaper per kilogram and more in demand. Also black bread remains fresh for an exceptionally long time due to the hard crust).

Across from this bakery shop is the confection place. Here is a kid's dreamland of sweets and chocolate. Although owing to its climate, chocolate costs four times as much as in the US (for four ounces one must pay sixty kopecks). Chocolate is much in demand since Russians have a vicious sweet tooth. Here there is always a crowd. Further down we come to the only department store in Minsk, the "SUM" which means "State Universal Store." Here one may buy anything sold in the smaller specialized stores and sign on the list for refrigerators, vacuum cleaners, and even cars, none of which can be bought anywhere outright.

The waiting list for refrigerators (1952-58, 112 million sold) is three months; also the same for vacuum cleaners. For cars the waiting list is anywhere from six months to a year, depending upon which of the three existing types one puts a down payment on. The "Moskavich," which costs 2,500 rubles, is presumed to be the best, so the waiting list is almost a year for that. However the "Victory" and "Volga" are a little cheaper and so one can expect it after only a six or seven month wait. Cars are bought more or less to order here. Their styles are not very impressive. The Moskavich looks like a box on wheels, while the Volga looks like a 1938 Studebaker, which, by the way, is what it is modeled after: "American reward aid."

Motorcycles and television sets can, however, be bought on the spot for ready cash. A good high powered motorcycle costs 350 rubles and their quality is apt to be better than the more complex automobile. Television sets cost anywhere from eighty rubles for a six-inch by six-inch screen to 350 rubles for a well made television of twenty-inch screen. Other models, light table models, cost 190 and 145 rubles. Here ready made suits of rough material can be bought. The cheaper, a double breasted blue for about 110 rubles or a better made three button suit for 250 rubles. A jacket costs forty rubles or two pairs of pants for not less than fifteen rubles. There are a few cheap ones, however in stock. They usually cost thirty rubles.

Just before we come to "Stalin Square," the end of the central district along the Prospect, we find the two "automats" or stand-up cafes. These cafes are located across the Prospect from one another, the internal and external structure is exactly the same in each. Both places serve the same dishes at the same prices. Why these were not built at opposite ends of the central district or even the square, for instance, is not known. Although, it would of course be more convenient. The reason is that the architectural plans for all the cities in the Soviet Union come directly from

Moscow, which, as one can imagine, is a big responsibility for the architect since in the USSR one pays for a mistake with one's head. It seems that the logical reason for the outward architecture is that in building the street so it is the simplest, it is therefore the safest way. Another characteristic and interesting structure in Minsk is the trade union building. This houses an auditorium, offices for the training and costuming of the amateur group who perform here periodically, and a small dance hall. There is not, as one might assume, an office of any trade union. They do not exist as we know them (since strikes or negotiations for higher pay or better working conditions are not allowed. Of course, suggestions may be made by any worker but these are all handled through the local Communist Factory Committee and are passed along or shelved as it suits the committees). An imposing structure, it looks like a Greek temple with figures atop the V shaped roof supported by large white marble columns all around. However, a close look reveals not naked Greek gods but, from left to right, a surveyor complete with scope, a bricklayer holding a bucket, a sports woman in track suit, and a more symbolic structure of a man in a double breasted suit holding a brief case, either a bureaucrat or an intellectual, apparently.

The rest of the Prospect for the remaining miles is enclosed with the so familiar square shaped five storied apartment houses, ending at Victory Square. It may be that at the present time sixty per cent of all living is in apartments. In twenty years ninety per cent of all living quarters will be in these many storied barracks. The building spree is in full swing, although at the 22nd Congress, Khrushchev announced that so many building projects were started in 1960-1961 that for a year after the finish of the Congress only special important projects will be allowed to be begun in order to give a chance for the completion of sites already started. This is not the only reason, for the demand for raw materials and prefabricated parts far exceeds the supply and in desperation, Khrushchev called a halt to the construction plans of the present Seven-Year Plan - this means especially on apartments, for which there is a dire need.

Most factory workers do not consider themselves in line for an apartment even if they are on the list for at least four years. Their estimates are based on experience.

20. Tourist Permits and Tourists

At the 22nd Party Congress, Khrushchev in his seven hour keynote speech (which was, for all practical purposes, the only speech, since all others followed in support of the first speech) revealed that in 1960, 700,000 people in the Soviet Union went abroad. This is a gross over-estimate, including engineers and technicians sent abroad, which make up twenty per cent of this total. All others are delegations of intelligent students, all scientific workers. The 250,000 "tourists" who do manage to go abroad are carefully selected from applicants. The main requisite is "is he loyal and politically prepared?" Any worker at our plant could apply for a tourist trip under the "limited number rules" applying to delegations. For one hundred and forty rubles he can go to China for two weeks from Minsk or for eighty rubles go to Czechoslovakia. For more, if he passes the requisitions, he can even get to England. The hitch is (1) that he must be OK'd by the Comm-Bureau, (2) he must account for the presence of excess money, since speculation is not allowed in the USSR, and (3) he must leave behind close relatives, preferably a wife and children, or mother and father. This last is actually the most important. The Russians know that a person will not ordinarily leave a delegation or group of tourists to seek asylum if he knows he'll never see his family again, not alive anyway. Individual tourists who go abroad when and where they want to because of their own desires is unknown in the Soviet Union. Passports abroad are issued only after a six month exhaustive investigation by the K.G.B.

Even trips to many cities of the Soviet Union are forbidden, even to those who would like to travel there to see relatives. All cities above Leningrad toward the Finnish border fall into this category. Breast on the Polish Border, Odessa, main seaport, some cities in the Ukraine and Siberia connected with industry, all cities along the Southern border of the USSR from Moldavia to India are forbidden without a pass. All cars, trucks and other private vehicles are stopped at police check points to these areas. Train and plane and bus terminals are not allowed to sell tickets to these places without being shown a passport or being shown a valid pass whose owner's address is in the forbidden city. Persons already living in these cities may travel freely to and from them. However, they may not bring others in without passes. Passes are given out by the local K.G.B. offices and one must apply directly to it.

21-22. Passports

It may be explained that in the Eastern European custom all citizens upon reaching the age of sixteen years are given a grey-green "passport" or identification papers. On the first page is a photo and personal information. On the following four pages are places for the registering of addresses, this including rented rooms. On the next four pages are places for making particular remarks as to the conduct of the carrier, a place better kept blank. The next three pages are for registering the places of work, then the next page is for marriage licenses and divorce stamps. These "passports" are changed for a small charge every five years. A lost passport can be replaced after a short investigation for ten rubles. All persons regardless of nationality are required to carry these at all times in the Soviet Union. Nationalities are all marked on the passport: for instance a Ukranian is Urkanian, a Jew is marked Jew, no matter where he was born. An immigrant is marked as to place of birth, as in the case of the many immigrants in the U.S.S.R. Also on these pages are marks for special remarks usually of a criminal nature. Immigrants have a short autobiography painted such as:

Gary W. O'Brien

Carlos Ventera, born in Buenos Aires, 1934, resident Buenos Aires until 1955, occupation student, immigrated to U.S.S.R. 1956. This is enough to insure that any and all who reads the passport that, Carlos, along with any other of his fellow immigrants, will be given the proper treatment and attention, so that he never gets too far away from his registered address without a good reason or too high at his work. But otherwise immigrants in the U.S.S.R., a relative few French, Spanish, and Eastern European, are treated with more respect than the Russians treat each other, particularly in the matter of being awarded an apartment. Any immigrant, no matter how unimportant he may have been in his native country, has much less to worry about concerning getting an apartment and being assigned to work than his Russian born counterpart; this is part of the nation wide drive to impress all foreigners as to the high level of life in the U.S.S.R.

23. Collective Farms and Schools

Twelve miles outside of Moscow is a "show" collective farm for the foreign tourists who ask to see a genuine, average collective farm. On it is almost every imaginable help to man possible, including automatic milers, feeders, and even automatic floor cleaners. The collective farms at this place, along with their counterparts at the same sort of place south of Leningrad, have well built apartment houses with food and clothing stores built right into the first floors.

For the benefit of everyone who doesn't want to be dubbed, I suggest you take the Moscow to Breast highway for twenty-four miles until you come to Uesteech where, by asking directions, you can in five minutes find a real collective farm, a village of the small black mud and scrape wood houses, seen throughout the Soviet Union and although it's fifty minutes from the Kremlin, it doesn't have electricity or gas. Inside plumbing is unknown and the only automation is that done with a broom. There are

45,000 collective farms in the Soviet Union of these types as well as 7,400 State farms run directly by the government. Collective farmers and their families number 65.5 million people or 31.4% of the total population.

True, the collective farmers may own chickens or pigs or even a cow, as well as his own piece of land, usually one-half of an acre, but the isolation and agonizingly hard work in summer and fall affects these "advantages." Nowadays, although still without electricity, "collective farms" have wire-fed radio programs and speakers in every home. This is part of the propaganda system instigated by Stalin to bring the cultural level of outlying collective farms up to the level of the city dweller. Therefore, although there are no lights, there is always the incessant blare of the loudspeakers. School attendance for the children of collective farmers is compulsory as it is for all children up to the age of maturity, that is up to the age when they receive their passports, sixteen. Public schools are in general, box shaped three story affairs with no particular decoration. Teachers receive eighty rubles a month in these general educational institutions. Discipline from the student's viewpoint is strong. Starting school at seven years, he is taught to keep his pioneer school costume, which all students must wear, in neat appearance, is thought to stand rigidly at attention when any adult enters the room or when the teacher asks a question. His studies, particularly foreign languages, are apt to be harder and more complex than their American counterparts. Science is also stressed as well as patriotism and Soviet history. An attitude toward his studies of complete seriousness is instilled in him at an early age and young Russian students are apt to appear rather more bookish than Americans.

Since most women work for a living in the U.S.S.R., (with or without husbands) they usually leave their non-school age children in the care of the local "children's garden." These are highly organized State-created care centers for children. Here babies are fed and cared for, their health is checked periodically by doctors, diets are recommended and baths given, all for thirty rubles a month. Young children are given pre-school preparation by trained day school teachers who receive fifty rubles a month in pay. A director of such a school may receive one hundred rubles a month. 3,050,000 children in 1960 were cared for by these establishments. After the U2 incident on May 1, 1960 and the following exchanges between the American government and the Soviet governments, Premier Khrushchev invited then President Eisenhower to come to the Soviet Union and become a director of one of these "children's gardens," since, he said in a speech at the Kremlin in July 1960, Eisenhower doesn't know how to run his country.

24. Vacations

Public care centers for young and old are an established principle in the U.S.S.R. Thousands of neat homes, sanatoriums, and hospitals are scattered around the Black and Caspian Seas, the "resort area" of the Soviet Union. For any worker to get a reservation for one of these places he should apply to the Factory Committee for a "petovkoo" or ticket reservation. After showing that he has the right to his three weeks vacation, (thirty days for persons engaged in dangerous occupations or mining), he may buy the "Petovkoo" from Minsk to the Black Sea, Yalta resort area, for three weeks at a cost of seventy to one hundred rubles, depending upon class of service available. If a member of the trade unions (a worker pays one per cent of his pay earnings as dues a month), he may only have to pay fifty per cent of the total cost, if it is at a trade union built house of rest or Republican Sanatorium. Service at these places include three good balanced meals a day, the attention of doctors and nurses, sports and sailing facilities, private beaches, excursions and all necessities.

More modest workers can, however, afford journeys to rest homes nearer home, in the case of Minsk, to Zhoonovich located in pine forest three hours from Minsk. Here the same services minus the beaches, fruit and sun can be had for as little as twenty-five rubles for two weeks.

Other rest homes include Liovod and Naroch located one hundred miles north-west of Minsk on the shores of twenty mile long Lake Naroch, deep in the pine forest of Belorussia, where hare-hunting and fishing can be had as well as the usual rest home services for thirty-five or forty rubles by any workers whose vacation time comes up. The only is restriction is sometimes lack of space, especially in summers, but that is not an obstacle to one who plans in advance. Russian workers always take advantage of these cut prices and fairly good services to escape the rigors and dust of Taria factories, at least for a while anyway.

25. Student Quarters and Institutes

The capital of Belorussia has twelve institutions of higher learning including a university and poly-technical institution. These institutions are engaged in turning out highly trained specialist for the national economy. The city has many secondary schools, colleges, vocational, and factory schools. These schools teach a rigorous five year course of vocational and political subjects. Hostels for students are located near their respective institutes. Non-residential students live here. Often these numbers exceed the rooms and many have to rent rooms in the city. All rooms, fifteen by fifteen feet, house five to six students with just enough room to allow metal beds to be placed around the walls and a table and chairs in the middle. There is not room enough for closets so clothing is kept in suitcases under beds. Here, except during the three month summers vacation, students live and study for five years. Common rooms with stoves are also located at the rate of one room to eight students, living quarters for cooking. The cleanliness of linen and rooms as well as the entire dormitory falls upon the students. The number of students in the U.S.S.R. in 1960-61 was 2,396,000: U.S. figures, 1,816,000 or 102 per 10,000. All students in higher educational institution receive "stipends" or grants of money at the rate of forty rubles a month, regardless of chosen vocations. For excellent to outstanding grades, a student may receive the maximum of fifty rubles per month. Thus all students are paid to study in the Soviet Union unlike the United States where students must pay tuition to learn. This is the reason why the Soviet Union turns out almost three times as many engineers, 159,000 in 1959, twice as many agronomist, 477,200, technicians, and other specialists. This is why the Soviet Union has more doctors per 10,000 of population (18.5 in 1960) than any other country in the world (U.S.A. (12.1) 1960). Regardless of the lack of dormitories and allied living conditions of the students that we have in the U.S., we would definitely learn from the rigorous and highly specialized educational system of the Soviet Union: a system which jointly and carefully instills political as well as vocational training into each and every student just as at the factories and plants. Each and every institution has its corps of party chiefs, sectional, and class, for teachers and professors as well as for students.

26. Population Figures and Textbooks

At the 22nd Congress in October 1961, Khrushchev prophesied that by 1980, one out of every five persons living in the Soviet Union will have a higher education. This is an unheard of figure, but it is possible under the system in the Soviet Union.

Foreign languages also hold positions of favority in the Soviet educational plan. Much more so than in the U.S., in scientific fields of vocation, two foreign languages are compulsory over a five year period: in engineering and also medicine at least one language is compulsory. The studied languages in order of importance and popularity are English, German, French, Italian, and Spanish with Far Eastern languages following. The textbooks from which these languages are learned are very interesting in themselves. They combine politics and education at once, a very common occurrence. An example is that texts in English or German for instance are given on the life of Lenin, founder of the Soviet State, or the structure of the Communist Party of the Soviet Union. Formerly the life of Stalin was a favorite subject to fill a textbook. These books are no longer in circulation. A good textbook for English speaking students studying Russian is the one by Nina Potronova, Chairman of the U.S.S.R. Society of Friendship with the United States and England. This book published in 1959 by the Moscow publishing house Lulovski Blvd, 29, Moscow is a good start for anyone interested in the highly expressive Russian language. Political texts are kept to a minimum in this book and only make up about twenty per cent of the text. Most of the millions of text books printed in the Soviet Union every year are published at the Central Moscow Publishing House, a truly gigantic and monopolistic enterprise printing 69,000 titles in 1959 and 1,169,000 copies. Here foreign books are printed in the Russian language and others into any one of the one hundred of languages of minority groups in the U.S.S.R. Ninety per cent of the population of the U.S.S.R. speak Russian. However national languages are protected and propagated by law. Of the 208,827,000 million people in the Soviet Union, 114,114,000 count Russian as their national language; next is Ukranians 37,253,000, and Belorussians 7,913,000, and Ubekstans 6,015,000. The remaining population figures are distributed among eighteen minority and sixty factional groups, some of which have as few as 4,000 people speaking the tongue. Also there are 60,000 persons in the Soviet Union who are not of Soviet origin. Of these the leaders are Yugoslavs 5,000, Albanians 4,800, Afgans 1,900, Uangols 1,800, Italians 1,200, (unintelligible) 1,000, Spanish 1,000, and Argentinians (estimated) 4,000. (Since the figures for Argentine immigrants are not given, 1960 figures for the Soviet Union, pages 74-75.)

27. Figures for Books and Foreign Books

Fifty per cent of all the 69,000 titles printed in the U.S.S.R. in 1959 were technical or industrial textbooks. Only twenty per cent of these titles were for light reading. Of those most concerned war stories reflecting the struggle and victory of the Soviet armed forces over the Nazis during the Second World War as well as heroic novels about opening up the virgin lands in Siberia and the wild country east of the Urals. As was described by Irving Levine in his book "Main Street U.S.S.R," love stories are few and far between with them apt to be "boy loves-tractors-loves girl," episode or how Ivan increased production at his machine to win the admiration of Natasha, the shop foreman. Foreign novels are very popular in the U.S.S.R. because of the comparability racy lines. However foreign writers seem to be chosen because they write about the decay and immorality of their respective country. Every foreign book seems to be chosen to show that if capitalism isn't dead or dying it should.

American authors include Jack London, Ernest Hemmingway, and others. Some of these writers are often very popular in the U.S.A. but not for the same reasons. Jack London wrote what we consider adventure stories while the Russians consider them to be reflective of present day life. Ernest Hemmingway wrote, "Old Man and the Sea," a deeply touching story of man's struggle against nature and the sea, where here it is considered an indictment of capitalist society, although Hemmingway, unlike Jack London, was never a Socialist.

For a person reading detective stories by foreign writers, one gets a very depressing feeling and is overwhelmed by the grayness and dullness of the life depicted in them. Other foreign authors including Leonard Frank, German nihilist William Goodwin, "Things As They Are," English, and more classical writers such as Alexander Drue, "Count Margo," French author. "Sherlock Holmes and Captain Blood" are also known and read in the U.S.S.R. but such titles are few and hard to find. Dickens however, is in profusion wherever one goes. Mark Twain books are also found in quantity. Such novels of three hundred to four hundred pages sell for 1.50 rubles or less. Spy stories rank high in fiction publication and therefore are popular with the plots more often than not American or West German spies chased and captured in the end by the young, handsome, Soviet courier espionage agent.

Newspapers and magazines are also a giant undertaking with the printing, if not the information agencies, less centralized and controlled. In 1959 periodicals and magazines numbered 4,029 titles and 10,000,000 copies.

28. Newspapers

Newspapers numbered 10,603 trade union, republican, city and collective farms papers, with thirteen and one half billion copies. Foreign newspapers are not allowed in the country except representative Communist Party papers such as the "Worker," United States; "Daily Worker," England; "Humanity," France; "New Germany," East Germany; "The Daily Berliner," West Germany; etc.

The main publications in the U.S.S.R. are "Pravda," "Truth," organ of the Communist Party of the U.S.S.R. and Isvestia, "The News," organ of the Council of Ministers of the Soviet Union. It may be noted that the Chairman of the Council of Ministers and the First Secretary of the Communist Party of the U.S.S.R. is one man, Nikita S. Khrushchev. All republican and city newspapers take their cue from these two leading dailies, reprinting articles passed to them by TASS, the Soviet news agency, government controlled. All newspapers are organs of one or another ministry or their subsidiaries. In Minsk, the newspapers are "Soviet Belorussia," organ of the Central Committee of the Communist Party of Belorussia. Sport newspapers are the organ of the Ministry of Physical Culture and the railroads' newspapers are the organ of the Ministry of Transport, etc. The name of the organ of control is printed at the top of the first page. Russian newspapers from "Pravda" right on down consist of four pages except on spy events where the number is increased from four pages for two kopecks to six pages for three kopecks. Advertising is unknown and unnecessary in a government controlled economy where prices are raised and lowered as the Seven Year Plan fluctuates up and down. The first page in all Soviet language is developed to Party news and speeches. The second is to production notices and local industrial achievements such as the opening of a new dam as the overfalling or overfulfilling plans at a plant. The third page is filled with foreign news items. Often covered and credited to A.P. or Reuter's news agencies, they usually concern strikes and clashes with police, crime and race incidents in capitalist countries as well as other "News," slanted to give a bad impression that all countries except those who are members of the Socialist camp or their fellow travelers such as Cuba, who are painted as prosperous democracies fighting against imperialism from without, and capitalist spies and agents from within.

29. Films

Films carry the propaganda ball where books and newspapers leave off, with 90,872 movie houses in the U.S.S.R., with collective farm clubs bringing the total to 118,000 movie houses. The average number of times a Soviet citizen goes to the movies, per year, including men, women, and children, is 16.5 times (page 319.) There is a joke current in the Soviet Union as to why N. S. Khrushchev received his third hero of the Soviet Union medal, the highest order in the Soviet Union. The answer is for his part in the film "Our Nikita Khrushchev," a documentary circulated in the summer of 1961, of old films showing Khrushchev in his younger days as a Commissioner on the Eastern front or touring Industries after the war. Half of the hundreds of films made in 1959-1960 were either revolutionary, historical, or war stories. Others were virgin land or Far North adventure stories. Most every Republic has its own studio which shoot pictures concerning their respective places. In Belorussia it's the Bele films on "Soviet Street." It employs scores of operators, technicians, writers, costume films, but no permanent (non-amateur) actors. All of these have finished the artist and operators higher school of film making in Leningrad, a 3-or-4 year course and have diplomas in their respective fields. During the week of October 9-15 the following movies were shown in Minsk: "Too Live," a revolutionary film of the 1917s; "Clear Sky," the film presented at the film festival in Moscow in July 1961 which took first place; a film about the post Stalin era - it condemns repression of the main character, an ex-prisoner of war who is driven out of the party because he didn't die as all good soldiers must but was captured instead (this film is very symbolic of the new government line condemning some of the tactics of Stalin and his clique); "The Fair," a West German film against militarism; and "The Poor Street," a Bulgarian film about the resistance in the Second World War.

Foreign films make up quite a large percentage of movies shown here since the young Soviet film industry is not well subsidized and cannot turn out half of the demand for films.

German, Italian, and French films as well as more numerous films from the "People's Republics" are popular here. American films are few, although well liked for the technical skill and production. American films shown in 1959-1960 were "Rhapsody" with Elizabeth Taylor, "Eve" with Joan Crawford, "The Seventh Voyage of Sinbad" made in 1959, and "Serenade of Sun Valley" made in the 40s. Others were "Vienna Waltz" about the life of the composer, and "Old Man and the Sea," a technicolor film of

Ernest Hemmingway's book. "War and Peace" was also shown to vast audiences in two serials.

Prices for seats in movie houses, unlike the United States, change for adults and children and also for the location of rows, with the center rows costing fifty Kopecks in the evening and front row seat thirty kopecks. Shows until five o'clock are ten Kopecks cheaper per seat, until the prices change. Showings are at posted times on the tickets and doors are opened for only five minutes while spectators take their designated seats. Nobody even has to stand because tickets are sold only according to the number of seats in the hall, per showing.

31-32. T.V. and Radio

Television is organized and shown in order not to interfere with work in industries. Monday to Friday programs start at six in the evening, quite enough to allow any work to get home in time for the start but not enough to allow him to take time off to watch television or become a television addict as we have in the U.S. Programs finish at eleven in the evening so that all the workers can get enough sleep. On Saturdays, they start at three to compensate for the shop work day and end at twelve or twelve-thirty. Sunday programs start as early as ten-thirty in the morning and end at twelve o'clock. Programs are varied but include as always, more than thirty-three percent pure Soviet politics but often there are good films, reruns of movies, and cartoons for the kids. The best programs, however, of all are the ballet performances from Moscow and Leningrad. Bolshoi theaters and symphonic music concerts are often used to break the monotonous run of politics and dry facts and figures. A show for a Sunday evening is like the one show in Minsk on October 22, 1961: 6:30 Sports; 7:25 Soviet Army Show; 8:25 a feature length film "Baltic Sky," Second Party; 10:30 at the 22nd Congress of the Communist Party of the Soviet Union "News"; 11:00 performance by people's artist of the U.S.S.R. G.

Glebove, who sings songs of the motherland; 11:50 news; and 12:00 sign off with the playing of the National Anthem and the anthem of Belorussia. Television however is not a force as it is in the U.S. because of the poor programs and the cost of television. A good one costs three hundred and fifty rubles and the light table models for one hundred and ninety rubles, rarely bought in, are quickly bought up. There were 103,200 television sets in Belorussia in 1960. The really penetrating voice of modern society comes from radio (unitelligible), and extensive. It is the means by which the Kremlin reaches into every nook and cranny to the most outlying collective farms or villages. While three million television sets were sold from 1952-1958 in the Soviet Union (facts and figures, page 343), over twenty-nine million radio sets were sold and this figure is brought up considerably when one considers the fact that whole collective farms, which may not have a radio in the place, have programs fed to reproducers in each home from points many miles away in keeping with the general plan to bring the cultural level of these collective farms up. And in the Soviet Union there are 45,000 collective farms and 7,400 State farms with 65,500,000 on them, or 31.4% of the total population (facts for 1961, page 27). So radio may be said to be the all encompassor. Programs start in Minsk at six and may end so late as two a.m. However, twenty-four hours a day broadcast are made to all parts of the Soviet Union from Moscow. There are 18.5 million radios and reproducers in Belorusse which can turn all stations to its one channel in a matter of minutes. This was when Gagarin made his epoch making trip into space, the entire Soviet Union was blanked out with nothing but reports and intermittent music for a solid day. In this way the government gets the most propaganda value out of its achievements. Again when Herman Titov made his flight for two days, this process was repeated. Also all stations are immediately turned to the Kremlin whenever Premier Khrushchev makes a policy speech. All stations in the Soviet Union are regularly turned every hour on the hour to the "news" from Moscow. Unlike the U.S.A. where small independent stations can operate, the Soviet Union rigorously imposes control over all it State broadcasting stations which, like industries, are all State financed and built. The radio and television station in Minsk is a four storied cement building located at no.6 Kalinina Street near the small River "SVISHLICH." Behind it stands the impressive five hundred feet steel radio towers, the highest structure in Belorussia. This radio tower and building are enclosed with high fences and a patrolling armed guard with a dog. Entrance into the courtyard must be through the building itself and persons cannot enter without a special pass shown to an armed guard. Performers are taken to a separate studio near the city center where production and performers are fed back to the station and them to the broadcasting towers. In this way the all important communications system is guarded against sabotage or "takeovers" of the sort often achieved by Latin American counter-revolutionary and malcontents elements.

Near the television tower, four blocks East on "Dolgabroadckay" Street stands two more towers approximately two hundred feet high each. They are not engaged in broadcasting, quite the opposite in fact. These very apparent landmarks, with high power cables strung between them, are jamming towers, used to blank out high frequency broadcast from abroad. The main target of these jamming towers is the Munich and Washington transmitters of the "Voice of America" programs, although they are sometimes employed to disrupt the B.B.C. and French broadcasts in Russian. These towers are likewise guarded by armed guards and entrance to the wire enclosed block house and tower area is forbidden except by passes. The amount of voltage used by these towers is known to be tremendous when one considers that needed lighting at workplaces is only grudgingly turned on even on the cloudy days. It is ironical and sad to think of the tremendous waste and effort the Soviet government goes to in order to keep other peoples ideas out. But the jamming frequencies are only half those of the "Radio Moscow" propaganda programs which may be heard on any shortwave radio in the United States without jamming. These "Radio Moscow" programs ensure peoples in eighty-one countries that the Iron Curtain no longer exists, never did exist, and is in general a fictitious slander against the Soviet Union thought up by reactionaries, sick!!!

33. Opera and Museums

Opera is also a favorite entertainment in the U.S.S.R. with thirty-two operas and ballet houses throughout the fifteen republics. As compared with one in the United States, the Metropolitan Opera House in New York, that is because Russians have their own operas written by their own Russian composers, while we have none. Here any person can tell you about such splendid operas as "Reiglo," "The Clown," "Queen of Spades," and "Traviate," while in the U.S. most citizens are sadly lacking in this field of art due not to the fallacy that we are uncultured as the Russians think, but due to the fact that we simply do have the facilities to put such productions on. Although there are those who prefer to remain tied to their T.V.s and comedy shows.

Comedy and drama theater number fifty-three with eleven in Belorussia. Plays are put on by amateur and professional groups in the Russian language or the languages of the republics. In Minsk the Belorussian drama theater on "VOIADARSKAYA" Street has a troupe of fifty-five professionals earning from ninety to one hundred and forty rubles a month putting on four plays a week in the Belorussian language. Sets and costume are always well made in any productions I saw, but the scripts are apt to be overloaded with politics in the dramas.

Museums exist for the education and learning of the population. Of these twenty-six are historical revolutionary, eighty-nine historical, one hundred and seventy-one memorial (the House of Shikovski in Moscow near the American Embassy), four hundred twenty-one of local or regional interest, and one hundred twenty-two art museums as well as sixty-eight more of different kinds bringing the total to exactly 907. There are thirty-seven in Minsk. In the year 1959, forty-three million people visited these places of interest as well as 7,200,000 who visited the famous permanent exhibition of Soviet achievements in Moscow's "SKOLHIKEY" Park. Here a huge display covering twenty-five acres was set up in 1955. It advertises real and imagined progress for tourist and Russians like. In it are sputniks and jet airliners, a tractor exhibition house in a building 300 feet long, housing and industrial samples. The light consumer industry is shown more as the Russians would like it to be than as it is with pocket radio (there are none made in quantity in the U.S.S.R.). Automatic washing machines with two spinners (from 1952-1958) - there were 1.2 million made and sold. All simply one spinners and modern vacuum cleaners (1950-1958), 500,000 sold. However this doesn't keep Russians from hoping that some day these things will be in mass production, and undoubtedly they shall be.

Another means of distributing propaganda are through the Agitpunks, or in English "agitation points." These are located at desks or in small offices open sixteen hours a day. They are manned by "volunteer" Communist and Young Communist Party members. They are for the distribution of pamphlets, bulletins and other party literature, for the more or less informal meetings of groups of Communist Party members. Formed in the early 1920s, they were then points of armed workers located near to each other who would could down "white" uprisings or conveniently arrest anyone in the neighborhood. Now their functions have slightly changed but it's still known that any party member may come in and report disloyal comments at an unguarded moment on the part of any citizen: there is always a telephone handy here. In Minsk there are only twelve movie houses but fifty-eight agitpunks in the telephone book. They can be recognized at a distance by red flags and banners dropped over the doors and windows of the respective building.

34. Young Communist League

The Young Communist League or YCL embraces all young people from the age of sixteen until they outgrow the children's Pioneer League. Ninety per cent of all persons between the ages of sixteen to twenty-six belong to this organization, although they may attain a Communist Party membership as early as nineteen or twenty years. Signed on as soon as they receive their "passport" at sixteen, they receive a YCL party ticket and must pay a small due of seventy or eighty kopecks a month. After this they are obligated to attend YCL meetings, go on harvesting trips on weekends during the fall to collective farms to help bring in the potato and grain, and to keep their studies up to high standards. A violation of conduct or refusal to tow the line will result in expulsion from the League and is a block to personal progress in the Soviet Union since membership is considered a reference in hiring in factories or institutions reviewing requests for a place at higher educational institutions. Expulsions are fairly common, about twenty per cent being expelled before reaching the age where they may be chosen for Communist Party membership. A young student may become rather popular and powerful by being elected to the post of YCL secretary in his classes at school or at work. A sure way to success is to remain at this post in one's local school or institute keeping high standards of marks and discipline until chosen for party membership. In this way young people get a taste of what the Party can do for them if they have the right attitude.

35. Y.C.L. and People Police

At our shop, the YCL secretary is Arkadia _____ a tall, handsome, langly Russian of twenty-four with a broad grin. He reminds one of a Texas or Oklahoma boy. His father is a minor bureaucrat while his mother works as a nurse. Therefore they have a full three room apartment. Arkadia has worked at this factory for years after serving his three years in the navy in the Black

Sea. He was only recently elected to the post of YCL secretary in our shop, after the former person received CP membership. Usually an easy-going fellow if you don't get him rallied, he takes his YCL duties seriously collecting dues on every other pay day (which are on the fifth and twentieth of the month) of one per cent of the total paycheck, of one per cent of eighty rubles, eighty Kopecks. He checks off names and is responsible for turning in the cash to the factory YCL committee. He is responsible for posting directives handed down by the YCL factory committee for helping to draw up the list of Droozhniks who shall have the duty during this month. Droozhniks are "volunteer" civilians who patrols streets and parks as peace and order keepers. They are given a special card which they carry and when on duty wear red arm bands. They help to subsidize the police in its more routine work, such as walking a beat in a usually quiet district. Droozhniks always walk in groups of threes and fours, often women and girls are seen in this capacity. This custom is relatively new and is not generally used except on Saturdays and Sundays when there are boisterous groups as teenagers and a large number of drunks to be seen. Both these types of groups are on the downgrowth at least, partly due to these "volunteer" efforts. Besides helping to draw up the list of Droohniks is their respective shops, the YCL secretary is expected to set high examples of work and political "preparedness" to their fellow members and to help the shop and section leaders get to know his workers.

In Minsk the Young Communist headquarters is a long grey cement four story building on "KAPASNO ARMI" Street or in English, "Red Army Street." Inside, the building is honey combed with two hundred rooms, an auditorium, and meeting hall. Three hundred people are permanently employed here to do the work of the YCL. Also here is the Central Committee of the YCL of Belorussia. They review cases of expulsion and direct YCL party organization. The actual political influence of this committee is almost nothing compared to the Central Committee. YCL in all cities are directed by the CP headquarters in their respective cities.

36. Central Committee and Ministries

The headquarters of the Central Committee of the CPB is located on "Karl Marx Street," an eight storied yellow metal and brick structure. It is rectangular shaped with straight shape lines and almost none of the gaudy decorations found on most buildings in the city. "The First Secretary of the Central Committee of the CP of Belorussia" is the imposing title carried by a short stocky man in his late 50's, K.T. Mazoorof. Rarely seen on the streets, he and his family occupy a huge eight-room apartment on the top floor of a government apartment house on prospect Stalin. Entrance to this apartment is guarded night and day by one uniformed policeman who checks passes and keeps unauthorized persons out. Here is also the residence of several ministers such as the Minister of Education, B. Poroshebed, and the Minister of Administration, E. Zhezhel. Mazoorof controls and directs all activities in his republic with authority no United States governor has ever enjoyed, while his authority cannot be controlled or challenged by court orders or injunctions as it often is in the United States. Mazoorof is responsible directly to Moscow and the party presidium chaired by Khrushchev. He appears in the reviewing box in the center of his cronies, on May 1st and November 7th holidays, where waves a congenial hand occasionally without the trace of a smile. He isn't elected to his post in a general election anymore than Khrushchev is elected to the post of premier, but rather appointed from the members of the Supreme Soviet of the Republic who are elected on the one candidate ticket which is prepared and authorized in the first place, by the Central Committee of the Communist Party of the respective republics. Therefore the Central Committee chooses the members of the Supreme Soviet from whose members replacements for vacated seats in the Central Committee are filled. Replacement may be required in the case of "death, derangement, higher appointment to the Central Committee of the Soviet Union, or expulsion from the party" under the Party constitution, government procedure in the Central Committee.

37-39. Corruption in the USSR

Corruption in the U.S.S.R. takes a major form in embezzling and greasing of palms as in any purely bureaucratic society. In 1961, the death penalty for embezzlement of State funds in large sums was reenacted as an answer to widespread pilfering of goods, crops and embezzling of money and State bonds. On any collective or state farm there is a certain percent of State goods illegally appropriated by the collect farmers for their own private use to make up for low wages and therefore low living conditions, often sold to private individuals, stores or at the open market type of bazaars. These goods may consist of only a pilfered lamb or piglet or may run in scores of sheep or cows hidden in backwater swamps or thick pine forest and sold by the appropriator piecemeal or in wholesale lots to crooked store supervisors, who are supposed to buy State meats and crops at government prices, but pocket the differences in prices from the black market without making entrances in their books that such merchandise was brought for State prices. Such practices are so common that without them many stores would be almost empty if they had to rely on the sporadic, poor quality meats brought in from the State slaughterhouses at high prices. The directorship of even a small fruit or milk store opens up wide opportunities for lucrative enterprising by person with a slight business sense. It is almost impossible for authorities to act on such going on because of difficulties in obtaining proof in acceptable amounts since such going on are usually in small amounts. Materials such as electric appliances and dining tables are often ridden with speculation which often leads to poor goods or bad foods brought in and sold under the counter. Examples are horse meat used to subsidize a "beef stew."

Most of the bureaucratic apparatus can be detoured by a well placed ten spot. Persons occupying most of the housing ministry and passport and visa offices expect remuneration for the life and death services which all Russians seek namely, to receive permission for an apartment, and official visas to live in such an apartment, and compulsory laws in the Soviet Union. Without a city "visa" stamp a person cannot work in that city. Once a position or work is decided or taken it is a very difficult process to secure permission and work in order to receive an apartment in another city, therefore to live in another city. In such instances the administrator of an apartment house may expect 60-100 rubles for his stamp of approval on a request blank for an apartment or into an apartment already occupied by a family who are expecting to leave one city for another. The usual method of getting a room or apartment without having to wait on the so called housing list which may take five to seven years to receive a one room "apartment." In any bureaucratic society a class of desk administrators is always born who expect their palms greased and who exploit their position for self-purposes. However in the U.S.S.R. such practices take on a particularly potent nature, since it is not simply a matter of receiving rare services or conveniences but a matter of getting the fundamental things of life - a simple room, a work stamp, permission to see a relative in a city inside a restricted zone such as border zones or military base and rocket base zones. In order to receive permission to leave one city and live in another because of individual choice, a person must receive permission from the local passport agency in the city from which he is leaving and from the city to which he is going. Then he must show that he has received a place of living in that city to which he is going, as well as permission to move (from the military authority if he is militarily obligated) from the police and security agency in case he has government or secret work. He must show that his specialty or profession will be used in the city to which he goes. All this creates piles of paperwork and photos, references, documents, and notarized declarations but the main obstacle to moving in the U.S.S.R. is getting a place to live, since it would be years if one simply applied for a place in the housing line. Even if one can live until with friends or relatives for the time being, they could rent a nook from somebody, they could not work because without a living visa stamps on one's "passport." It is against the law for any directors or administrators of any enterprise, store or office, to give work to that person since without a living visa one cannot get a "work stamp." Even renting a room to a person who cannot get a living visa to that room is against the law (speculating). So although moving from one city to another is quite legal now (after the war it wasn't) it is a long process of red tape, greasing palms and struggling against bureaucratic procedure. That is why few people actually do change cities or exercise paper rights. The structure and procedure of Soviet society control the flow of people and their occupations and hence value, to the State. Any Russian will tell you he can change jobs or move to another city any time he wants to. This is true, however he must meet certain requirements in order to receive new work, although he may indeed quit any job he likes. Up until 1950 a person could not quit a job without police and State security permission. It was simply compulsory to work at the job one had been assigned to. Nowadays it is more common that foremen enforce a Soviet law making permissible the holding of any workers who cannot be replaced. In the event a worker does not chose to remain at his place of work or chooses to refuse a certain job, he can be tried by a peoples court and sent to a work camp or prison for terms ranging up to three years.

40. Virgin Land Volunteers

Such work laws safeguard the State from "sabotage" of State property. Work stamps and passes as well as permission from proper authority in regards to living passes and the "work passes" is the indirect control influx and outflux of what Marx called "Scruples of Labor," which in a capitalist society has no control and is determined by mode and matter of production and economic conditions which are always fluctuating. Therefore it is not the liberation of the proletarian masses but rather the administration of State machinery which regulates population and labor moves in a geographic sense and isolates instances of backflow of labor in specialized economic areas, which leads to unemployment in capitalist countries due to automation and over production, both of which can be carefully controlled by the State, which builds and operates all enterprises in the U.S.S.R. In such cases, as there are, of overflow of labor, the excess is portioned off by the "living visa" system, and since there is no place for them to live and the extra workers realize there is no place for the workers. The "virgin land" program is instrumented, and surplus labor is promptly shipped off to a promised room and work. This is one of Khrushchev's favorite plans and has been a spectacular failure, mostly owing to the quick subsiding of enthusiasm of the young people (for most part) seeing conditions of five to a room hostel erected, "towns" of concrete blocks with unpaved streets in village conditions, 1,000 miles from their mothers and families in the overcrowded, lack of work-demanding cities (mostly Moscow, Leningrad, Kiev and a few of the other big population centers). Conditions for leaving the Virgin land center and young back home are simple: get up and go, but few do, because they must pay their own way back, a cost of sometimes two hundred rubles or more and also face the same conditions which drove them from the cities in the first place.

41. Elections

When elections are initiated in the U.S.S.R. a whole huge, mechanical apparatus is started, not only to ensure victory, but to safeguard the State from any voice of dissent, either in absenteeism or opposition. All eligible voters (that is from the age of sixteen up) are registered well beforehand by "agitators," who go around to every door in their district getting names and notifying all voters of their duty to the Motherland in voting. In the case of the elections held throughout the Soviet Union on March 18,

1962 to "elect" the Supreme Soviet including Khrushchev, the People's Movement (House of Representatives) and the Soviet of Nationalities, the agitator came on January 24 and February 20. On election day all voters go to the polls (usually a school) and vote. They are given a ballot which they drop into a box. On the ballot is the single name of the candidates for each post. That's all anybody does, ever does, to "vote." This system ensures a ninety-nine per cent turnout and predetermined victory. In each polling place there is a booth for secret balloting (crossing out the candidate and writing in your own). Under Soviet law anyone can do this. Nobody does this for the obvious reason that anyone who enters the booth may be identified. There is a Soviet joke about the floor dropping out from anyone stepping into the booth. But the fact is if the entire population used the polling booth they could beat the system. However years of mass discipline and fear have made the people afraid to attempt any such demonstration. And with no means of communication at the hands of a would-be candidate, there is no way for communication with the people and wiping up support for a black horse candidate.

42. The Army

Universal military training has been in force in the U.S.S.R. for several years. Unlike the U.S., drafting always takes place at nineteen years of age, all other reasons for exemption notwithstanding. Periods of service are from two years in the North to three years in the South. Climactic conditions vary so much that many young men elect to the relatively sunny South to serve for three years, rather then to the nine month bitter cold winters of camps in Siberia or Sakhalin in the far North-East. Clothing issues are scarce in the beginning and in getting one's clothes cleaned, and dirty clothes thrown into a common pile to be cleaned off and steamed and brought back in a common pile with the result that a soldier never gets the same jackets and trousers twice. Barracks are usually bare and damp, even in Minsk, where they are located in the older parts of town behind high walls. Passes are never given except on holidays and sometimes on Sundays or after manoeuvres. Leave of thirty days as our armed forces guarantee in their contracts are unknown. However the greatest difference is pay. After Marshall Mikalyn became commander in chief of the Soviet armed forces in the early 1950's, pay was summarily cut for common soldiers (privates) from 3.30 rubles old money to three rubles new money, a loss of 29.7 rubles (new). Three rubles are enough to buy twelve packs of cigarettes, twenty cigarettes to a package whereas thirty rubles was enough for a soldier to save up for his discharge. The pay of a lath worker in Minsk is eighty rubles new money. The drop of money was less felt in the officers' ranks since they lose only a ten per cent cut up to the rank of Major.

And no loss of pay for major and above. A lieutenant in the Russian army gets one hundred eighty rubles. A full soldier gets around three hundred rubles but also gets "duty expense" pay, like our travel pay. Discipline in the Russian army is supposed to be the most rugged in the world since top sergeants can hand out up to fifteen day sentences to any private any time he wants to without a court martial for minor offenses. Duties at a base camp or barracks may be more like a prison than an American base as we know it, with soda fountains, clubs where alcoholic drinks are served, a snack bars, and PX's. As soldiers are never allowed to wear civilian clothes (this is against military law) we might think such life to be exceedingly drab even for a soldier but Russians have such drab lives on the outside that there is no conflict of color between civilian and military life. When I told about the basic features of American military life in the U.S. marine Corp, the ex-soldier I knew usually laughed and said we have no discipline but I'm quite sure the ohs and ahs were signs of admiration when I spoke of our "undisciplined" army, especially the complete absence of political lectures under our system of separation of Army and State, and also the fact that at the end of each work day we could put on civies and pile in the car and drive up to town to a movie or a dance, army discipline without a wall, with money in our pockets and our own military obligation clearly understood and in our own hands.

43. Army

44. Taxes

45. Destruction of Monument to Stalin in 1961

The New Era

In Minsk there was a thirty-five foot monument to Stalin which stood even after the first denunciation of Stalin by Khrushchev, unlike the monument of Stalin in Leningrad which was torn down immediately.

This impressive bronze and marble structure has stood for as long as it was due to the efforts of diehard Stalinists such as Colonel Petrokof head of the O.V.E.E.R. Office in Minsk and others. However, after the 22nd Congress meeting when Khrushchev again denounced Stalin on November 5 two days before the November 7 revolutionary celebrations, a force of one hundred men descended upon the then Stalin Square (now Lenin Square) and with bulldozer and piledriver commenced to tear up (not salvage) the structure. They must have been very enthusiastic because next day they had removed the ten ton bronze figure of a man revered by the older generation and laughed at by the sarcastic younger generation.

The most remarkable thing about the destruction of this giant monument was that work was ceased on the 6th of November but started again on the 7th, the very day the big parade of workers came by. The monument was right across from the reviewing stand as it was built to be. In full view of all the dignitaries and workers going by, the destruction of Stalin and the symbolic ending of Stalinism (Khrushchev hopes) was concluded.

But Belorussia as in Stalin's native Georgia is still a stronghold of Stalinism and a revival of Stalinism is a very, very possible thing in those two republics.

1.3 Commission Exhibit 25 (*Notes Written on Holland –American Line Stationary*, 16 H 106-122)

I have often wondered why it is that the communist, capitalist and even the fascist and anarchist elements in America, always profess patriotism toward the land and the people, if not the government; although their movements must surely lead to the bitter destruction of all and everything.

I am quite sure these people must hate not only the government but the culture, heritage and very people itself, and yet they stand up and piously pronounce themselves patriots, displaying their war medals, that they gained in conflicts between themselves.

I wonder what would happen if somebody was to stand up and say he was utterly opposed not only to the governments, but to the people, to the entire land and complete foundations of his socially.

I have heard and read of the resurgent Americanism in the U.S., not the ultra-right type, but rather the polite, seemingly pointless Americanism expressed by such as the "American fore group" and the freedom foundation.

And yet even in these veiled, formless, patriotic gestures, there is the obvious "axe being ground" by the invested interests of the sponsors of their expensive undertaking.

To where can I turn? To factional mutants of both systems, to odd-ball Hegelian idealists out of touch with reality religious groups, to revisionist or too absurd anarchism. No!

To a person knowing both systems and their factional accessories, there can no mediation between the systems as they exist today and that person.

He must be opposed to their basic foundations and representatives.

And yet it is immature to take the sort of attitude which says "a curse on both your houses!"

There are two great representatives of power in the world, simply expressed, the left and right, and their factions and concerts.

Any practical attempt at one alternative must have as its nucleus the traditional ideological best of both systems, and yet be utterly opposed to both systems.

For no system can be entirely new, that is where most revolutions industrial and political, go astray. And yet the new system must be opposed unequivocally to the old. That is also where the revolutions go astray.

At the turn of the century in America, in the emerging industrial revolution, private enterprise triumphed because it offered a new, efficient and promising future while still observing the idealistically democratic ideals of its overthrown predecessor, i.e. rural small enterprise.

And at about the same time the Tsarist Russian aristocracy was overthrown by the peasants and workers and the road laid open for the gaining of power by the Bolsheviks because they too, offered a bright new future without violating historical traditions of Russian working class life.

In history there are many such examples of the nucleus of the new order rooted in the idealistic tradition of the old.

The Industrial revolution horrored the present atomic age and yet it has developed as an intricate part of its system its own shortcomings.

Automation for instance.

Automation may be compared to the run away robot who displays so many facilities that it is obvious it is run away. Rather it is the much more subtle aspects of Industrialization and mechanization which brings the greatest hardships upon the people, a general decay of classes into shapeless socialites without real cultural foundations, regimentation, not so much of people since industrialization actively provides for more free movement of classes around each other, but rather of ideals although those regimented ideals have more freedom of expression throughout all the classes.

The biggest and key fault development of our era is of course the fight for markets between the imperialist powers themselves, which lead to the wars, crises and oppressive friction which you have all come to regard as part of your lives.

And it is this prominent factor of the capitalist system which will undoubtedly eventually lead to the common destruction of all the imperialistic powers. Already many lesser imperialistic countries have become dependent upon other factors than domination of colonies through force. They have been divested of their former colonies by the great imperialist countries or in some cases even given up their colonies themselves as unprofitable and many cases even given up their colonies themselves as unprofitable and many cases the oppressed peoples rose up and physically threw the colonist out and this process is continuing even today as we all can see. But what is important to remember

is that the old system of capitalism even within itself is revising and what is most evident, forming imperialistic economic coalitions, such as the common market.

In the communist experiment several factions and unavoidable developments have emerged which Marx and Engels could not possibly have forseen. There emerges with increasing clarity two monumental mistakes which Marx and Engels made, not to mention the very keystone of Marx's economic theory "the doctrine of surplus value" which has always been unshakey and controversial.

The first mistake is fairly well known at this stage in the communist development, the "withering away of the state" as it was called. Marx envisualized that the abolition of classes would lead to the gradual reduction of the state apparatus. However, this is not the case and is better observed than contemplated. The state rather becomes more extensive in that while the powers of central ministries are delegated they are not reduced in the dividing of an organ of state power into smaller units at lower levels. So although the ministers have actually disappeared, to Moscow they have become more entranced than ever at lower levels. Thus in dividing power you multiply units and in everyday life you become more and more dependent on these organs of state power wherever you turn, before you meet them and they touch the lives of people more and more, and a new bureaucracy, rather than a withering away of the state. In Russia in the last two years there has been a shift of power from the capital of Moscow to the so-called "Republics" but the state apparatus, simply grows into a greater maze throughout the republics. Thus in Minsk, the capital of Belorussia, the ministry of Interia became responsible in the 1960 for determining the eligibility of applicants for hard-to-get exit visas to leave the USSR formally, the official prerogative of Moscow alone. But now that this state ministry in Moscow has "withered away", it becomes all the more difficult to get an exit visa since now one has to the area, city and republican state capital committees of bureaucrats and on top of all that a last final O.K. has to come from incredibly the Moscow Ministry of Foreign Affairs!! The withering away of the state as Marx envisualized was an unforseen mistake pointed out by many critics of Marx.

The second mistake of Engels and Marx made is much more obscure but fundamentally just as important.

In the late 1800's Engels wrote Anti Duhring which rightly criticized Eugen Duhring, a German idealist, who was supposedly not consistent enough in his materialism for the dialectal materialist Marx. In his critical analysis of Duhring, Engels said with much heavy sarcasam that Duhring only changed a word in his putting forward of his social revolutionary ideas, that a changed word 'was the word community from the word state' whereas Duhring wanted Social Democracy at a local or community level. Marx and Engels advocated a centralized <u>state</u> which would later "wither away!"

But in this Engels was mistaken again.

As history has shown time again the state remains and grows whereas true democracy can be practiced only at the local level. While the centralized state, administrative, political or supervisual remains, there can be no real democracy, a loose confederation of communities at a national level without any centralized state whatsoever.

In equal division, with safeguards against coalitions of communities there can be democracy, not in the centralized state delegating authority but in numerous equal communities practicing and developing democracy at the local level.

There have already been a few organizations which have disclosed that they shall become effective only <u>after</u> conflict between the two world systems leaves the country without defense or foundation of governments, organizations such as the Minutemen for instance. However, they are preparing to simply defend the present system and reinstate its influence after the mutual defeat of both systems <u>militarily</u> which is more or less taken for granted.

These armed groups will represent the remaining hard core of fanatical American capitalist supporters.

There will undoubtedly be similar representation of this kind by communist groups in communist countries.

There will also be many decided religious segments putting forward their own alternatives and through larger memberships than the Minutemen, etc.

There will also be anarchist, pacifist and quite probably fascist splinter groups. However all these, unlike the Minutemen and communist partisan groups, will be unarmed.

The mass of survivors however will not belong to any of these groups. They will not be fanatical enough to join extremists, and will be too disillusioned to support either the communist of capitalist parties in their respective countries after the atomic catastrophe.

They shall seek an alternative to those systems which have brought them misery.

But their thinking and education will be steeped in the traditions of those systems. They would never accept a 'new order' any more than they would accept the extremist, etc. completely beyond their understanding. Logically, they would deem it necessary to oppose the old systems but support at the same time their cherished traditions.

I intend to put forward just such an alternative.

In making such a declaration I must say that in order to make this alternative effective supporters must prepare now in the event the materialist situation presents itself for the practical application of this alternative.

In this way the Minutemen and their narrow support of capitalism have been most far-sighted. However, they present only a suicide force whereas what is needed is a constructive and practical group of persons desiring peace but steadfastly opposed to the revival of forces who have led millions of people to death and destruction in a dozen wars and have now at this moment led the world into unsurpassed danger.

We have lived into a dark generation of tension and fear.

But how many of you have tried to find out the truth behind the cold war cliches!!

I have lived under both systems. I have <u>sought</u> the answers and although it would be very easy to dupe myself into believing one system is better than the other, I know they are not.

I despise the representatives of both systems whether they be socialist or Christian Democrats, whether they be Labor or Conservatives they are all products of the two systems. When I first went to Russia in the winter of 1959 my funds were very limited, so after a certain time, after the Russians had assured themselves that I was really the naïve American who believed in communism, they arranged for me to receive a certain amount of money every month. OK, it came technically through the Red Cross as financial help to a Russian political immigrate but it was arranged by the M.V.D. I told myself it was simply because I was broke and everybody knew it. I accepted the money because I was hungry and there were several inches of snow on the ground in Moscow at that time but what is really was payment for my denunciation of the U.S. in Moscow in November 1959 and a clear promise that for as long as I lived in the USSR life would be very good. But I didn't realize this, of course, for almost two years.

As soon as I became completely disgusted with the Soviet Union and started negotiations with the American Embassy in Moscow for my return to the U.S., my "Red Cross" allotment was cut off.

This was not difficult to understand since all correspondence in and out of the Embassy is censored as is common knowledge in the Embassy itself.

I have never mentioned the fact of these monthly payments to anyone.

I do so in order to state that I shall never sell myself intentionally, or unintentionally, to anyone again.

As for my fee of $---- I was supposed to receive for this---- I refuse it. I made pretense to accept it only because otherwise I would have been considered a crack pot and not allowed to appear to express my views. After all who would refuse money?!?

1.4 **Commission Exhibit 100** (*Self-Questionnaire,* 16 H 436-437)

Version One

1.Q. Why did you go to the USSR? I went as a mark of disgust and protest against American political policies in foreign countries, my personal sign of discontent and horror at the misguided line of reasoning of the U.S. Government.

Q.A. What about those letters? I made several letters in which I expressed my above feelings to the American Embassy when in October 1959, I went there to legally liquidate my American citizenship and was refused this legal right.

Q.2.B. Did you make statements against the U.S. there? Yes.

Q.2.C. What about your type recording? I made a recording for Radio Moscow, which was broadcast the following Sunday, in which a spoke about the beautiful capital of the Socialist work and all its progress.

3. Did you any break law by residing in or taking work in the USSR? I did in that. I took an oath of allegiance to the USSR.

4. Isn't all work in the USSR considered State work? Yes of course and in that respect I also broke US Law in accepting work under a foreign state.

5 What about statements you made to UPI agent Miss Mosby? I was approached by Miss Mosby and other reporters just after I had formally requested the American Embassy to legally liquidate my U. S. citizenship, for a story, they were notified by the U. S. Embassy, not by me. I answered questions and made statements to Miss Mosby in regard to my reasons for coming to the USSR, her story was warped by her later, but in barest essence it is possible to say she had the truth printed.

6. Why did you remain in the USSR for so long if you only wanted a look? I resided in the USSR from October 16, 1959 to Spring of 1961, a period of 2 ½ years. I did so because I was living quite comfortably. I had plenty of money, an apartment rent-free, lots of girls, etc. Why should I leave all that?

7A Are you a communist? Yes basically, although I hate the USSR and socialist system, I still think Marxism can work under different circumstances.

7BQ. Have you ever know a communist? Not in the U.S.A.

8. What are the outstanding differences between the USSR and USA? None, except in the US the living standard is a little higher, freedoms are about the same, medical aid and the educational system in the USSR is better than in the USA.

Version Two

1.Q Why did you go to the USSR? I went as a citizen of the U.S. (as a tourist) residing in a foreign country, which I have a perfect right to do. I went there to see the land, the people and how their system works.

Q.A. What about those letters? I made no letters deriding the U.S.!! In correspondence with the U.S. Embassy I made no anti-American statements, any criticism I might have made was of policies not our government.

2.QQ Did you make statement against the U.S. there? No.

2 What about that tape recording? I made a recording for the Moscow Tourist Radio travel log, in which I spoke about sight-seeing and what I had seen in Moscow tourist circles. I expressed delight in all the interesting places. I mentioned in this respect the University, Museum of Art, Red Square, the Kremlin. I remember I closed this two minute recording my saying I hoped our peoples would live in peace and friendship.

3. Did you break laws by residing or taking work in the U.S.S.R? Under U.S. law a person may lose the protection of the U.S. by voting or serving in the armed forces of a foreign State or taking an oath of allegiance to that State. I did none of these.

4. Isn't all work in the U.S.S.R. considered State work? No. Technically only plants working directly for the State, usually defense, all other plants are owned by the workers who work in them.

5. What about the statements you made to U.P.I. agent Miss Mosby in 1959? I was approached just after I had formally notified the U.S. Embassy in Moscow of my future residence in the USSR by the newspaper agencies in Moscow including U.P.I., A.P.I., and Time Inc., who were notified by the Embassy. I did no call them. I answered questions and gave statements to Miss Mosby of U.P.I. I requested her to let me OK her story before she released it, which is the polite and usual thing. She sent her version of what I said just after she sent it. I immediately called her to complain about this, at which time she apologized but said her editor and not her had added several things. She said London was very excited about the story (there is how I deduced she had already sent it) so there wasn't much else I could do about it. And I didn't realize that the story was even more blown out of sharp once it got to the U.S.A. I'm afraid the printed story was fabricated sensationalism.

6. Why did you remain in the USSR for so long if you only wanted a look? I resided in the USSR until February 1961 when I wrote the Embassy stating I would like to go back. (My passport was at the Embassy for safekeeping) They invited me to Moscow for this purpose. However it took me almost one-half year to get a permit to leave the City of Minsk for Moscow. In this connection I had to use a letter form the head Consular to the Russian authorities in Minsk (the Russians are very bureaucratic and slow about letting foreigners travel about the country hence the visa). When I did get to Moscow the Embassy immediately gave me back my passport and advised me as to how to get an exit visa from the Russians for myself and my Russian wife. This long and arduous process took months from July 1962 until ____, ____1962. Therefore you see almost one year was spent in trying to leave the country. That's why I was there so long, not out of desire!

7. Are you a communist? Have you ever known a communist? No, of course not. I have never known a communist, outside of the ones in the USSR, but you can't help that.

8. What are the outstanding differences between the USA and USSR? Freedom of speech, travel, outspoken opposition to unpopular policies, freedom to believe in God.

Newspapers, Thank you sir, you are a real patriot!!

Gary W. O'Brien

1.5 **Commission Exhibit 102** (*Speech Before*, 16 H 442-443)

1. Americans are apt to scoff at the idea that a military coup in the US, as so often happens in Latin American countries, could ever replace our government but that is an idea that has grounds for consideration. Which military organization has the potentialities of executing such action? Is it the army, with its many conscripts, its unwieldly size, its scores of bases scattered across the world? The case of General Walker shows that the army, at least, is not fertile enough ground for a far right regime to go a very long way. For the same reasons of size and deposition, the navy and air force are also to be more or less disregarded. Which service then can qualify to lunch a coup in the USA? Small size, a permanent hard core of officers and a few bases are necessary. Only one outfit fits that description and the U.S.M.C. is a right wing, infiltrated organization of dire potential consequences to the freedoms of the U.S. I agree with former President Truman when he said that "The Marine Corps should be abolished".

2. My second reason is that undemocratic, country-wide institution known as segregation. It is, I think, the action of the active segregationist minority and the great body of indifferent people in the South do the United States more harm in the eyes of the world's people than the whole world communist movement. As I look at this audience there is a sea of white faces before me. Where are the Negroes amongst you (are they hiding under the table?) Surely if we are for democracy, let our fellow Negro citizens into this hall. Make no mistake, segregationist tendencies can be unlearned. I was born in New Orleans and I know.

In Russia I saw on several occasions that in international meetings the greatest glory in the sport field was brought to us by Negroes. Though they take the gold medals from their Russian competitors, those Negroes know that when they return to their own homeland they will have to face blind hatred and discrimination. The Soviet Union is made up of scores of naturalist Asians and Euro-Asian Armenian and Jews, whites and dark skinned peoples. Yet, they can teach us a lesson in brotherhood among peoples with different customs and origins.

3. A symbol of the American way, our liberal concession, is the existence in our midst of a minority group whose influence and membership is very limited and whose dangerous tendencies are sufficiently controlled by special government agencies. The Communist Party U.S.A. bears little resemblance to their Russian counterparts, but by allowing them to operate and even supporting their right to speak, we maintain a tremendous sign of our strength and liberalism. Harassment of their party newspaper, their leaders, and advocates is treachery to our basic principles of freedom and speech and press. Their views no matter how misguided, no matter how much the Russians take advantage of them, must be allowed to be aired. After all, Communist U.S.A. has existed for 40 years and they are still a pitiful group of radicals.

4. Now-a-days – most of us read enough about certain right wing groups to know how to recognize them and guard against their corrosive effects. I would like to say a word about them, although there is possibly few other American born persons in the U.S. who know as many personal reasons to know and therefore hate and mistrust communism. I would never become a pseudo-professional anti-communist such as Herbert Philbricks or McCarthy. I would never jump on any of the many right wing bandwagons because our two countries have too much to offer to each other to be tearing at each other's truths in an endless cold war. Both our countries have major shortcomings and advantages. But only in ours is the voice of dissent allowed an opportunity of expression. In returning ___ to ___ to the U.S., I hope I have awoken a few who were sleeping, and others who are indifferent.

I have done a lot of criticizing of our system. I hope you will take it in the spirit it was given. In going to Russia I followed the old principle "Thou shall seek the truth and the truth shall make you free." In returning to the U.S., I have done nothing more or less than select the lesser of two evils.

1.6 **Commission Exhibit 98** (*A System Opposed to the Communist,* 16 H 431-434)

A System Opposed to the Communist

In that the State or any group of persons may not administer or direct funds or value in circulation, for the creation of means of production.

A. Any person may own private property of any sort.
B. Small business or speculation on the part of a single individual be guaranteed.
C. That any person may exchange personal skill or knowledge in the completion of some service, for remuneration.
D. That any person may hire or otherwise remunerate any other single person for services rendered, so long as that service does not create surplus value.

A System Opposed to the Capitalist in that:

No individual may own the means of production, distribution or creation of goods or any other process wherein workers are employed for wages, or otherwise employed, to create profit or surplus profit or value in use or exchange.

A. In that all undertaking of production, distribution or manufacturing or otherwise the creation of goods must be made on a pure, collective basis under the conditions :

1. equal shares of investment be made by members.
2. equal distribution of profit after tax be made to all investors.
3. that all work or directive or administrative duties connected with the enterprise be done personally by those investors.
4. That no person not directly working or otherwise directly taking part in the creational process of any enterprise have a share of or otherwise receive any part of the resultant profit of it.

Stipend
Agronomist

The Atheian System

A system opposed to communism, socialism and capitalism.
Democracy at a local level with no centralized State.

A. That the right of free enterprise and collective enterprise be guaranteed.
B. That Fascism be abolished.
C. That nationalism be excluded from every-day life.
D. That racial segregation or discrimination be abolished by law.
E. The right of the free, uninhibited action of religious institutions of any type or denomination to freely function.
F. Universal suffrage for all persons over 18 years of age.
G. Freedom of dissemination of opinions through the press or declaration or speech.
H. That the dissemination of war propaganda be forbidden as well as the manufacturing of weapons of mass destruction.
I. That free compulsory education be universal till 18.
J. Nationalization or communization of private enterprise or collective enterprise be forbidden.
K. That monopoly practices be considered as capitalistic.
L. That the combining of separate collective or private enterprises

into single collective units be considered as communistic.

M. That no taxes be levied against individuals.

N. That heavy guaranteed taxes of from 30% to 90% be leveled against surplus profit gains.

O. That taxes collected by a single ministry subordinate to individual communities. That taxes be used solely for the building or improvement of public projects.

1.7 **Commission Exhibit 97** (*Notes Regarding the Communist Party of the United States*, 16 H 422-436; see also CE 779, 17H 647-648)

The Communist Party of the United States has betrayed itself!

It has turned itself into the traditional lever of a foreign power to overthrow the Government of the United States, not in the name of freedom or high ideals, but in servile conformity to the wishes of the Soviet Union and in anticipation of Soviet Russia's complete domination of the American continent.

The Forresters and the Flynns of the subsidized Communist Party of the United States have shown themselves to be willing, gullible messengers of the Kremlin's Internationalist propaganda.

There can be no international solidarity with the arch-betrayers of that most sublime ideal.

There can be so sympathy for those who have turned the idea of communism into a vile curse to western man.

The Soviets have committed crimes unsurpassed even by their early day capitalist counterparts, the imprisonment of their own peoples, with the mass extermination so typical of Stalin, and the individual suppression and regimentation under Khrushchev.

The deportations, the purposeful curtailment of diet in the consumer slighted population of Russia, the murder of history, the prostitution of art and culture.

The communist movement in the U.S., personalized by the Communist Party U.S.A., has turned itself into a "valuable gold coin" of the Kremlin. It has failed to denounce any actions of the Soviet Government when similar actions on the part of the U.S. Government bring pious protest. Examples:

Denounced	Not Denounced
United States	Russian
Atomic Bomb Test	Atomic Bomb Test
Cuba	Hungary
N.A.T.O. Manoeuvres	Warsaw Pact Manoeuvres
U-2	Sobel
Congo	Eastern Germany
Negro Lynching	Genocide

Only by declaring itself to be, not only dependent upon, but opposed to, Soviet domination and influence, can dormant and disillusioned persons hope to unite to free the radical movement from its inertia.

Through the refusal of the Communist Party U.S.A. to give a clear cut condemnation of Soviet political acts, progressives have been weakened into a stale class of fifth columnists of the Russians.

In order to free the hesitating and justifiable uncertain future activist for the work ahead, we must remove that obstacle which has so efficiently retarded him, namely the devotion of Communist Party U.S.A. to the Soviet Union, Soviet Government, and Soviet Communist International Movement.

It is readily foreseeable that a coming, economic, political or military crisis, internal or external, will bring about the final destruction of the capitalist system. Assuming this, we can see how preparation in a special party could safeguard an independent course of action after the debacle, an American course steadfastly opposed to intervention by outside, relatively stable foreign powers, no matter from where they come, but in particular and if necessary, violently opposed to Soviet intervention.

No party of this type can attract into its ranks more than a nominal number of fundamental radicals.

It is not the nature of such an organization to attract such membership as, let's say, the Republicans or even the Socialist Party, but it is possible to enlist the aid of disenchanted members of the Socialist Party and even some from more "respected" (from a capitalist viewpoint) parties.

But whereas our political enemies talk loudly now, they have no concept of what total crisis means.

The faction which has the greater basis in spirit and the most far-sighted and ready membership of the radical futurist will be the decisive factor.

We have no interest in violently opposing the U.S. Government. Why should we manifest opposition when there are far greater forces at work to bring about the fall of the United States Government than we could ever possibly muster.

We do no have any interest in directly assuming the head of Government in the event of such an all-finishing crisis. As dissident Americans we are merely interested in opposing foreign intervention which is an easily drawn conclusion if one believes in the theory of crisis.

The emplacement of a separate, democratic, pure communist society is our goal, but one with union-communes, democratic socializing of production and without regard to the twisting apart of Marxist communism by other powers.

The right of private personal property, religious tolerance and freedom of travel (which have all been violated under Russian "Communist" rule) must be strictly observed.

Resourcefulness and patient working towards the aforesaid goals are preferred rather than loud and useless manifestations of protest. Silent observance of our principles is of primary importance.

But these preferred tactics now may prove to be too limited in the near future. They should not be confused with slowness, indecision or fear. Only the intellectually fearless could even be remotely attracted to our doctrine and yet this doctrine requires the utmost restraint, a state of being in itself majestic in power.

This is stoicism and yet stoicism has not been effective for many years and never for such purpose.

There are organizations already formed in the United States which have declared they shall become effective only after the military debacle of the United States. Organizations such as the Minutemen, or the opposite of stoical organizations. But these performers who are simply preparing to re-defend in their own backyards a system which they take for granted will be defeated militarily/ a strange thing to hear from "patriots". These armed groups represent hard core American capitalist supporters. There will also be small armed communist and probably Fascist groups. There will be anarchist and religious groups at work.

However, the bulk of the population will not adhere to any of these groups because they will not be inclined to join any of the old factions with which we are all so familiar.

But the people will never accept a new order presented by politicians or opportunists.

Logically, they will deem it necessary to oppose those systems of Government against whom they have been educated but they will be against anything resembling their former capitalist masters also.

Steadfastly opposed to the revival of the old forces they will seek a new force.

This will be the sentiment of the masses.

But any organization cleverly manipulating words may sway the masses.

There is where a safeguard in necessary.

And not only a safeguard, but a safety valve, to shut off opportunistic forces from within, and foreign powers from without.

There can be no substitute for organization and procurement work. Towards the aforesaid ideals and goals.

Work is the key to the future door but failure to apply that key because of possible armed opposition in our hypothetical, but very probable crisis, is as useless as trying to use force now to knock down the door.

Armed defenses of our ideals must be an accepted doctrine after the crisis just as refraining from any demonstrations of force must be our doctrine in the meantime.

No man, having known, having lived, under the Russian Communist and American capitalist systems, could possible make a choice between them. There is no choice. One offers oppression, the other poverty. Both offer imperialistic injustice, tinted with two brands of slavery.

But no rational man can take the attitude of a "curse on both your houses." There are <u>two</u> world systems, one twisted beyond recognition by its misuse, the other decadent and dying in its final evolution.

A truly democratic system would combine the better qualities of the two upon an American foundation, opposed to both world systems as they are now.

This is our ideal.

Membership in this organization implies adherence to the principle of simple distribution of information about this movement to others and acceptance of the idea of stoical readiness in regards to practical measures once instituted in the crisis.

1.8 **Commission Exhibit 93** (*Notes On His Background,* 16 H 337-346)

Military and Far East

I served in the USMC from October 1956--September 1959, during which time I served in San Diego, California October 1956--April (1957); Camp Pendleton April--May 1957; Jacksonville, Florida May--June 1957; Santa Anna California June--August 1957. And in Japan, August 1957--November, 1958; Santa Anna, El Toro Air Base December 1958--September 1959. One month on leave during December, 1958.

My stay in the Far East included eight months in Japan from September 1957 to November 1957 and from May--October 1958. During December 1957 to May 1958, I was stationed at Subic Bay near Manila, Philippine Islands.

I served in Electronics School Jacksonville, Florida, and advanced radio school Biloxi, Mississippi. I also received my high school level diploma at the same time as my schooling in Biloxi, Mississippi.

A. Discharge DD 214

B. Diploma – Jacksonville, Florida School

C. Diploma – Biloxi, Mississippi School

D. Certificate of high school completion

Resident of USSR

I lived in Moscow from October 16, 1959 to January 4, 1960 during which time I stayed at the Berlin and Metropoles Hotels. I then lived in Minsk from January 5, 1960 to July 1962. I visited Moscow during June 1961 and June 1962 for a few weeks. In Minsk, I was granted a small apartment at Kalinnin Street, later re-named Komunist Street. I worked at the Belorussian Radio and T.V. plant as a metal worker.

A. Clippings

Marxist

I first read the Communist Manifesto and first volume of Capital in 1954 when I was fifteen. I have studied 18th century philosophers, works by Lenin, after 1959 and attended numerous Marxist reading circles and groups at the factory where I worked, some of which were compulsory and others which were not. Also in Russia, through newspapers, radio and T.V., I learned much of Marx, Engels and Lenin's works. Such articles are given very good coverage daily in the USSR.

After my stay in the Soviet Union, upon my return to the USA, I continued to receive my subscription from "Komkrin Inc.," Soviet ideological and informative literature, "Agitator" newspaper, Soviet "Belowsi," "Krockill," satirical political magazine, and the CPUSA newspaper "Worker." Also I receive the well known Soviet Journal "Ogonxok." I also received literature from the Soviet Embassy, Washington, D.C.

A. Proof of subscriptions to Soviet Journals
B. Subscriptions from 1962 of Worker

Gary W. O'Brien

Russian

I learned the Russian language during my almost three years' residence in Moscow and Minsk, USSR, October 1959 - July 1962. I studied Russian elementary and advanced grammar from text books with an English-speaking Russian intourist teacher by the name of Rosa Agafonava, Minsk, January - May 1960. I am totally proficient in speaking conversational Russian. I can read non-technical Russian text without difficulty and can to a less extent write in the Russian language.

A. Letter of proficiency

Organizer

I am experienced in street agitation, having done it in New Orleans in connection with the F.P.C.C. On August 9, 1963, I was accosted by three anti-Castro Cubans and was arrested for "causing a disturbance." I was interrogated by the intelligence section of the New Orleans Police Department and held overnight, being bailed out the next morning by relatives. I subsequently was fined $10. Charges against the three Cubans were dropped by the judge.

On August 16, I organized a four man FPCC demonstration in front of the International Trade Mart in New Orleans. This demonstration was filmed by WDSU TV and shown on the 6:00 news.

On August 17, I was invited by WDSU-Radio to appear on the August 17 radio program, Latin American Focus, at 7:30 PM. The moderator was Bill Stuckey who put questions to me for half and hour about FPCC attitudes and opinions.

After this program, I was invited to take part in a radio debate between John Butler of "Inca," anti-communist propaganda organization representative, and Carlos Bringuier, Cuban exile Student Revolutionary Directorate delegate in New Orleans, This debate was broadcast at 6:05 to 6:30, August 21. After this program, I made a three minute T.V. newsreel, which was shown the next day (August 22).

I received advice, direction, and literature from V.T. Lee, National Director of the Fair Play for Cuba Committee, of which I am a member. At my own expense, I had printed "Hands Off Cuba" handbills and New Orleans branch membership blanks for the F.P.C.C. Local.

A. Letter from V.T. Lee

B. FPCC membership card

Radio Speaker and Lecturer

On August 22, I was invited by Gene Murret, who is studying for the Catholic priesthood to give a lecture on Russia. Gene Murret is the son of my mother's sister, Mrs. D. Murret, 757 French Street, New Orleans, Louisiana. This lecture took place July 27, 1963, 7:00 PM at The University Jesuit House of Studies, Spring Hill Station, Mobile, Alabama. Over fifty student priests, all of whom were college graduates taking four years subsequent course for the priesthood, attended. Several of the college's professors were also present. This lecture lasted for one hour ten minutes after which there was twenty minutes of questions from the audience. This lecture took place in auditorium where women are not allowed, so an all-male audience attended. The moderator of this lecture was Paul Piozza, Jesuit.

Gary W. O'Brien

LECTURE

A. invitation

B. comments later

RADIO

NO RECORDS

Photographs

I have worked in the Jaggers-Chiles-Stoval Co. 522 Browder Street, Dallas, Texas. I have worked from October 1, 1962 to April 1, 1963. I am proficient in the photographic arts known as reverses, transparacial, line, modifications, squats, blowups and miniaturizations. I have submitted and been commended for photo work for the Party. I am familiar with layout and artwork and am acquainted with cold metal and hot metal processes in printing.

A. Tax returns of JCS

B. Letters commending photo work by Party

1.9 **Excerpts from Commission Exhibit 18** (*Political Entries in Oswald's Address Book*, 16 H 37-40; See also CE 2465, 25 H 638; and Holloway, *op. cit.*, pp. 291-308)

Page 1

Wm. B. Reily & Co. 640 Magazine Gen. Ofcs 524-6131

Page 2

Walker LA -14115

SMU Hillcrest Bank Danials to Dicksns

Page 4

John B. Connally Fort Worth, Texas Sec. of Navy

Page 6

684-3271 Imm. & Nat. Service 1402 Rio Grand Bldg. 251 No. Field St. Dallas, Texas

Page 7

Mosgorispolkom

American Pass 1733242 11 Sept. 1959

Page 8

U.S. Department of Justice Immigration and Naturalization Service P.O. Box 2539

Page 9

Russ. Am. Mikhal A. Menshikov New York

Sec. Navy Fort Worth Fred Korth

Washington DC Soviet Embassy Ofc. 1125 6th NW

Sety to Ambass NA 88549 Ofc. 1706 18th NW AD 23092

PE8-1951 Ft. Worth T.V. Stn

Page 11

Gary W. O'Brien

N.Y. Russ.Em. Worker Socialist Party Re typing papers

907? Bldg. Pauline Bates ED-55006

Page 12

Editorial Director PO Box 2119 UPO New York, N.Y.

Account No. 38210

Page 16

"Worker" P.O. Box 28 Madison Square Garden Station New York 10, N.Y.

Imm. card no. A12530645

Page 17

Immigration x Naturalization Service 1402 Rio Grande Bldg. 251 No. Field St. Dallas Texas Riverside Phone 8-5611 EXT. 2644

Page 18

George Bouhe 4740 Homer St. TA-72280

Anna Meller 5930 1 / 2 La Vista TA3-2219

Paul Gregory 3513 Dorothy Lane PE1-16309

Page 19

PE8-1951 KUTV

Page 20

Jaggers-Chiles-Stovall 522 Browder RI-15501

Page 21

New U.S. Passport DO92526 June 25, 1963

Page 27

Rosa Agadonova Hotel Berlin Mak Savoy

Amer. Embassy Tel. Moscow 52-00-08 Chaikovsky St. D2-20-08 1/21 D2-0010 9-6 bus. Aksonov, Colonel Ministry of Internal Affairs of the USSR

Page 28

ACLU Box 2251 Dallas 1

A. Ex. K-4200 384 1-2 Dinner Room 384 Jelisavcic "Maasdam" Holl-amer:

Page 30

George DeMohrenschildt 6628 Dickens EN31365

Page 32

Everett Glover LA-83901

Page 33

Agzdanova Hotel Savoy K 41980

U1 Zakharova Street House No. 11, apt. 72 Golovachev, Pavel

Page 34

Gary W. O'Brien

Peter Gregory Continental Life Blg. ED6-8449 1503

Mrs. Max Clark WA4-9377 Russian specker

Elena Hall 4760 Trail Lane Dr. WA-63741

Gary & Alex Taylor 3519 Fairmount #12 LA-10692

Page 35

Lyudmir Dmitreivena Hotel "Berlin" Savoy Gomam Demka 20233 (Bus.)

mother of U.S. Embassy doctor Mrs. Hal Davison 4047 Tuxedo Rd. Atlanta, George

Natalia Alekseevna

Pages 36-40

Aleks. Romanovich Ziger Krasnaya Street Minsk House 14, Apt. 42

West German Embassy B. Gruzinskaya Street 17 Miss Kaisenheim

Kalashnaya Lane 6 Dutch Embassy

Van Hattum

Page 43

Inderedko Inter. Rescue Com. 251 Park Ave. South New York OR-44200

Page 45

Kon. Narokhsov Tel 2-6311 Comrade Dyadeve Room 279 20575 Sharapov

Kuznetsova, Rosa Intourist Hotel "Minsk" 92-463 House 130, Apt. 8

Page 46

Communist Party U.S.A. 23 West 26th Street New York

Ruth Koefer 306 Pine St. New Orleans 18, La

H. Warner Kloepfer UN 60389 UN 62741 Ex 276

Page 47

Mexico City: Consulado de Cuba Zamora y F. Marquez 11-28-47 Sylvia Duran

Embassy of the Soviet Union, 15 61 55 (15 60 55) Department of Consular Matters

Cubano Airlines Paeso de la Reforma 56 35-79-00

U.S. Embassy Lafragua 18 46 94 00

Page 54

Nat. Sec.Dan Burros Lincoln Rockwell Arlington, Virginia

American Nazi Party Hollis sec. of Queens N.Y.

(Newspaper) Nat. Socialist Bulletin

Page 60

Gary W. O'Brien

Petrikov 8 Lunacharskogo Street Argentine Embassy

Ruth Paine 2515 W. 5th Street Irving, Texas BL-31628

Page 61

Johnson-Moscow Miss Mosby The Ass. Pr. 13 Narodnaya Street, Moscow 726430

Unit. Pr. 726681 with Mosby Mr. Goldberg

Page 62

Lev Setyaev-Radio Moscow B3-65-88 (work) Novo-Peschanaya 23/7, Apt. 65

Rimma

Page 65-68

N.O. T.V.-W.D.S.U. 1. Burns, Rottman 523-5033 2. Bill Stuckey 529-2274

Page 70

Horace Twiford 7018 Suhley Houston Texas WA35492

Texas school depository Mr. Truly RI-73521

Page 71

Ministry of Finances of the USSR 9 Kuybysheva Street 792

Page 74

Elena Hall 4760 Trail Dr. WA-63741

Page 76

Nov. 1 1962 FBI Agent R11-1211 James P. Hosty MU8605 1114 Commerce St

Dallas

Page 77-80

Rimma Sherakava Intourist Moscow Sherakov 2-05-75

Page 82-86

Cuban Student Directorate 107 Decatur St. New Orleans La. Carlos Bringuier

N.O. City Editor "Cowan" David Crawford reporter

117 Camp 107 Decatur 1032 Canal

Nat. Progressive Youth Organization 80 Clinton St. N.Y. 2, N.Y. "Advance" Youth Organ.

Page 88

Philidelphia

Russ-Amer. Citizenship Club 2730 Snyder Av.

Russ. Lan. School 1212 Spruce

Russian Daily Paper Jefferson Bldg.

Russian Lan. Trn. 216 S. 20

Russ. Broth-hood Organ. 1733 Sprin Grdn.

Gary W. O'Brien

Rear

Book 1984 Orwell

Rear 3

Embassy Newspapers OVIR Rimma

Ruth LA71701

Rear 4

Leslie Welding Co.

Box 2915

Appendix Two - The Letters

2.1 To the Socialist Party of America, October 3, 1956 (Gray Exhibit No. 1, 20 H 25-26)

Dear Sirs: I am sixteen years of age and I would like more information about your youth League. I would like to know if there is a branch in my area, how to join, etc. I am a Marxist, and have been studying socialist principles for well over fifteen months I am very interested in your YPSL. Sincerely.

2.2 To Robert Oswald, Spring 1959 (CE 296, 16 H 824)

Dear Robert. Well, I just got back off a short maneuver, to camp Pendleton. The C Rations are still lousy, in case you've forgotten.

How is the boy and how is Vida?

Well, pretty soon I'll be getting out of the corps and I know what I want to be and how I'm going to do it, which I guess is the more important thing in life.

I know I haven't written in a long time please excuse me. Well there really isn't too much news here, but I would like to hear from you and the family. Write soon. Your brother.

2.3 To Marguerite Oswald, undated, Postmarked September 19, 1959 (CE 200, 16 H 580)

Dear Mother: Well, I have booked passage on a ship to Europe. I would have had to sooner or later and I think its best I go now. Just remember above all else that my values are different from Robert's or yours. It is difficult to tell you how I feel. Just remember this is what I must do. I did not tell you about my plans because you could hardly be expected to understand.

I did not see Aunt Lillian while I was there. I will write again as soon as I land.

2.4 To the American Embassy, Moscow, n.d. (CE 913, 18 H 109)

I, Lee Harvey Oswald, do hereby request that my present citizenship in the United States of America, be revoked.

I have entered the Soviet Union for the express purpose of applying for citizenship in the Soviet Union through the means of naturalization.

My request for citizenship is now pending before the Supreme Soviet of the U.S.S.R.

I take these steps for political reasons. My request for the revoking of my American citizenship is made only after the longest and most serious considerations. I affirm that my allegiance is to the Union of Soviet Socialist Republics.

2.5 To the USSR Supreme Soviet, October 16, 1959 (Given by President Boris Yeltsin to President Bill Clinton, June 22, 1999, The U.S. National Archives and Records Administration. Translation from article "Americans won't find anything - Yeltsin

passed Kennedy file to Clinton," by Maxim Zhukov and Aleksei
Alekseyev)

I, Lee Harvey Oswald am asking to be granted citizenship of the
Soviet Union. My visa is valid from 15th of October and expires
on 21st of October. My citizenship should be granted before this
date. In the meantime I am waiting for your decision about my
citizenship.

Currently, I am a citizen of the United States of America. I
wan citizenship because I am a Communist and working class
person. I have lived in a decadent capitalist society where the
workers are slaves. I am 20. I served in U.S. marines for three
years. I served in occupation forces in Japan. I have seen American
militarism in all of its forms.

I do not want to return to any other country outside of the
Soviet Union borders.

I wish to reject my American citizenship and accept the
responsibility of a Soviet citizen.

I saved up some money while serving for two years as a private
in the American military service in order to come to Russia with
one purpose to obtain citizenship. I do not have enough money
to live here indefinitely or to return to any other county I do not
want to go to any other country. I am asking you to consider my
request as soon as possible.

**2.6 Note found among Oswald's personal papers in Hotel
Berlin, Moscow after his attempted suicide on October 21,
1959** (Nechiporenko, *op. cit.,* pp. 35-36)

I, Lee Harvey Oswald, hereby request Soviet citizenship. This
request, written by me, has been carefully and seriously thought

out, with full understanding of the responsibilities and duties connected with it. While my citizenship is being processed, I also ask that I be granted asylum in the Soviet Union as a Communist and Marxist.

2.7 **To Robert Oswald, November 8, 1959** (CE 294, 16 H 814)

Dear Robert, Well, what should we talk about? The weather perhaps? Certainly you do not wish me to speak of my decision to remain in the Soviet Union and apply for citizenship here, since I am afraid you would not be able to comprehend my reasons. You really don't know anything about me. Do you know for instance that I have waited to do this for well over a year? Do you know that I (Example of Russian writing) speak a fair amount of Russian which I have been studying for many months.

I have been told that I will not <u>have</u> to leave the Soviet Union if I did not care to. This then is my decision. I will not leave this country, the Soviet Union, under any conditions. I will never return to the United States, which is a country I hate.

Someday, perhaps soon, and then again perhaps in a few years, I will become a citizen of the Soviet Union, but it is a very legal process. <u>In any event</u>, I will not have to leave the Soviet Union and I will never leave.

I received your telegram and was glad to hear from you. Only one word bothered me. The word "mistake." I assume you mean that I have made a "mistake." It is not for you to tell me this. You cannot understand my reasons for this very serious action.

I will not speak to anyone from the Unites States over the telephone since it may be taped by the Americans.

If you wish to correspond with me you can write to the below address, but I really don't see what we could talk about. If you want to send me some money, that I can use, but I do not expect to be able to send it back.

2.8 To the American Embassy, Moscow, November 3, 1959 (CE 912, 16 H 108)

I, Lee Harvey Oswald, do hereby request that my present United States citizenship be revoked.

I appeared in person at the consulate office of the United States Embassy, Moscow, on October 31st, for the purpose of signing the formal papers to this effect. This legal right I was refused at that time.

I wish to protest against this action, and against the conduct of the official of the United States consular service who acted on my behalf of the United States government.

My application, requesting that I be considered for citizenship in the Soviet Union is now pending before the Supreme Soviet of the U.S.S.R. In the event of acceptance, I will request my government to lodge a formal protest regarding this incident.

2.9 To Robert Oswald, November 26, 1959 (CE 295, 16 H 815-822)

Dear Robert, I shall begin by answering your question on why I and my fellow workers and communists would like to see the present capitalist government of the U.S. overthrown.

Do you remember the time you told me about the efforts of your milk company to form a union? Try to see <u>why</u> workers must form unions against their employers in the U.S. It is because the government supports an economic system which exploits all its workers; a system based upon credit which gives rise to the never ending cycle of depression, inflation, unlimited speculation (which is the phase America is in now) and war. In this system art, culture, and the spirit of man are subjected to commercial enterprising. Religion and education are used as a tool to suppress what would otherwise be a population questioning their government's unfair economic system and plans for war. Science is neglected unless it can be directly used in making war or producing more profit for the owners of businesses. These are some of the reasons. Look around you, and look at yourself. See the Segregation, see the unemployed, and what automation is, remember how you were laid off at Convair.

I remember well the days we stood off shore at Indonesia waiting to suppress yet another population, when they were having a revolution there in March 1958. I can still see Japan and the Philippines and their puppet governments. More important I can see the American in uniforms, men who were there because they were drafted or because they were adventurous or unemployed in civilian life. I will ask you a question Robert, what do you support the American government for? What is the Ideal you put forward? Do not say "freedom" because freedom is a word used by all peoples through all of time. Ask me and I will tell you I fight for <u>communism</u>. This word brings to your mind slaves or injustice. This is because of American propaganda. Look this word up in the dictionary or better still, read the book which I first read when I was 15, "CAPITAL", which contains economic theories and most important, the "Communist Manifesto."

I will not say your grandchildren will live under communism. Look for yourself at history, look at a world map! America is a dying country. I do not wish to be a part of it, nor do I ever again wish to be used as a tool in its military oppressions.

This should answer your question, and also give you a glimpse of my way of thinking.

So you speak of advantages. Do you think that is why I am here? For personal, material advantages? Happiness is not based on oneself, it does not consist of a small home, of taking and getting. Happiness is taking part in the struggle, where there is no borderline between one's own personal world, and the world in general. I never believed I would find more material advantages at this stage of development in the Soviet Union than I might of had in the U.S.

When I talked to a reporter I gave most of my reasons. However the story I found out later was badly slanted and left out very real reasons. The reporter was interested only in a colorful story. I have been a pro-communist for years and yet I have never met a communist. Instead I kept silent and observed, and what I observed, plus my Marxist learning, brought me here to the Soviet Union. I have always considered this country to be my own.

I left you out of the matter because I did not want to get you into any sort of trouble because of me. Also this decision is one which I only could make and you would not have been able to understand me.

You probably know little about this country so I will tell you about it. I did find, as I suspected I would, that most of what is written about the Soviet Union in America is for the better part fabrication. The people here have a seven hour work day now and only work till three o'clock on Saturdays with Sundays off. They have socialism, which means they do not pay for their apartments or for medical care. The money for these comes from the profit they help to create in their labor, which in U.S. goes to capitalist. Here in Moscow, there is a housing shortage because of the war but it's not bad now. There is no unemployment here and in fact a slight shortage of manpower even with a 250,000,000 population. This is because this country is building at a pace which will put it first in all fields of endeavor in 15 years. Most important is the fact they do not work for employers at all, a milkman or a factory supervisor are both socially equal. This does not mean they have the same salary of course. This just means that their work goes for the common good of all.

These people are a good, warm, alive people. These people would never think of war. They wish to see all peoples live in peace, but at the same time, they work to see the economically enslaved people of the West free. They believe in their Ideal and they support their government and country to the full limit.

You say you have not renounced me. Good I am glad, but I will tell you on what terms I want this arrangement.

I want you to understand what I say now, I do not say lightly, or unknowingly, since I have been in the military as you know, and I know what war is like.

1. In the event of war, I would kill any American who put a uniform on in defense of the American government--any American.

2. That in my own mind, I have no attachments of any kind in the U.S.

3. That I want to, and I shall, live a normal happy and peaceful life here in the Soviet Union for the rest of my life.

4. That my mother and you are (in spite of what the newspapers said) not objects of affection, but only examples of workers in the U.S.

You should not try to remember me in any way I used to be, since I am only now showing you how I am. I am not all bitterness or hate; I came here only to find freedom. In truth, I feel I am at last with my own people. But do not let me give you the impression I am on another world. These people are as much like Americans and people the world over. They simply have an economic system and the Ideal of communism, which the U.S. does not have. I would never been personally happy in the U.S.

I wish you would do me one favor since that other bad newspaper story went over, I have been thinking I would like to give people, who are interested, the real reasons. If you would give the contents of this letter (except that which is for your benefit) to some reporter, it will clarify my situation. Use your own judgment however.

I have no money problems at all. My situation was not nearly as stable then as it is now. I have no troubles at all now along that line.

It is snowing here in Moscow now, which makes everything look very nice from my hotel window. I can see the Kremlin and Red Square and I have just finished a dinner of (words in Russian) meat and potatoes. So you see the Russians are not as different from you and I.

2.10 To Robert Oswald, n.d., Received December 17, 1959 (CE 297, 16 H 825)

Dear Robert, I will be moving form this hotel, and so you need not write me here. I have chosen to remove all ties with my past, so I will not write again, nor do I wish you to try to contact me. I'm sure you understand that I would not like to receive correspondence from people in the country which I fled. I am starting a new life and I do not wish to have anything to do with the old life.

I hope you and your family will always be in good health. Lee

2.11 **To the American Embassy, Moscow, n.d.** (CE 931 18 H 131-132)

Dear Sirs: Since I have not received a reply to my letter of December, 1960, I am writing again asking that you consider my request for the return of my American passport.

I desire to return to the United States, that is if we could come to some agreement concerning the dropping of any legal proceedings against me. If so, than I would be free to ask the Russian authorities to allow me to leave. If I could show them my American passport, I am of the opinion they would give me an exit visa.

They have at no time insisted that I take Russian citizenship. I am living here with non-permanent type papers of a foreigner.

I cannot leave Minsk without permission, therefore I am writing rather than calling in person.

I hope that in recalling the responsibility I have to America that you remember your's in doing everything you can to help me since I am an American citizen. Sincerely.

2.12 **To the American Embassy, Moscow, Postmarked March 5, 1961** (CE 940 18 H 151)

Dear Sirs: In reply to your recent letter. I find it inconvenient to come to Moscow for the sole purpose of an interview.

In my last letter I believe I stated that I cannot leave the city of Minsk without permission.

I believe there exits in the United States a law in regards to resident foreigners form Socialist countries, traveling between cities.

I do not think it would be appropriate for me request to leave Minsk in order to visit the American Embassy. In any event, the granting of permission is a long drawn out affair, and I find there is a hesitation on the part of local officials to even start the process.

I have no intention of abusing my position here and I am sure you would not want me to. I see no reason for any preliminary inquiries not to be put in the form of a questionnaire and sent to me.

I understand that personal interviews undoubtedly make to work of the Embassy staff lighter than written correspondence. However, in some cases other means must be employed. Sincerely.

2.13 **To Robert Oswald, May 5, 1961** (CE 298 16 H 826)

Dear Robert It's been a long time since I have written you, more than a year; a lot has happened in that time.

I am now living in the city of Minsk which is located about 400 mile S-W of Moscow. Minsk is the capital city of the Soviet State of Belorussia. I shall have been living here already a year and three months. I came to live in Minsk after I wrote my last letter to you. I have been working at the local radio-television plant as a metal-smith.

On April 30 of this year; I got married. My wife is nineteen years old, she was born in the city of Leningrad, which is the second largest in the U.S.S.R., her parents are dead – and she was living with her aunt and uncle here in Minsk when I first met her.

Not too long ago I received a letter from mother but I lost the address. I would like you to send it to me if you write.

We have a small flat near our factory and are living nicely. In general I have found the living conditions here to be good but there are a lot of things still to be done. I hope to send you some things from here if you like. The Soviet Union is one of the most interesting county's I have seen in my travels. You should try to visit us some time I some times meet American tourists here especially in the summer. Well that's about all for now hope to hear from you soon. Regards to Vatta and Kathy.

2.14 To the American Embassy, Moscow, May 16, 1961 (CE 252, 16 H 705-707)

Dear Sirs: In regards to your letter of March 24. I understand the reasons for the necessity of a personal interview at the Embassy. However, I wish to make it clear that I am asking not only for the right to return to the United States, but also for full guarantees that I shall not, under any circumstances, be persecuted for any act pertaining to his case. I made it clear from my first letter, although nothing has been said, even vaguely, concerning this in my correspondence with the Embassy. Unless you honestly think that this condition can be met, I see no reason for a continuance of our correspondence. Instead, I shall endeavor to use my relatives in the United States, to see about getting something done in Washington.

As for coming to Moscow, this would have to be on my own initiative and I do not care to take the risk of getting into an awkward situation unless I think it worthwhile. Also, since my last letter I have gotten married.

My wife is Russian, born in Leningrad. She has no parents living and is quite willing to leave the Soviet Union with me and live in the United States.

I would not leave here without my wife so arrangements would have to be made for her to leave at the same time as I do.

The marriage stamp was placed on my present passport after some trouble with authorities so my status so far as the USSR is concerned is the same as before, that is, "Without Citizenship."

So with this extra complication I suggest you do some checking before advising me further. I believe I have spoken frankly in this letter. I hope you do the same in your next letter. Sincerely yours.

2.15 To Robert Oswald, May 31, 1961 (CE 299, 16 H 827-829)

Dear Robert, I was glad to hear from you, and really surprised that you have a new son, that is really great. Congratulations to you and Vada.

My wife's name is Marina. I am sorry I forgot to write it last time. Marina works in a pharmacy at one of the hospitals here. (almost all girls and women in the U.S.S.R. have some kind of profession and work at it.) She sends her regards to you and Vada and the kids.

I'm glad you have a good job and are thinking about the future. My work here also is not too bad, but in the USSR there is no unemployment so a job is not an exceptional thing.

There's nothing you can send me, thanks anyway, maybe you could send something, real small to Marina as a wedding present I think she would get a kick out of something from the states. And let us have some pictures of the new baby, I still have Cathy's picture, but I guess she is all grown up by now. Also a picture of the house, since here 90% of living is done in apartments house's, like we have, they are comfortable, but still a house is a home.

I can't say whether I will ever get back to the States or not, if I can get the government to drop charges against me, and let the Russians to let me out with my wife, then maybe I'll be seeing you again. <u>But,</u> you know it is not simple for <u>either</u> of those two things. So I just can't say for now. I am in touch with the American Embassy in Moscow so if anything comes up I'll know.

Well, that's about all for now. Say hello to Robert Lee Jr. for me. Your brother.

2.16 **To Robert Oswald, June 26, 1961** (CE 300, 16 H 831-832)

Dear Robert. Received your letter yesterday and was glad to hear from you and we were very interested in the Pictures. Marina says you don't look very much like me in the picture, but I told her we look like two peas in a pot.

I assume the government must have a few charges against me, since my coming here like that is illegal. But I really don't know exactly what charges.

In a few days you should get a package from us. I'm sorry It shall be so modest, we bought some perfume and other stuff but the post office would not accept them because they are breakable.

I see you have a new car It sure is nice looking. What kind is it? A Ford? When did you get it?

Marina says she would like to see America and meet you and the family.

I received a letter from ma yesterday she is working on a ranch in Cromwell Texas. Do you see her?

Well that's all for now.

2.17 **To Robert Oswald, July 14, 1961** (CE 301 16 H 833)

Dear Robert, On the 8th of July I and my wife went into the American Embassy. I cannot write you what went on there, because the Russians read all letters going in and out. But anyway I have the American Passport and we are doing everything we can to get out.

You don't know what a test this is. I could write a book about how many feeling have come and gone since that day.

The Russians can be cruel and very crude at times. They gave a cross-examination to my wife on the first day we came back from Moscow, they knew everything because they spy and read the mails, but we shall continue to try to get out. We shall not retreat. As for the package, we never received it. I suppose they swiped that to, the bastards.

I hope someday I'll see you and Vada but if and when I come, I'll come with my wife. You can't imagine how wonderfully she stood up. Write often. Your brother.

2.18 **To the American Embassy, Moscow, July 15, 1961** (CE 1122, 22 H 87)

Dear Sirs: As per instructions I am writing to inform you of the process and progress of our visas.

We have proceeded to the local "OVEEP" office and the results are not discouraging. However, there have been some unusual and crude attempts on my wife her place of work. While we were still in Moscow, the foremen at her place of work were notified that she and I went into Embassy for the purpose of visas. Then there followed the usual "enemy of the people" meeting in which in her absence she was condemned and her friends at work warned against speaking with her. However, those tactics are quite useless and my wife stood up well, without getting into trouble.

We are continuing the process and will keep you informed as to the overall picture.

2.19 **To Robert Oswald, September 10, 1961** (CE 305, 16 H 838-840)

Dear Robert, Well, apparently I was too optimistic in my last letter: since you say you thought I would be coming home soon.

The Russians are holding me up now, and are giving me some trouble about the visas, so for now I can only wait. In general, for an ordinary Russian it's impossible to leave the USSR, simply because he wants to. However, I and my wife have the possibility because of the fact I am still an American citizen and have the U.S. passport.

My Russian documents are good until Jan. 4, 1962. Therefore you can expect that they will let me go before that date, since I will not extend the length of time of these documents after Jan. 4 1962. However the Russians have been known to hold people, against international law, and against their wills, but as I say 'time will show'. Marina did not write that letter herself, but the words were hers. I only translated them into English. Marina doesn't know any English at all, and at home we always speak Russian.

Robert Lee sounds like he is growing into a fine boy and Cathy is also quite a grown up little lady, already 4 years old. It hardly seems possible, I remember when mother phoned me to say she was born, on Aug. 21st or 22nd, I was in Calf. We were getting ready to leave for Japan, and we did leave a few days later. A lot has changed since then!!

Well I hope everything is alright and your back isn't giving you any more trouble. Keep writing. Enclosed are some views of Minsk. Your brother.

2.20 To the American Embassy, Moscow, October 4, 1961 (CE 2747, 26 H 123)

Dear Sirs: I am hereby requesting the Offices of the American Embassy and the Ambassador of the United States, Mr. Thompson, to act upon my case in regards to my application to the Soviet authorities for an exit visa.

This application was made on July 20, 1961, and although three months have already elapsed I have not received this visa. There was no difficulty with the application itself or with the supporting documents including my valid American passport

No. 1733242 which was returned to me on July 8, 1961 at the American Embassy in Moscow, where it had been kept for safekeeping.

I have made repeated inquiries to the proper offices in Minsk but I have, as yet, to receive a satisfactory answer.

I believe there is justification for an official inquiry, directed to the department of "Internal Affairs, Prospect Stalin 15, Minsk," and the offices of the "address and passport office." Ulitsa Moskova, Colonel Petrakef director.

Also I believe it is doubly important for an official inquiry, since there have been systematic and concerted attempts to intimidate my wife into withdrawing her application for on visa. I have notified the Embassy in regard to these incidents b the local authorities in regard to my wife. These incidents had resulted in my wife being hospitalized for a five day period on September 22, 1961 for nervous exhaustion.

On July 11, 1961, I executed a petition to classify status of alien for issuance of immigration visa, on behalf of my wife. I assume there has been no difficulty with it.

I think if is within the lawful right, and in the interest of, the United States government, and the American Embassy, Moscow, to look into this cases on my behalf.

2.21 To Robert Oswald, October 22, 1961 (CE 306, 16 H 842-843)

Dear Robert, Well, it's been a month or more since I've written and also a long time since I've heard from you.

Our deal about the exit Visa is still going on, something is holding it up, mostly about my wife since she is a Soviet citizen, but as also, it's hard to get out of this place, in general.

Marina is in the city of 'Kharkov,' about 600 miles south east of Minsk, on her vacation, she's living with her aunt, we both agreed a change of scenery was good for her, she comes back on the 1st of November: From 'Kharkov' she sent me beautiful gold and silver cup with inscription "To my Dear Husband on his birthday 18/X/61." Very nice, huh? She is sweet, when is your birthday anyway sometime in July isn't it?

How are the kids?

How is Vada doing?

Did you get my last letter with some pictures of Minsk in it?

I think around New Years, if I'm still unlucky enough to be here, I'll call you on the telephone OK? How's the hunting out at the farm? Still good I bet.

I got a letter from the Embassy the other day, they are keeping in touch as to developments with the exit visa.

Soon, on Nov 7-8 the big revolution day holidays will come off. They'll be a lot of red flag waving and fireworks like on the 4th of July in the States. Well, that's about all for now. Write soon. Your brother.

2.22 **To Robert Oswald, November 1, 1961** (CE 309, 16 H 852-853)

Dear Robert, I got your birthday card a few days ago thanks for the thought. Marina came back from her vacation on Oct. 28 so everything is back to normal here.

Well, it looks like I'm going to be a papa at the beginning of March. Of course, we want a boy, but you can never tell.

Our visas have still not come through although we have already waited for four months. These people are never too quick to grant visa to anybody.

We hear over the radio today that the present Russian government has decided to remove Stalin's body from the hall on Red Square, this is big news here and it's very funny for me. It shows what these people are made of, one day a hero lying in state, and another day "somebody's doormat." They employ a lot of "doublethink" over there, and so when I listen to the radio or to some of the political commissars we have here, I always think of George Orwell's book "1984" in which "doublethink" is the way of life also.

In any case, everything over here is very interesting, and the people are generally simple and nice.

I haven't been doing too much hunting lately. I'm more of a "home-body" now. Ha-Ha.

Well, that's about all the news from Minsk. Your brother.

2.23 To the American Embassy, Moscow, November 1, 1961
(CE 2744, 26 H 120)

Dear Sirs: I am writing to clarify one point in regard to my residence in the USSR and my eventual return to the United States of America.

My Soviet document which is for foreign residents in the Soviet Union was granted to me in Moscow on January 4, 1960 and was valid until January 4, 1961 for one year. On January 4, 1961, the document was extended with my written permission until January 4, 1962.

I have stated to Soviet official that I shall not under any circumstances request or permit the extension of this document again.

However, the Soviet officials say that if I have not received an exit visa for which I applied on July 20, 1961, they shall themselves, and without my permission, extend this document.

I am of the opinion that the forceful and unrequested extension of this document would be unlawful.

Am I correct in assuming that the American Embassy supports the view that the forceful and unrequested extension of this temporary document for residence in the Soviet Union of a citizen of the United States would be unlawful?

The document in question was shown at the American Embassy by me on July 8-11 and I believe its contents are known as well as its temporary nature and makeup.

However, in case you do not have information on it, here are the features: dlya Lits Bez grashdanstiva N. 311479, extended until January 4, 1962, at the passport office of the city of Minsk.

In regards to I and my wife's application for exit visas, we have still not been granted exit visas and still have not received any answer to our applications, although I have repeatedly gone to the officials in Minsk in regard to our requests for permission to leave the country. They have failed to produce any results and are continuing to try to hinder my wife in relation to her application.

In the future I shall keep the Embassy informed as to our progress. Thank you.

2.24 To the American Embassy, Moscow, December 1, 1961 (CE 2744, 26 H 120)

Dear Sirs: I am writing in regard to a letter which I sent to the Embassy on November 1, in which I asked: "Does the American Embassy feel that in the light of the fact that my temporary Soviet document for residence in the Soviet Union expires on January 4, 1962, that the deprivation of an exit visa after this date and therefore the foreseeable holding of me against my expressed desires is unlawful?"

I would like a written reply to this question before the expiration date of January 4, 1962 in order to have a basis for my refusal to give my permission for the legal extension on this document. Sincerely.

2.25 To Senator John Tower, n.d. Sent to Senator Tower's office on or before January 26, 1962 (CE 1058, 22 H 6)

Dear Senator Tower: My name is Lee Harvey Oswald, 22, of Fort Worth up till October 1959, when I came to the Soviet

Union for a residential stay. I took a residential document for a non-Soviet person living for a time in the USSR. The American Embassy is familiar with my case.

Since July 20th 1960, I have unsuccessfully applied for a Soviet Exit Visa to leave this country the Soviets refuse to permit me and my Soviet wife, (who applied at the U.S. Embassy, Moscow, July 8, 1960 for immigration status to the U.S.A.) to leave the Soviet Union. I am a citizen of the United States of America (passport No. 1733242, 1959) and I beseech you, Senator Tower, to raise the question of holding by the Soviet Union of a citizen of the U.S., against his will and expressed desires. Yours very truly.

2.26 To the American Embassy, Moscow, January 5, 1962 (CE 2744, 26 H 119)

Dear Sirs: This letter is to inform the Embassy of the expiring of my former document of residence in the USSR: dlya Lits Bez grazhdanstva N. 311479 expiration date January 4, 1962, and the granting of a new document: vid na shitelestvo dlya Inostraneta AA 549666, expiration date July 5, 1962.

As I have already informed the Embassy, exit visas for myself and my wife have already been granted. I can have mine anytime, but it will be good for 45 days only. Since I and my wife wish to leave the USSR together, I shall delay requesting my visa until such time as documentation from the Ministry of Foreign Affairs of the USSR and the American Embassy is completed on my wife.

I'd like to be sure we can leave as soon as all documents are finished since there will be an addition to the family in March.

Gary W. O'Brien

I would like to make arrangements for a loan from the Embassy or some organization for part of the plane fares. Please look into this and notify me. Yours truly.

2.27 To the American Embassy, Moscow, January 16, 1962 (CE 256, 22 H 717-718)

Dear Sirs: In reply to your informative letter of January 5.

Since I signed and paid for an immigration petition for my wife in July. 1961, I think it's about time to get it approved or refused.

I hope you will inform me if any other documents are needed and not wait until the last minute.

The enclosed affidavits are as close as I can come to meeting the requirements under the law. Section 212A15© Form OSL-845, I hope they will suffice for now.

You suggest that because of the documentation necessary I go to the United States alone.

I certainly will not consider going to the U.S. alone for any reason. Particularly since it appears my passport will be confiscated upon my arrival in the United States.

I would like for all documentation to be completed, at or by, the Embassy in Moscow. We have not had an easy time getting our exit visas from the Soviet authorities, as the Embassy well knows. I would not like this whole thing repeated because of a lack of this or that on anybodies part. I'm sure you understand.

Also, we will have a child in March and although the Russian processing in this case will be to write in age, sex and place of birth of the child, on my wife's travel passport (a process of four days, in Moscow). I would like to know what you will require in this event. Sincerely.

2.28 To the International Rescue Committee, New York, N.Y., January 26, 1962 (CE 2680, 26 H 36-37)

Dear Sirs: I'd like to request your aid in helping myself and my wife get resettled in the U.S.A. I am a citizen of the United States. I have lived in the Soviet Union since October 1959. My wife is a Soviet citizen, born in the USSR in 1941.

She has been classified under the immigration act of the United States and is eligible to enter the U.S.A. as my wife, for permanent residence.

However, in making the move, it incurs money expenses and inconveniences, this is where your fine organization can help.

Since July 1961 I and my wife have been working and waiting to get Soviet exit visas to leave the Soviet Union for the U.S.A. After all this time our visas have finally been granted. Thank God, but our troubles are not finished, only if organization steps in.

I would direct you to contact the American Embassy, Moscow, U.S.S.R. for information in regards to our case. A sum of $1000 is necessary.

Our need is urgent, please render all assistance you can. Sincerely.

2.29 **To John B. Connally, Secretary to the Navy, January 30, 1962** (Cadign Exhibit No. 2, 19 H 248)

I wish to call your attention to a case about which you may have personal knowledge since you are a resident of Ft. Worth as I am.

In November 1959, an event which was well publicized in the Ft. Worth newspapers concerning a person who had gone to the Soviet Union to reside for a short time (much in the same way E. Hemingway resided in Paris).

This person in answers to questions put to him by reporters in Moscow criticized certain facets of American life, the story was blown into another turncoat sensation with the result that the Navy Department gave this person a belated dishonorable discharge, although he had received an honorable discharge after three years service on September 11, 1959 at El Toro, marine corps base in California.

These are the basic facts of my case.

I have and always had the full sanction of the U.S. Embassy, Moscow, USSR, and hence the U.S. Government. In as much as I am returning to the USA this year with the aid of the U.S. Embassy, bring with me my family (since I married in the U.S.S.R.) I shall employ all mean to right this gross mistake or injustice to a bonafide U.S. citizen and ex-service man. The US government has no charges or complaints against me. I ask you to look into the case and take the necessary steps to repair the damage done to me and my family. For information I would direct you to consult the American Embassy, Chikovski St. 19121, Moscow, U.S.S.R.

2.30 **To Robert Oswald, January 30, 1962** (CE 314, 16 H 865-867)

Dear Robert. Well, I haven't heard from you for quite awhile either you're not writing or your letters aren't getting through to me.

I told you in my last letter that we have been finally been granted exit visas for leaving the Soviet Union will probably be in the States in the spring.

You once said that you asked around about whether or not the U.S. government had any charges against me, you said at that time "no." Maybe you should ask around again. It's possible now that the government knows I'm coming they'll have something waiting. Mother wrote me a letter the other day in which she informed me that the Marine Corps had given me a dishonorable discharge in Nov. 1959. Did you know this?

Of course, this is not too bad since it relieves me of reserve duty but still I should take this into account.

I wrote a letter to John B. Connally Secretary of the Navy who lives in Ft. Worth asking about my dishonorable discharge. Maybe you could ask him to look into the case since I don't know whether the Russians will let that letter through.

You said you were sending us something but we still haven't gotten anything. Don't worry packages are very slow coming and going.

The Embassy said they will see about a loan for us when we leave so it seems our money problem will not be too acute.

Marina still has a month to go so by the time you get this letter you'll be pretty close to being an uncle. March 1 is the big day. Marina sends her love to all, as I do hope to see you all soon. I really don't know where we'll settle. I'd sort of like New Orleans.

How's the hunting up out the farm? How's the weather and all?

If you find out any information about me, please let me know. I'd like to get ready on the draw so to speak. We'll keep writing until we get ready to leave so don't quit writing. Your brother.

2.31 **To Marguerite Oswald, February 1, 1962** (CE 192, 16 H 562)

Dear Mother Today I received 2 letters from you one from the 12th and the other from the 17th. As for the gifts we sent you, the can is of candy, eat it in good health.

As to your questions about the money problem I don't know if giving the story to the newspaper is too good, maybe you'd better hold off for awhile about that. I'll tell you when.

We will probably fly into the US on an airplane and I see no reason for you to come to New York to meet us. I want you to understand that although you can aid is in certain, small ways this business about coming to the U.S. is relatively simple, don't make it more complicated than it is.

About all for now, write soon.

Marina sends her love.

2.32 To Marguerite Oswald, February 9, 1962 (CE 193, 16 H 564-565)

Dear Mother Well it won't be long now until the baby is born and until we will be seeing you. In the meantime you can do two things for me: file an affidavit of support on behalf of Marina (this has to be done in the U.S.A.). It's a technical point regarding U.S. permission to enter the United States and can be done at the office of emigration and naturalization.

Also you can see about sending me some clippings or columns from the Ft. Worth papers for the months of Nov. 1959, I want t know just what was said about me in the Ft. Worth newspapers so I can be forwarded. If you don't have the clipping yourself, you can always get back issues of newspapers by apply as their offices or the public library.

I received your package of newspapers and magazines, Thanks!! Cutting those editorials was also good thinking on your part. It gave me a lot of news.

I suppose it is almost spring in Vernon by now, huh?

What is the latest news in Vernon?

Please write soon, we are getting your letters and so we always wait for more ha-ha.

When you write please write Minsk 29 (zone). This helps me get your letters quicker. Love from us both.

2.33 **To Robert Oswald, February 15, 1962** (CE 315, 16 H 870-872)

Dear Robert. Well, I have a daughter, June Marina Oswald, 6 lbs. 2 0z. born Feb. `15, 1962, at 10 AM. How about that?! We are lucky to have a little girl, don't you think?

But then you have a head start on me, although I'll try to catch up. Ha.Ha.

This makes you an Uncle, congratulations!

The chances of coming to the states are very good, as I already told you. We received the Soviet exit visas. I can leave the country at any time. But here are still formalities concerning Marina's <u>entrance visa</u> into the U.S. These are granted by the US government; and they have assured me they are getting all the papers together (they are quite a lot) and certified accepted.

How are things at your end? I heard over the Voice of America that they released Powers, the U2 spy plane fellow. That's big news where you are I suppose. He seems to be a nice, bright American-type fellow, when I saw him in Moscow. You wouldn't have any clippings from the Nov. 1959 newspapers in Ft. Worth, would you? I am beginning to get interested in just what they <u>did</u> say about me and my trip here. The information might come in handy when I get back. I would hate to come back completely unprepared.

The American Embassy in Moscow has offered us a loan to pay for the price of the airline tickets, so we have nothing to worry about temporary along that line.

Have you heard from Pic at all, what's he doing now? Still in the air force do you know?

Well, I guess that all for now.

P.S. I received a letter from you dated Jan. 3, I did not get it until Feb. 5, the censors are so stupid over here it sometimes takes them a month to censor a letter before letting it through. Love to Vada, Cathy and little Robert Jr. he and June will play together I'm, quite sure.

P.P.S. when writing me in Minks please include zone no. example Minsk 29, Communistecheski St. House 4, Apt. 24 Oswald. P.S. Enclosed 2 photo pictures. Your Brother.

2.34 To Marguerite Oswald, February 15, 1962 (CE 194, 16 H 567-568)

Dear Mother Well I have a little girl (6 lbs) daughter, June Marina Oswald born at 10:00 AM February 15, How about that?

Marina feels OK she only took an hour and a half to give birth at the hospital. The possibility of our coming to the United States is very good although, of course, it'll be another couple of months.

Marina's exit visa to leave the U.S.S.R. is good until Dec. 1, 1962 so we have no worries about the visas running out before everything is arranged.

The American Embassy in Moscow sent me an application for a loan (which I requested) so they will make the money available to us as soon as everything is arranged for Marina.

The only thing holding us up now is the "affidavit of support" for Marina, which I already told you about, once that is in, we can leave the U.S.S.R. any time we want.

How are things at your end?

If you don't have that letter from the Marine Corps, telling about the discharge how about getting a copy, I would like to have some material upon which to start, before going into the discharge matter further with the Marines.

That's about all for now. Love from all Three of us. P.S. Enclosed 3 pictures of Marina and I.

2.35 To Marguerite Oswald, February 24, 1962 (CE 195, 16 H 570-571)

Dear Mother Well, I suppose you've already received out letter about the birth of little June Lee Oswald (not June Marina) she weighted 7 lbs at birth which was on Feb, 15th. Mother and child are doing well, she left the hospital on Feb. 24th.

We will probably wait for a period of two or more months while little June gains weight for her trip to the U.S. I don't think it is too advisable to leave earlier than May. Our visas are good.

How's everything at our end? OK?

The weather is rather cold here yet I guess in Texas it must be pretty hot by now.

Did you get those newspaper clipping I asked for?

I hope you've already made out that affidavit of support for Marina by now, like I asked.

That's about all for now.

2.36 **To Robert Oswald, n.d.** (CE 316, 16 H 874)

Dear Robert, Received a letter from you not too long ago dated Feb. 8. I suppose by now, you've received my letter telling about the birth of my daughter on Feb 15th only in that letter I said her name would be June Marina Oswald but we finally registered her as June Lee Oswald so that's that.

Marina and June are both well Marina left the hospital on Feb. 24th.

We'll probably be in the States in May since we want to wait for little June to gain weight and strength.

In another month or so it will start to thaw out here although I suppose it's already hot in Texas. I heard a "voice of America" program about the Russians releasing Powers. I hope they aren't going to try him in the U.S. or anything.

Thanks a lot for your offer of taking us in when we get back to the States. It's a nice gesture and I'll see about [whether] I'll take you up on it or not. That's about all for now loves to the family.

P.S. little June looks just like Robert Jr. at 2 months.

2.37 **To the United States Marine Corps, March 22, 1962** (CE 823, 17 H 723)

Dear Sirs: In reply to your notification of the granting of an Undesirable discharge and your conveying of the process at which at was arrived.

I would like to point out in direct opposition to your information that I have never taken steps to renounce my U.S.

citizenship. Also that the United States Department has no charges or complaints against me whatsoever.

I refer you to the United States Embassy, Moscow, or the U.S. Department of State Washington, D.C. for the verification of this fact.

Also I was [not] aware of the finding of the board of officers of 8 August 1960. I was notified by my mother in December (1961).

My request to the Secretary of Navy, his referral to you and your letter to me, did not say anything about a <u>Review</u>, which is what I was trying to arrange.

You mention "reliable information" as the basis for this <u>undesirable</u> discharge. I have no <u>doubt</u> it was newspapers speculation which forward your "reliable information."

Under U.S. law governing the use of passports and conduct abroad I have a perfect right to reside in (any) county I wish to.

I have not violated: Section 1544, Title 18, U.S. Code, therefore you have no <u>legal</u> or moral right, to reverse my <u>honourable</u> discharge from the U.S.M.C. on September 11, 1960 into an <u>undesirable</u> discharge.

You may consider this letter a request by me for a full <u>review</u> of my case in the light of these facts, since by the time you receive this letter I shall have returned to the USA with my family and shall be prepared to appear in person at a reasonable time an place in my area, before a reviewing board of officers.

If you choose to convene a review board you <u>may</u> contact me through the below address in the United States after May 15th 1962. 7313 Davenport St. Fort Worth, Texas, Sincerely.

2.38 **To American Embassy, Moscow, March 23, 1962** (CE 249, 16 H 697-698)

Dear Sirs: Regarding your letter of March 9, in which you suggest I come to Moscow.

Although there are several reasons for such a trip, I don't feel they are too pressing so simply for the sake of my convenience, I'll wait until such time as you formally invite us to the Embassy for the final formalities, just before we leave the Soviet Union.

I have received notification from the San Antonio, Texas, office of immigration, that my wife's visa petition was accepted, they also wrote that they shall notify the Embassy in Moscow so I assume you will shortly give the go-ahead for us to leave.

In case your letter [to] this effect crosses mine, I assure you that as soon as we complete our personal affairs, we shall follow your instructions, as given in your letter of March 9th, and come to Moscow. I received the notification from Texas on March 15th. Sincerely.

2.39 **To Marguerite Oswald, March 27, 1962** (CE 1315, 22 H 487)

Dear Mother In the last few days I have received 5 letters from you dated Feb. 25 clippings and Mar 1st also in one letter some more clippings thanks a lot for them I'm glad you know about the baby also.

They seemed to write a lot about me in the papers <u>Rob talked too much </u>but I'm glad <u>you </u>supported me in your own way.

<u>I had written a letter to the Secretary of the Navy in Jan. 1962</u>. I got a reply yesterday from some General telling me about the reversal of my <u>honourable </u>discharge into an <u>undesirable </u>one.

We should be in the States in May at the latest <u>the Embassy has agreed to loan $500</u> for the trip, and also they accepted my affidavit of support so yours won't be necessary after all.

However, <u>don't try to get that businessman's friend of your's to cancel his affidavit, it may come in handy some day.</u>

As you say <u>my</u> trip here would make a good story about <u>me</u>. I've already thought about that for quite a while now, in fact, <u>I've already made 50 pages of longhand notes on the subject.</u>

All is well with Marina and the baby, her length at birth was 50 centimetres (I don't know how many inches that is but everything is normal, right down to June's little fingernails.

I don't think we'll be at this address much longer so it is not advisable for you to write here.

The reasons for the delay in some letters and the speed in others is because of the Russian censor who reads all letters.

I was not aware you sent me other letters to me in the Hotel when I lived in Moscow as I left there for Minsk after I wrote that letter.

I cannot say where we will go at first probably directly to Vernon.

2.40 To Marguerite Oswald, March 28, 1962 (CE 196, 16H 573-574)

Dear Mother Today I received the affidavits from Mr. Phillips.

You asked [whether] I'll be staying at your place (or) Robert's in Ft. Worth. I don't think I'll be staying at either but I will be visiting both. I'll want to live on my own and finally will probably live in Ft. Worth or New Orleans. We will undoubtedly come by ship to the U.S. which will be a two week trip. I'll let you know when we leave the Soviet Union. I still don't know our exact date of departure yet as there are still a few things to be done before we shove off.

As I said in my last letter we shall be coming probably in April. I already told you I received those clippings and so forth O.K.

The money situation is pretty good although I'd like to have enough to fly to the states, but that's too lightly at this time, still it's not very important as regards the _mode_ of transportation.

June Lee, feels fine, she already weighs 11 lbs. and is 1 ½ months old. Marina feels very well also.

We are in constant touch with the Embassy so all is well. That's about all for now. P.S. Marina sends her love. P.P.S. Today we also received your card.

2.41 To Robert Oswald, April 12, 1962 (CE 317, 16 H 877)

Dear Robert, Well spring has finally come to Minsk with the snow melting and above-freezing temperatures.

It looks like we'll be leaving the country in April or May, only the American side is holding us up now. The Embassy is as slow as the Russians were.

How is everything at the house?

I got a letter from the Marine Corps not (too) long ago. Then I sent them a request for a re-hearing on my undesirable discharge. I told them I would be back in the U.S. after May 25 and they could contact me through your address.

Now that winter is gone, I really do not want to leave until the beginning of fall since the spring and summer here are so nice. Marina and June are all right. June already weighs 11 lbs or so, she's real cute.

Marina sends her "hello" to the family. That's about all for now. Your brother.

2.42 **To Marguerite Oswald, April 22, 1962** (CE 197 16 H 576)

Dear Mother, Well as you see we shall have not gotten off yet, the hold up is from the Embassy which is apparently trying to get us money from other sources than itself for our tickets to the U.S. probably they'll approach you for money again. Don't pay any attention to them.

June is getting big now already 2 ½ months old she's real cute I know you'll like her.

Who is Mr. Phillips? Since you work at a new place now do you still have contact with him? When will the elections for governor be in Texas?

Do you get any word from Pic?

Write soon. Love.

2.43 To the American Embassy, Moscow, n.d. (CE 250, 16 H 700)

Dear Sir; Having been informed by you over the telephone on April 9 that all necessary papers have been completed in relation to my wife's American entrance visa, I assume to the hold-up to our leaving the USSR arises out of the transportation problems, i.e. the money problem.

My relations in the U.S. have informed me that the Embassy has approached them, on my behalf, for money for tickets to the U.S.

I assure you my relations are quite unable to assist in this matter, that is why I had to apply to the Embassy for a loan.

I request that solicitations to my relatives be stopped.

Also, I request that my approved loan application be honoured, as soon as possible, so that my wife and I can leave the U.S.S.R.

In regards to when you finally do call us to Moscow, whether by telegram or letter, you should not fail to specify through which point of exit <u>my</u> exit visa should be made out to, of course. It should be the same as my wife's designated point of exit. Sincerely.

2.44 To Robert Oswald, May 1, 1962 (CE 318, 16 H 800-801)

Dear Robert, Well we have finally gotten the word from the U.S. Embassy and shall leave for Moscow tomorrow we will be 10-14 days in Moscow and then leave for England where we shall board a ship for America. The transatlantic trip will take another two weeks so all in all it'll be another month before where actually arrive in American, probably in New Orleans. We'll inform you as soon as we arrive. This will be the last letter you get from us from the USSR. In case you hear about our coming, or the newspapers hear about it (I hope they won't), I want to warn you not to make any comment whatsoever about us. None at all!! I know what was said about me when I left the U.S. as mother sent me some clippings from the newspaper; however, I realize that it was just the shock of the news which made you say all those things. However, I'll just remind you again not to make any statements or comments if you are approached by the newspapers, between now and the time we actually arrive in the U.S. Hope to see you soon. Love to family.

2.45 **To Marguerite Oswald, May 30, 1962** (CE 198, 16 H 578)

Dear Mother, Well, here we are in Moscow getting ready to leave for the U.S.A. I'll be sending you a telegram or otherwise informing you as to where we shall embark and so forth, everything is O.K. so don't worry about us we shall be leaving from Holland by ship for the U.S. on June 4th however I expect to stay over in new York for a day or so and also Washington D.D. for sightseeing.

See you soon. Love.

2.46 **To the United States Marine Corps (Brief in Support of Application for Review of Discharge or Separation from the Armed Services of the United States) June 18, 1962** (CE 780, 17 H 653-657)

A review of my file will show that a recommendation to separate me from the Marine Corps. Reserve was concurred in by a board of officers at Glenview Illinois, to become effective from September 13, 1960, or I year 2 days from the time <u>I was honorably discharged from active duty</u> at H&HS, Macs, El Toro Calif. on 11 September 1959.

Referral of my case to this board was premised on the purported fact that I had renounced my American citizenship with intent to become a permanent citizen of the Union of Soviet Socialist Republics.

<u>Since this was the sole reasons I was separated from the Marine corps. Reserve and summarily given a Undesirable Discharge I do hereby request:</u>

That the board does convene to review this case.

This is a case which comes under the heading: NAVEXOS 15(e)(4), i.e. <u>a discharge improperly issued</u>. In this case there is no question as to service, which as the naval records show, was of <u>strictly honourable nature.</u>

This case is a question of loyalty revolving out of my residence in the Soviet Union.

In requesting a review of this case, I can show: I had not violated any laws or regulations pertaining to my prolonged residence abroad and that I am a loyal U.S. citizen. (End)

<u>Statement of Plaintiff</u> (I request that this statement be made part of the record.)

I have been informed that a board of Inquiry was convened at Naval Air Station, Glenview, Illinois to determine my fitness to remain a member of the U.S.M.C.R.

Gary W. O'Brien

I was separated from the U.S.M.C.R. with a undesirable discharge superseding my original honourable discharge of 11 September 1959 given at H&HR Marine Corps Air Station, El Toro, Santa Anna, California.

This board was given to consider weather I had gone to the Union of Soviet Socialist Republics with the object of becoming a permanent citizen of that country.

Since I was not in the United States at the time of the convening of the board and since I was completely unable to communicate with anyone in the outside world through the Iron Curtain, this board found against me.

My relatives, who were notified of the convening of this board, could not conceivably present evidence of my behalf against such vaguely defined charges, without any knowledge of my whereabouts.

It was only on July 8, 1961, that I was able to put in a appearance at the American Embassy, Moscow after escaping from the detention of the city to which the Russian authorities had sent me. Subsequent events, through the active support of the U.S. Embassy, will see myself and my Russian wife in the U.S. very shortly.

As far as the case in question is concerned I can understand how, without any inquiry directed towards me, a conclusion of disloyalty might possibly be arrived at.

However, whether my choice of permanent or temporary residence my be in the U.S.S.R., or in the United States, grounds for such arbitrary action as was instigated against me cannot be judged as being fair or impartial.

I must point out that I have not violated any laws under the U.S. Code Section 1544 title 18.

1 may say that even the most prolonged residence abroad is an accepted custom, and absolutely legal (so long as other pertinent regulations have not been violated).

In introducing the letter from the U.S. Embassy, Moscow, I have it in mind the last paragraph Nov. 13, 1961, which states: "meanwhile your retention of your present Soviet passport or an extension thereof does not prejudice in any way your claim to American citizenship", signed Joseph B. Norburg, American consular: whereas in the letter from the Embassy of January 31, 1962, you see I am present in the Soviet Union only because of the technical difficulties in getting my family out of the Soviet Union.

The tone of the letter, while not an affidavit, hardly reflect the opinion of the American Embassy that I am undeserving, through some sort of breech of loyalty, of their attentions.

In presenting a notarized affirmation of valid U.S. citizenship I have had to present my valid U.S. passport and valid Soviet residential document to the notary. ("This paragraph to be disregarded." Lee H. Oswald, June 14, 1962).

In presenting my case I have avoided notarized affirmations, which would under the circumstances, have to be in Russian. However I request in view of my particular case and my location that par: 12(B) NAVEXOS P-70 be in force throughout the proceeding.

Affirmation of contains of affidavit can be had by contacting that naval bureau, office or officer who can give such affirmation of contents (12(A) NAVEXOS P-70).

Since there are no other possible way to present my case, in consideration of the nature of the charge which was brought against me, I would like to include a request for re-enlistment regardless of the finding's of the Board, in accordance with par: 15(e)(5). I request that the Board consider my sincere desire to use my former training at the aviation fundamentals school, Jacksonville, Florida, and Radar operators school, Biloxi, Miss., as well as the special knowledge I have accumulated through my experience <u>since my release from active duty</u>, in the naval service.

I made the foregoing statements as part of my application with full knowledge of the penalties involved for willfully making a false statement.

2.47 To the Socialist Worker's Party, New York, N.Y., August 12, 1962, (Dobbs Exhibit No. 9, 19 H 575)

Dear Sirs. Please send me some information as the nature of your party, its policies, etc., as I am very interested in finding out all about your programme. Sincerely.

2.48 To the Soviet Embassy, Washington, D.C. n.d. (CE 986, 18 H 486)

Dear Sirs: In regard to my wife's Russian passport, <u>N.KU37790</u>, which we sent to your embassy on July 20th for registration as is required by your law.

We have not received this passport back as yet, please look into this.

Also, please give me information as how I can subscribe to "Pravda" or "Isvestia," Russian Language newspapers on some other Russian Language magazines such as "Ogonyok."

I assume you have received my wife's passport, and will return it after the registration of her address.

I would like for the Embassy to send us any periodicals of bulletins which you may put out for the benefit of your citizens living, for a time, in the U.S.A. Thank you. Sincerely.

2.49 To *The Worker* and Its Defense Committee, n.d. (Tormey Exhibit No. 1, 21 H 674)

Dear Sirs, Enclosed a small example of my modest skill, If you may happen to need any head-line-photo work on a small scale, I will be honored to do it. For your of course, there will be no charge. Sincerely. Instruction:

Just send me any size, small reproduction of what you want done for instance, the below size reproduction was also needed on the prints enclosed (Gus Hall).

I can make black on white (positive print), or white on black (negative print) any size you desire.

2.50 To Pioneer Publishers, New York, January 1, 1963 (Dobbs Exhibit No. 7, 19 H 573)

Dear Sirs, Please send me the following publications; by J.B. Cannon; 1. The Coming American Revolution - .10; 2. The End of the Comintern - .10; 3. 1948 Manifesto of the 4th International - .15.

Also I would like to know whether you have the English words to the song the 'International'. Thank you.

2.51 **To Marina Oswald found April 10, 1963** (CE 1, 16 H 1-2) (English translation)

1. This is the key to the mailbox which is located in the main post office in the city on Ervay Street. This is the same street where the drugstore, in which you always waited, is located. You will find the mailbox in the post office which is located 4 blocks from the drugstore on that street. I paid for the box last month so don't worry about it.

2. Send the information as to what has happened to me to the Embassy and include newspaper clippings (should there be anything about me in the newspapers). I believe that the Embassy will come quickly to your assistance on learning everything.

3. I paid the house rent on the 2d so don't worry about it.

4. Recently I also paid for water and gas.

5. The money from work will possibly be coming. The money will be sent to our post office box. Go the bank and cash the check.

6. You can either throw out or give my clothing etc. away. Do not keep these. However, I prefer that you hold on to my personal papers (military, civil, etc.)

7. Certain of my documents are in the small blue valise.

8. The address book can be found on my table in the study should you need the same.

9. We have friends here. The Red Cross will help you.

10. I left you as much money as I could, $60 on the second of the month. You and the baby can live for another 2 months using $10 per week.

11. If I am alive and taken prisoner, the city jail is located at the end of the bridge through which we always passed on going to the city (right in the beginning of the city after crossing the bridge).

2.52 To V.T. Lee, n.d. (Lee (Vincent T.) Exhibit No. 1, 20 H 511)

Dear Sirs; I do not like to ask for something for nothing but I am unemployed.

Since I am unemployed, I stood yesterday for the first time in my life, with a placard around my neck, passing out fair play for Cuba pamphlets, etc. I only had 15 or so.

In 40 minutes they were all gone. I was cursed as well as praised by some. My home-made placard said:

HANDS OFF CUBA!

VIVA FIDEL!

I now ask for 40 or 50 more of the five basic pamphlets. Sincerely.

2.53 To V.T. Lee, May 26, 1963 (Lee (Vincent T.) Exhibit No. 2, 10 H 512-513)

Dear Sirs. I am requesting formal membership in your Organization. In the past I have received from you pamphlets etc. both bought by me and given to me by you.

Now that I am in New Orleans, I have been thinking about renting a small office at my expense for the purpose of forming a FPCC branch here in New Orleans.

Could you give me a charter? Also I would like Also I would like information on buying pamphlets, etc. in large lots as well as blank F.P.C.C. applications etc.

Also a picture of Fidel, suitable for framing would be a welcome touch.

Offices down here rent for $30 a month and if I had a steady flow of literature I would be glad to take the expense.

Of course I work and could not supervise the office at all times but I'm sure I could get some volunteers to do it.

Could you add some advice or recommendations?

I am not saying this project would be a roaring success <u>but I am willing to try.</u>

An office, literature and getting people to know you are the fundamentals of the F.P.C.C. as far as I can see so here's hoping to hear from you. Yours respectfully.

2.54 **To V.T. Lee, n.d.** (Lee (Vincent T.) Exhibit No. 4, 20 H 518-521)

Dear Mr. Lee. I was glad to receive your advice concerning my try at starting a New Orleans F.P.C.C. chapter. I hope you won't be too disapproving at my innovations but I do think they are necessary for this area.

As per your advice, I have taken a P.O. Box (No. 30061).

Against your advice, I have decided to take an office from the very beginning.

As you can from the circular, I had jumped the gun on the charter business but I don't think it's too important. You may think the circular is too provocative but I want it to attract attention, even if it's the attention of the lunatic fringe. I had 2000 of them run off.

The major change in tactics you can see from this small membership blank, in that I will charge $1.00 a month dues for the New Orleans chapter only, and I intend to issue N.O. F.P.C.C. membership fee.

However, you will lose nothing in the long run because I will forward $5.00 to the national F.P.C.C. for every New Orleans Chapter member who remains a dues paying member for 5 months in any year.

It's just that the people I am approaching will not pay 5 dollars all at once to a committee in New York which they cannot see with their own eyes.

But they may pay a dollar a month to their own chapter, after having received their membership card from my hand to theirs.

Also I think such a dues system binds the members closer to the F.P.C.C.

I will promise only a membership card and a chapter vote to future members, that is, I don't expect you to extend them national F.P.C.C. mailing for their one dollar a month.

As you will notice on the membership blank, there is a place for those who do wish to subscribe to the national mailings for the fee of $5.00. That fee will go directly to you in New York.

As soon as any member has paid dues adding up to five dollars in any year, I will forward that fee to you and then you may handle it as if it was a usual application for membership in the national F.P.C.C.

In any event, I will keep you posted and even if the office stays open for only 1 month, more people will find out about the

F.P.C.C. than if there had never been any office at all, don't you agree?

Please feel free to give advice and any other help. Yours truly.

2.55 To *The Worker*, June 10, 1963 (Johnson (Arnold) Exhibit No. 1, 20 H 257-258)

Dear Sirs, As a long time subscriber to the worker, I know I can ask a favor of you with full confidence of its fulfillment.

I have formed a "Fair Play for Cuba Committee" here in New Orleans. I think it is the best way to attract the broad mass of people to a popular struggle.

I ask that you give me as much literature as you judge possible sin (like the one enclosed) and pamphlets in my office.

Also please be so kind as to convey the enclosed "honorary membership" cards to those fighters for peace Mr. Gus Hall and Mr. B. Davis. Yours fraternally.

2.56 To the Soviet Embassy, Washington, D.C., July 1, 1963 (CE 13, 16 H 30)

Dear Sirs: Please <u>rush</u> the entrance visa for the return of Soviet citizen, Marina N. Oswald.

She is going to have a baby in <u>October</u>; therefore you must grant the entrance visa and make the transportation arrangements before then.

As for my return entrance visa please consider it <u>separately</u>. Thank you.

2.57 To V.T. Lee, August 1, 1963 (Lee (Vincent T.) Exhibit No. 5, 20 H 524-5)

Dear Mr. Lee. In regards to my efforts to start a branch office in New Orleans.

I rented an office as planned and was promptly closed three days later for some obscure reasons by the renters. They said something about remodeling, etc., I'm sure you understand.

After that I worked out of a post office box and by using street demonstrations and some circulars work have sustained a great deal of interest but no new members.

Through the efforts of some Cuban-exile "gusanos" a street demonstration was attacked and we were officially cautioned by police.

This incident robbed me of what support I had leaving me alone.

Nevertheless, thousands of circulars were distributed and many, many pamphlets which your office supplied.

We also managed to picket the fleet when it came in and I was surprised at the number of officers who were interested in our literature.

I continue to receive through my post office box inquiries and questions which I shall endeavor to keep answering to the best of my ability. Thank you.

Gary W. O'Brien

2.58 To V.T. Lee, August 12, 1963 (Lee (Vincent T.) Exhibit No. 6, 20 H 526)

Dear Mr. Lee, Continuing my efforts on behalf of the FPCC in New Orleans, I find I have incurred the displeasure of the Cuban exile "worms" here. I was attacked by three of them as the copy of the enclosed summons indicates. I was fined ten dollars and the three Cubans were not fined because of 'lack of evidence' as the judge says.

I am very glad I was stirring things up and shall continue to do so. The incident was given considerable coverage in the press and local TV news broadcast.

I am sure it will be to the good of the Fair Play for Cuba Committee. Sincerely yours.

(Attached from Times-Picyuene)

Pamphlet Case Sentence Given

Lee Oswald, 23, 4907 Magazine, Monday was sentenced to pay a fine of $10 or serve 10 days in jail on a charge of disturbing the peace by creating a scene.

Oswald was arrested by First District police at 4:15 p.m. Friday in the 700 block of Canal, while he was reportedly distributing pamphlets asking for a "Fair Play for Cuba."

Police were called to the scene when three Cubans reportedly sought to stop Oswald. Municipal charges against the Cubans for disturbing the peace were dropped by the court.

2.59 To Arnold Johnson, August 13, 1963 (Johnson (Arnold) Exhibit No. 3, 20 H 261)

Dear Mr. Johnson – I wish to thank you for the literature which you sent me for our local branch of the "Fair Play for Cuba Committee" of which I am the secretary-president.

As you can see from the enclosed clipping I am doing my best to help the cause which I know you approve of.

Would you from time to time send us literature? Any at all will be greatly appreciated.

Please accept an honorary New Orleans branch membership as a token of esteem. Thank You.

2.60 To V.T. Lee, August 17, 1963 (Lee (Vincent T.) Exhibit No. 7, 20 H 529-530)

Dear Mr. Lee – Since I last wrote to you (Aug. 13) about my arrest and fine in New Orleans for distributing literature for FPCC, things have been moving pretty fast.

On August 16th I organized a FPCC demonstration of three people. The demonstration was given considerable coverage by WDSU-TV channel 6, and also by our channel 4 TV station.

Due to that I was invited by Bill Stuckey to appear on his TV show called 'Latin American Focus' at 7.30 p.m. Saturdays on WDSU – channel 6. After this 15 minute interview which was filmed on magnetic tape at 4.00 p.m. for rebroadcast at 7.30 I was flooded with callers and invitations to debate, etc. as well as people interested in joining the FPCC New Orleans branch.

That then is what happened up to this day and hour. You can I think be happy with this developing situation here in New Orleans. I would however like to ask you to rush some more literature particularly the white sheet "Truth About Cuba" regarding government restrictions on travel, as I am quickly running out. Yours truly.

2.61 To the Central Committee of the CPUSA, August 28, 1963 (Johnson (Arnold) Exhibit No. 4, 20 H 262-4)

Comrades; Please advise me upon a problem of personal tactics.

I have lived in the Soviet Union from Oct. 1959 to July 1962.

I had, in 1959, in Moscow, tried to legally dissolve in favor of Soviet citizenship, however, I did not complete the legal formalities for this.

Having come back to the U.S. in 1962 and thrown myself into the struggle for progress and freedom in the United States, I would like to know weather, in your opinion, I can continue to fight, handicapped as it were, by my past record, can I still, under the circumstances, compete anti-progressive forces above ground or weather in your opinion I should remain in the background i.e. underground.

Our opponents could use my background of residence in the U.S.S.R. against any cause which I join, by association, they could say the organization of which I am a member, in Russian controlled, etc. I am sure you see my point.

I could of course openly proclaim (if pressed on the subject) that I wanted to dissolve my American citizenship as a personal protest against the policy of the US government in supporting dictatorship, etc. But what do you think I should do? Which is the best tactic in general? Should I disassociate myself from all progressive activities?

Here in New Orleans, I am secretary of the local branch of the "Fair Play for Cuba Committee" a position which frankly I have used to foster communist ideals on a local radio show I was attacked by Cuban exile organization representatives for my residence etc. in the Soviet Union. I feel I have compromised the FPCC so you see that I need the advice of trusted, long time fighters for progress. Please advise. With fraternal Greeting. Sincerely.

2.62 To *The Worker*, New York, N., August 31, 1963 (Johnson (Arnold) Exhibit No. 5, 20 H 266-267)

Dear Mr. Best. As a commercial photographer I have, in the past, made blow-ups, reverses and other types of photo work for the "Worker."

Mr. Weinstock, in December 1962, expressed thanks for my modest work in a letter.

Mr. Tormey, of the Gus Hall - Ben Davis Defense Committee also has commended some photos I did for his committee.

I am familiar with most forms of photo and art work, and other phases of typography.

I am sure you realized that to a progressive person with knowledge of photography and printing, the greatest desire imaginable is to work directly for the "Worker".

However, I understand that there might be many loyal comrades who want the same thing, i.e. to work for the "Worker."

So if you say there are no openings I shall continue to hope for the chance of employment directly under the "Worker."

My family and I shall, in a few weeks, be relocating into your area.

In any event I'm sure you shall give my application full consideration. Thank you. Sincerely.

2.63 To the Socialist Workers Party, September 1, 1963 (Dobbs Exhibit No. 10, 19 H 577)

Dear Sirs, Please advise me as to how I can get into direct contact with S.W.P. representatives in the Washington - Baltimore area.

I and my family are moving to the area in October.

As you know, there is no S.W.P. branch in the New Orleans area where I have been living.

I am a long time subscriber to the Militant and other party literature which I am sure, you have a record. Thank you.

2.64 To Arnold Johnson, November 1, 1963 (Johnson (Arnold) Exhibit 7, 20 H 271-273)

Dear Mr. Johnson: In September I had written to you saying I expected to move from New Orleans, La., to the Philadelphia-Baltimore area. You advised me that I could contact you when I had gotten settled there and the party would contact me in that area.

Since than my personal plans have changed and I have settled in Dallas, Texas for the time.

Through a friend I have been introduced to the American Civil Liberties Union Local Chapter which holds monthly meetings on the campus of Southern Methodist University.

The first meeting I attended was on October 25th, a film was shown and afterwards a very critical discussion of the ultra-right in Dallas.

On October 23rd, I had attended a ultra-right meeting headed by General Edwin A. Walker who lives in Dallas.

This meeting preceded by one day the attack on i.e. Stevenson at the United Nations Day meeting at which he spoke.

As you can see, political faction between "left" and "right" is very great here.

Can you advise me as to the general view we have on the American Civil Liberties Union. And to what degree, if any, I should attempt to heighten its progressive tendencies?

The Dallas Branch of the A.C.L.U. is firmly in hands of "liberal" professional people (a member and two Law Professors conducted the Oct 25th meeting). However, some of those present showed marked class-awareness and insight. Respectfully yours.

2.65 To the American Civil Liberties Association, n.d. Received on November 4, 1963 (CE 783, 17 H 671)

Please enroll me as an associate member at $2.00.

Also, please notify me as to how I may contact ACLU Groups in my area. Thank you. (Occupation listed as "Photographer")

2.66 To the Soviet Embassy, Washington, D.C., November 9, 1963 (CE 103, 16 H 443-444) (Handwritten draft)

Dear Sirs: This is to inform you of recent events since my meetings with Comrade Kostin in the Embassy of the Soviet Union, Mexico City, Mexico.

I was unable to remain in Mexico indefinitely because of my Mexican visa restrictions which were for 15 days only. I could not take a chance on requesting a new visa unless I used my real name so I returned to the U.S.

I and Marina Nichilayeva are now living in Dallas, Texas.

The FBI is not now interested in my activities in the progressive organization FPCC of which I was secretary in New Orleans Louisiana since I no longer reside in that state.

The FBI has visited us here in Dallas, Texas on November 1st. Agent James P. Hosty warned me that if I attempt to engage in FPCC activities in Texas, the FBI will again take an "interest" in me. The agent also "suggested" that my wife could remain in the U.S. under FBI protection, that is she could defect from the Soviet Union. Of course, I and my wife strongly protested those tactics by the notorious F.B.I.

I had no planned to contact the Mexican City Embassy at all so of course they were unprepared. Had I been able to reach Havana as planned, the Soviet Embassy would have had time to assist me, but of course the stupid Cuban console was at fault here, I'm glad he had since been replaced by another.

2.67 To the Soviet Embassy, Washington, D.C., November 9, 1963 (CE 15, 16 H 33) (Typed)

Dear Sirs: This is to inform you of recent events since my meetings with Comrade Kostin in the Embassy of the Soviet Union, Mexico City, Mexico.

I was unable to remain in Mexico indefinitely because of my Mexican visa restrictions which was for 15 days only. I could not take a chance on requesting a new visa unless I used my real name so I returned to the United States.

I had not planned to contact the Soviet Embassy in Mexico. so they were unprepared, had I been able to reach the Soviet Embassy in Havana as planned, the embassy there would have had time to complete our business.

Of course the Soviet Embassy was not at fault, they were as I say unprepared, the Cuban consulate was guilty of a gross breach of regulations. I am glad he has since been replaced.

The Federal Bureau of Investigation is not now interested in my activities in the progressive organization "Fair Play for Cuba Committee" of which I was secretary in New Orleans (state Louisiana) since I no longer reside in that state. However the F.B.I. has visited us here in Dallas, Texas on November 1st. Agent James P. Hosty warned me that if I attempt to engage in F.P.C.C. activities in Texas, the F.B.I. will again take an "interest" in me.

The agent also "suggested" to Marina Nichilayeva that she could remain in the United States under F.B.I. "protection", that is she could defect from the Soviet Union, of course, I and my wife strongly protested those tactics by the notorious F.B.I.

Gary W. O'Brien

Please inform us of our Soviet entrance visas as soon as they come.

Also, this is to inform you of the birth on October 20, 1963 of a DAUGHTER, AUDREY MARINA OSWALD in DALLAS, TEXAS, to my wife. Respectfully.

Appendix Three - The Press Interviews

3.1 Aline Mosby, Notes of interview conducted in Moscow on November 13, 1959 (CE 1385, 22 H 701-710)

The cavernous Metropole Hotel lobby smells of sweet Russian to tobacco and heavy varnish, and it was noisy with foreign tourists when I hurried through the revolving door that November day in 1959. Falling snow was softening the harshes of the Soviet streets, but the atmosphere in Moscow and the hotel lobby was far from cold.

Mir y druzhba (peace and friendship) was the symphony that Premier Nikita Khrushchev was conducting at that time, and the once forbidding Soviet capital has an air of relief from cold war tension.

As foreign correspondent from United Press International, I had seen Soviets and Americans reaching out their hands to each other at the American Exhibition in Sokolniky Park that summer. I had toured the Soviet Union with the then Vice President Richard Nixon for friendly Russian receptions from Leningrad to Novosibirsk in Siberia.

The once-closed Soviet Union had just burst wide open to hordes of invading foreign tourists, and packs of them, cameras around their necks, chattered and milled around the Metropole reception desk. But I had come through the snow to the old-fashioned hotel to see another type of American tourist, a defector who did not want to be part of that gay crowd.

I had heard at the American Embassy that a young American named Lee Harvey Oswald, 20, had walked in Oct. 30 (1959), slapped his passport on the consular officer's desk and announced he'd 'had enough of the United States.' On Nov. 2 he had signed an affidavit saying 'I affirm my allegiance to the soviet socialistic republic.'

After calling all hotels where foreigners are placed by Intourist, the Soviet tourist agency, I finally found Oswald at the Metropole and, over the telephone, arranged to interview him in his room.

I went up in the creaky elevator to the second floor and down the hall, past the life-sized nude in white marble, the gigantic printing of Lenin and Stalin and the usual watchful floor clerk in her prim blue dress with brown braids wrapped around her head.

An attractive fellow answered my knock on the door of room 233.

"I am Lee Oswald", he said, with a hesitant smile.

When I murmured some pleasantry that it was nice of him to seem me, when others in his position had shunned the press, he said, "Yes, other reporters have been trying to get up here."

I couldn't tell if he as boasting or truthful.

The he said, "I think you may understand and be friendly because you're a woman."

I speculated whether he was flattering me because he resented men and the authority they stood for.

The young man I saw was 5 feet 9 inches tall, weighed about 150 pounds and had a slight build. He had a sallow complexion, brown eyes and dark brown hair parted on the side. He was inexpensively but well and neatly dressed in a suit, white shirt and tie, that all had the air of his "Sunday best."

He was polite, but not particularly cordial, and seemed a bit awkward. I selected a red plus chair by the window – he sat opposite me in another chair in the baroque room resplendent with gilt clock and chandeliers. It was the standard $30-a-day room with meals that all tourists must buy.

For two hours in that old Russian setting, I talked with Lee Harvey Oswald of Fort Worth, Texas, about his philosophy, his life and why he was there.

As he spoke he held his mouth stiffly and nearly closed. His jaw was rigid. Behind his brown eyes I felt a certain coldness. He displayed neither the impassioned fervor of a devout American Communist who at last had reached the land of his dreams, nor the wise-cracking informality and friendliness of the average American. Sometimes he looked directly at me, other times at the plush furniture. Now and then he gazed out the tall window, hung with lace curtains and gold draperies, to Sverdlovak Square and the Lenin Museum and the gold onion-shaped domes of the ancient Kremlin churches beyond.

He talked almost non-stop like the type of semi-educated person of little experience who clutches what he regards as some sort of unique truth. Such a person often does not expect anyone else to believe him and is contemptuous of other people who cannot see his "truth." A zealot, he is not remotely touched by what anyone else says. In fact, at time in my two hours with Lee Harvey Oswald I felt we were not carrying out a conversation, but that two monologues were being delivered simultaneously.

He was pleasant and well-mannered but he sounded smug and self-important and so often was that small smile, more like a smirk...

As the light already began to fade in the mid-afternoon over the Square, Oswald began by rather formally announcing his desire to stay in the Soviet Union. It sounded to me as if he had rehearsed these sentences, and they had the tone of childish defiance and pretentiousness.

"Soviet officials have informed me that either in the event of reception or acceptance of my first application, I won't have to leave," he began in good English with only a slight southern accent.

"They are investigating the possibilities of finding me an occupation. They think it would be best to continue my higher education."

He said he had "put in my application to the supreme soviet" for Soviet citizenship Oct. 16, the day after he arrived in Moscow. He added, "I had my first meeting with officials three days later."

Oswald said he was born Oct. 18, 1939 in New Orleans, where, like most of the south and southwest United States, a tradition of violence runs through the town like the Mississippi River.

Behind the lacy facades of its picturesque French quarter, New Orleans is a tough town. It is emotionally divided by the cleavages between its old rich, who gathered their money through cotton and land, the new rich who snared theirs through local politics which for years had a strong underworld cast; between the poor white ignorance of Louisiana's agriculture up-country and the much more sophisticated city, and, hanging over everything else, by the fierce, slashing hatreds between negro and white.

Oswald said "I lived for two years in New York…where I saw the luxuries of Park Avenue and the workers' lives on the East Side" and then his widowed mother took him and his two brothers to Fort Worth, Texas, back to New Orleans and Fort Worth again.

Oswald painted a verbal picture of a boy who grew up with an "old" mother and without the discipline, love and care of a father.

"My father died before I was born", he continued. "My mother works in shops mostly, in Fort Worth and around. I finished high school. I played baseball and football…"

I asked if he formed many friendships in school.

"Oh, I had a certain amount of friends, but I don't have any attachments now in the United States. I traveled a lot. We moved from one to city to the next. Besides, I was a bookworm."

And what did he read?

"Marx", he said. "I'm a Marxist," and had added that eagerly as if the label gave him pride and importance.

"I became interested about the age of 15. From an ideological viewpoint. An old lady handed me a pamphlet about saving the Rosenbergs."

He glanced out the lace-curtained window and was quiet for a moment.

"I looked at that paper and still remember it for some reason, I don't know why," he said.

"Then we moved to New Orleans and I discovered one book in the library, 'Das Kapital.' It was what I'd been looking for.

"It was like a very religious man opening the Bible for the first time," he said. His eyes shone like those of a religious enthusiast.

"I read the 'Manifesto'. It got me interested. I found some dusty back shelves in the New Orleans library, you know, I had to remove some front books to get at the books.

"I started to study Marxist economic theories. I could see the impoverishment of the masses before my own eyes in my own mother, and I could see the capitalists. I thought the worker's life could be better.

"I continued to indoctrinate myself for five years. My mother knew I was reading books but she didn't know what they were about.

"I would not care to live in the United States where being a worker means you are exploited by the capitalists. If I would remain in the United States, feeling as I do, under the capitalist system, I could never get ahead.

"I could not be happy. I could not live under a capitalistic system. I would have a choice of becoming a worker under the system I hate, or becoming unemployed. Or I could have become a capitalist and derived my profit and my living (sic.) under the exploitation of workers.

"I will live now under a system where no individual capitalist will be able to exploit the workers. I will feel that I'm working for all the people and not for an individual capitalist making a profit for himself" he said, rushing from one sentence to another.

"Communism is an aggressive ideal as well as an economic system. Capitalism is only an economic system, and can only be offensive. Capitalism will shrink but within the borders of the United States the country is also shrinking."

I did not quite understand that last remark, but I was too busy to take down his words in shorthand to puzzle through his train of thought.

"Capitalism has passed its peak. Unemployment is growing. An era of depression is on the way – uh, or perhaps not.

"The forces of communism are growing. I believe capitalism will disappear as feudalism disappeared. A young man in the United States looked forward as a millionaire, when he's young. When he gets old he looks forward as a worker.

"The hysteria in America has gotten worse. If practice makes perfect, the U.S. is getting better," he said sarcastically. "You know, fashions, mode, clothes, food – and hating communists or niggers. You go along with the crowd. I am against conformism in such matters, such as fashionably hating minority groups. Being a southern boy, I've seen poor niggers. That was a lesson, too. People hate because they're told to hate. Like school kids. In Little Rock they don't know the difference between a nigger and a white man but it was the fashion to hate niggers so they hated them. People in the United States are like that in everything."

I finally got a word in edgewise to inquire if he were a member of the Communist party.

"Communist?" he looked surprised. "I've never met a communist. I might have seen a communist once in New York, the old lady who gave me the pamphlet, save the Rosenbergs."

I asked him what he thought about communist party members in the United States, or even socialists.

"I don't want any socialist people to act for me" he said, his voice heavy with scorn. "I dislike them as I know them in the United States. You don't just sit around and talk about it. You go out and do it. I just haven't got out of university and read about Marx. I've seen all the workers on the east side.

"Of course, the conduct of America towards the communists is harsh" he added. "That was to be expected. My sympathies are with them as the underdog. That's natural, too.

"The Soviet Union had always been my ideal, as the bulwark of communism. The communists have been a minority in the United States, and have to rely on outside power and moral support from the Soviet Union. American communists can look to the Soviet Union as some sort of an ideal. The Americans are right in assuming that communism all over the world has ties with the Soviet Union, like the Catholic Church has ties with the Pope."

I tried to steer his conversation back to his mother and his early childhood. Did early poverty influence his decision to come to Moscow?

"Well-lll" he said in a sort of mock drawl, "My childhood allowed me to have a few benefits of American society. I was not completely hamstrung in enjoying life.

But seeing my mother always as a worker, always with less money than she could use...

"You see," he said, leaning forward and speaking slowly to emphasize his words, "my coming here, well, it was, uh, a matter of intelligence. I couldn't care to ramble. One way or another I'd lose in the United States. In my own mind, even if I'd be exploiting other workers. That's why I chose Marxist ideology."

Oswald also indicated that life as he saw it in the US Marine Corps convinced him that he should move to the other side of the Iron Curtain. For the Marine Corps, and for the United Stated policy, he showed deep hatred.

"After I finished high school, I joined the Marine Corps at 17" he said. "I was in Japan, Formosa, the Philippines. I was discharged when I was 20, in Santa Ana, California. I was a radar operator."

American Embassy officials had said Oswald told them he would reveal to the Soviets all he knew about American radar.

"I joined the Marine Corps because I had a brother in the Marines. I had a good conduct medal" he said.

Oswald did not have smooth relationships in the Marines, however. I later learned he had been tried twice before a military court for breaking regulations. At the end of his three years in uniform, he still was a private first class.

But he was skilled with guns. In classes he qualified as a sharpshooter, which is the second of three gradings for shooting ability in the Marine Corps.

The Marines put him on an inactive reserve list when he was discharged but later struck off his name as an undesirable.

But this he did not mention, of course, that snowy November day as we sat in his hotel room in Moscow.

This week a Fort Worth policeman who went to school with Oswald commented that "he was always opposed to any kind of discipline. He seemed to hold it against people up here – any authority." This apparently applied to his three years in the Marine Corps.

He said "In the Marine Corps I observed the leaders in certain foreign countries. The Russians would say 'military imperialism.' Well, the occupation of one country is imperialism, like Formosa. The conduct of American technicians there, helping drag up guns for the Chinese. Watching American technicians show the Chinese how to use them – it's one thing to talk about communism and another thing to drag a gun up a mountainside.

"If you live with that for three years, you get the impression things aren't quite so right.

"I guess you could say I was influenced by what I read, and by observing that the material was correct, both in civilian life and military."

Oswald said while in the Marines he continued to read Marxist books and laid careful plans to go to Russia.

"I thought it would give me a chance to observe that which I had read" he went on.

He said intensely, "When I was working in the middle of the night on guard duty, I would think how long it would be and how much money I would have to have. It would be like being out of prison. I saved about $1500.

"But for two years I've had it in my mind, don't form any attachments, because I knew I was going away. I was planning to divest myself of everything to do with the United States.

"I've not just been thinking about it, but wanting to do it. For two years, saving my money.

"I'm sincere in my ideal. This is not something intangible. I'm going through pain and difficulty to do this."

I asked him if his buddies in the Marines knew of his plans to give up his country.

"Nobody knew how I felt about things" he said "and I felt them very strongly. My superiors thought I was just interest in a foreign language. My commanding officer, a major, was studying Russian and we used to talk about it."

Outside the hotel, we could see Muscovites, bundled against the snow in heavy shubas and fur shapkas – queuing up for buses and hurrying through the swirling snow.

"Now that you're in Moscow," I said, "do you think Soviet society works as well in reality as Marx had it on paper?"

"Considering Russia of 50 years ago, I can see the Soviet society worker of today is remarkably well off," replied Oswald.

"Now I personally would not say every person who thinks of himself as a communist should migrate to Russia. The drawbacks are many. But the basic ideas that brought me here are sound. The United States has more light bulbs and hot water heaters, but I don't feel this will be the case in 20 or 30 years. I would like to spend the rest of my life getting a normal life here, and if that means a marriage and so forth, okay."

I asked me how he thought he would get along in a foreign country where he did not know the language.

"Oh, I've been in a lot of classes in Russian" he said. "I want to expand my reading and writing. I can get alone in restaurants but my Russian is very bad. The only barrier here is learning absolutely fluently the language." I have Soviet friends. I've gone to the museums and theaters. They are very sympathetic to me."

He thought a moment and chuckled.

"I am in essence an ignorant immigrant. I never thought I'd be an immigrant from the U.S. to some other country. Like a German living in America.

Two hours had passed. When he started in on the ebb and flow of communism again, I got up and said I had to go. I was tired of listening to what sounded like recitations out of Pravda.

As I put on my coat, I thought about how Oswald had appeared totally disinterested in anything but himself. He never once asked what I was doing in Moscow, or how we foreigners lived there.

I also thought about a boy trying to digest that Metropole hotel food every night, a stranger in a foreign land without family or close friends. Perhaps if he came to my apartment he would see other westerners, he might think twice of his decision…

"Thank you" he said of my casual invitation to come to dinner some night. It was obvious to me he had no intention of seeing me again…

…Oswald had kept saying he was "sincere" in his beliefs, and obviously he was concerned about how they were presented to the public and as to how he fared in the first limelight of his life. A rival correspondent was queried by his London office, about my interview on Oswald. The defector immediately telephoned me, not to suggest dinner, but to complain.

"We weren't poverty-stricken" he said indignantly. "I am here because I believe in Marxist ideals. It is a matter of ideology, You don't understand."

We never got to go to dinner. Once I saw Oswald at a Moscow theater across a lobby. I felt sorry for him and wanted to say hello, but before I could reach him he was swallowed up in the crowd pushing around the ice cream stand and snack bar.

I had a feeling that the Soviets would not want this confused young man around Moscow. I never saw him after that. Later we heard that following Soviet custom he had been shipped off to unglamorous Minsk.

Oswald never followed his plans that he so excitedly outlined to me to enter college and study…. He worked in a factory in Minsk. Then he married a petite blonde nurse, Marina, and they had a child. The Soviets, as could have been predicted, ignored his pleas to become a citizen of the first Communist state.

Nine months after his arrival in Moscow, Oswald, as also could have predicted, asked the Soviets in July, 1960, for an exit visa and applied to the U.S. Embassy for the return of his passport.

... [H]e probably was disillusioned with life in Russia, homesick and had found he could not leave his personal problems behind just by stepping behind the Iron Curtain. But most important of all, Oswald had discovered that he failed to find in Russia the glory that he ever found in his own country, and for which he had give up his passport.

When a Soviet exit visa was not forthcoming, Oswald, the lad who had scorned the U.S. government and marine corps, and vowed to me he would live forever in the Soviet Union, wrote to Sen. John Tower of Texas in January 1962...

With the Senator's help, the State Department decided to provide the usual loan of $435.71 for Oswald, his wife and child to return to Texas. They received a Soviet exit visa and left Moscow May, 1962.

Oswald was a man who had never been noticed, and who obviously still wanted to be. Back in New Orleans his unstable philosophy hopped form one notion to another. He campaigned with anti-Castro, then Castro forces. He applied for a passport to travel to Eastern Europe and Russia again.

On Aug. 21 he appeared on a New Orleans radio program, claiming to be the secretary of the New Orleans chapter of the "Fair Play for Cuba Committee," which the committee branded an outright lie as he was no secretary and there was no New Orleans chapter.

The program pointed up that Oswald had done a 180-degree switch from many ideas he had expounded to me. He also sounded to me more confident than when I knew him, and, at least, apparently he had learned a few more things about communism and the Soviet Union than he knew in 1959. But I still heard the smug cockiness in his voice during the interview.

xxxxxxxxxx

The night of Friday, Nov. 22, 1963 on a teletype in the UPI Paris bureau, where I now was stationed, I read a dispatch that police has arrested a suspect in the assassination of President Kennedy. The suspect had lived for a while in Russia and had a Russian wife.

My mind raced over the parade of defectors and twilight-zoners I had known in Moscow. Not Marty, surely, but Oswald –

During the night my office telephoned me at home that the suspect was "that Lee Oswald that you knew in Moscow." I was not surprised.

In a trunkful of papers and momentoes of Moscow, I found a tan notebook labeled, "Defector." My notes began, "Lee Harvey Oswald, Fort Worth, room 233, Metropole..."

He looked just the same in the newspaper photographs I saw in the morning. But I disagree with the captions which say "glaring at photographers defiantly..."

Oswald was not glaring angrily. I have a feeling that in a way he was enjoying every minute of it. There was the same tight-lipped secretive smirk he wore when he related his self-imposed mission to me that snowy day in Moscow so far from Texas.

That same little smile was on his face when he walked out of his cell for the last time to face reporters and photographers, but the smile changed to the grimace of pain and death.

If he was guilty, why did he not confess in jail? In my opinion he did not confess probably because he felt nobody would understand him. Nobody ever had.

For 24 hours – from the time somebody raised a rifle from the 5th floor window of a warehouse where Oswald worked, and aimed it at the passing figure of one of the world's most popular leaders, until his own death at the hand of an enraged strip tease club owner – Lee Harvey Oswald at last found a place in the sun he had been seeking.

3.2 **Priscilla Johnson (Recollections of Interview with Lee Harvey Oswald in Moscow, November, 1959 – dated December 5, 1963** (Johnson (Priscilla) Exhibit No. 5, 20 H 292-306)

I have frequently thought about Oswald in connection with doing an article on defectors to the Soviet Union. Most of the defectors who came to Moscow while I was a correspondent there (1958-1960) came because of personal troubles there were having at home. They did not come or purport to come for reasons of ideology. Oswald was such an exception to the general run of defectors that I had been thinking about him ever since, I thought that the unideological quality of most of the defectors was a symptom of what had happened to the Soviet Union itself. It no longer seems to appeal to potential defectors for ideological or idealistic reasons.

The type of person who is attracted to Soviet Russia today reveals a good deal about the Soviet Union itself. The Russians had wanted one or two defectors from the United States exhibition of 1959 to combat the negative propaganda they had been suffering from the more or less frequent defection of East bloc persons to the West. But they were not eager to have such defectors as Oswald. They can take them or leave them and at a moment of history like 1959 (the spirit of Camp David), could even be embarrassed by them. The motives of a man like Oswald might be jejeune but they are more idealistic than those of most defectors nowadays. Precisely because they are realistic however, people like Oswald are tricky and hard to handle. The Russians don't fully understand or trust the person who comes to them out of self-styled idealistic motives. This may be a mark of the Russians own low self-esteem. But above all, it shows how Soviet Society itself has changes since the 1920's and 1930's. From experience, Soviet officials know that such a person can become bitter and turn against them. A defector like Webster who came only because he was trapped in an unhappy marriage at home and fell in love with a Russian waitress is easier to deal with and not so hard on the hosts' self-esteem. Those are the thoughts I had about Oswald after I had interviewed him, considerably after I interviewed him, but years before the assassination; they were ideas I had noted down with the aim of writing a piece on how the changing profile of the defector was a clew to the changing profile of Soviet society itself. I thought, however, that I had not fully comprehended Oswald. As he was the key to the piece and the inspiration of it, I had not written the article. But I had thought of Oswald often.

The interview took place about November 12th or 13th, 1959, on what I believe was a Monday night.

Lee Harvey Oswald, 20, of Fort Worth, Texas, born in New Orleans, went to the United States Embassy on October 31, and

> dissolved my American citizenship as much as they would let me at that time – I did request that my citizenship be dissolved. The Embassy officials did not allow me to swear an oath renouncing citizenship. They refused to allow me to take the oath at that time. They said they would not allow me to act without confirmation of my Soviet citizenship. I relinquished my passport and they would not act unless my Soviet citizenship was confirmed.

This is what he said first. I asked him about the official Soviet attitude and he said:

> The Russians had confirmed that I would not have to leave the Soviet Union or be forced to go even if the Supreme Soviet refused my request for Soviet citizenship. They have said they are investigating the possibilities of continuing my education at a Soviet institute.

And then he said at 17 he entered the Marine Corps and been discharged in September, having spent 14 months in Japan, the Philippines, Indonesia and Formosa, that he was a radar operator, and that he had finished his high school education in the Marine Corps. His birthday was October 18, 1939. He said he had been in the Marines 2 years, 9 months, 3 days, overseas 1 year, 2 months, 24 days. He said he had been born in New Orleans, spent his childhood in Louisiana and Texas, spent 2 years in New York, and then gone back to Louisiana, enlisted in Dallas. He said his father died before he was born. "I believe he was an insurance salesman." (This, in response to my question as to what his father did. I was stuck by his vagueness). He said he had one brother, that the Marines had given him a good conduct medal, and that his mother was alone and living in Fort Worth. Then he said he had started learning Russian a year ago "along with my other priorities" for coming to the Soviet Union. He said he had been able to teach himself to read and write Russian from Berlitz, but that he still had trouble speaking the language. (I believe he spoke very little Russian at that time). I asked him what method of Berlitz he as using, and he said he has both practice in speaking the language and teacher, but he was either being vague or elusive as to how he learned Russian. Perhaps he was just bored with just telling me about it. I asked him how he financed his trip to the Soviet Union and he said he came in money which he saved while in the Marine Corps. I asked him if he had made or was going to make any formal statement about his defecting and the reasons for it, and he said he would not. He said that if the Embassy had not told people about his defection (the American Embassy) he would never have said anything to anybody. But since they had, he as giving me an interview because

> I would like to give my side of the story – I would like to give people in the United States something to think about.

(In retrospect, that is an important remark. It may have some bearing on his motives in the assassination. Also it reveals his sense that the Embassy might be persecuting him, might be spreading unpleasant reports bout him). He said

> Once having been assured by the Russians that I would not have to return to the United States, come what may, I assumed it would be <u>safe</u> for me to give my side of the story.

(So long as he felt there was a chance that he might have to go back to the United States, he apparently did not want to jeopardize his chances of staying in the Soviet Union by talking to a foreign correspondent). Until they assured him that he could remain in the Soviet Union "there was always the possibility that my visa would not be extended." Russians had told him that a special law had to be passed by the Supreme Soviet making him a Soviet citizen. There had been a Supreme Soviet Session in late October. It had taken no action on Oswald's citizenship and he appeared disappointed by that and worried. He said that Soviet officials had warned him that

> It is not my wish nor even that of Soviet officials but the over-all political atmosphere that will determine whether I can become a citizen.

My citizenship may take years but I am safe in the knowledge that I can have a prolonged stay.

Then I asked him what position the American Embassy had taken on his defecting and he said:

They warned me about the trouble I could get into: (1) At first they tried to discourage me; (2) I asked to be allowed to take an oath renouncing my citizenship and they made excuses so as to refuse to let me take the oath. They said I should come back fully knowing that I cannot get back into the Embassy without a passport.

(Oswald handed in his passport to the Embassy, in fact he could get into the Embassy as an obvious foreigner without the passport but this whole passage is indication of his bitterness at the Embassy).

(3) at the time I become a Soviet citizen then "my government" (the Soviet government) will handle my renunciation through the usual diplomatic channels.

Then I guess he said he was bitter that the American Embassy refused to take his oath.

I was there on Saturday, October 31st. They refused to take the oath on the ground that the consular officer needed time to get the papers together. I told them I wanted to go through with the formality then and there. I can't be too hard on them but they are acting in an illegal way. He (the U.S. Consul) is supposed to carry that formality through, On November 1st I wrote

a letter of protest to the American Ambassador
on the way Snyder carried out his duties and I get
this letter back.

And then he quoted the letter.

> It is a matter of principle of the American
> Government that the right of expatriation is a
> natural and inherent right of any person and that
> the manner prescribed by law for the renunciation
> of American citizenship is the execution of oath
> before a diplomatic or consular officer of the
> United States in the established form.

> You are again informed that you may appear
> at the Embassy at any time during the normal
> business hours and request that the Embassy
> prepare the necessary documents for the
> renunciation of citizenship.

(I don't know whether he showed this letter to me or cited it from
memory). Next, I asked him the attitude of the Russians. Were
they encouraging him or were they discouraging him to defect?
He replied:

> The Russians are treating it like a legal
> formality. The(y) don't encourage you and they
> don't discourage you. They do of course warn you
> that it is not easy to be accepted as a citizen of
> the Soviet Union. But even if I am not accepted
> I would not consider returning to the United
> States.

I then asked him about his finances, whether he had bought the $30 a day Intourist vouchers and whether he had be able to afford it. He said he bought ten day Intourist vouchers. He said

> I am paying the standard room and food rate.
> I want to make clear that they are not sponsoring
> me (financially).

And he repeated "they are investigating the possibility of my studying." He had indicated that he had been impatient to get out of the Marines to come to Moscow and I asked him whether he had ever been tempted by the idea of deserting the Marines. He said,

> I didn't desert because (1) it is illegal; (2) for
> financial reasons; and (3) you can't get a passport
> while you are in the Marines.

I asked him why he hadn't resigned from the Marines since he was in such a hurry to get to Russia, and he said "you can't resign of course (he laughed rather bitterly at this point) – that is for officers." He said, "I never seriously considered deserting." Then I asked him (I guess I had it in my mind that he was a publicity seeker), would you mind if anybody ever knew about your deciding to defect? He replied:

> My family and my friends in the Marine
> never know my feelings about communism
> though I spent 2 years preparing to come here.
> These preparations consisted mostly of reading.
> It took me two years to find out how to do it.

I asked me how he found out. He said it wasn't hard. I asked him if anybody helped him. He refused to name any person or institution who had helped him.

Question: Did Intourist know of his plans to defect at the time he arrived in the Soviet Union?

Answer: "I won't say."

But he said he had an interview with an official of the Soviet Government a few days after his arrival in Moscow. He would not say who the official was or what agency he represented. Oswald said he had left New Orleans September 19th, he thought. Anyway it was a Friday, by ship. He had spent 12 days sailing to Le Harvre, from there he booked a flight to Helsinki where he bought vouchers at $30 a day. (This implies he got a visa in Helsinki). From Helsinki he went by train to Moscow where for the first 10 days he had been living on Intourist vouchers.

> For the past 2 years I have been waiting to
> do this one thing. (Here he raised his voice and
> gestured.) For 2 years I was waiting to leave the
> Marine Corps and get enough money to come. I
> have had practical experience in the world. I am
> not an idealist completely. I have had a chance to
> watch American imperialism in action.

He told me he had become a Marxist when he was 15. (My query- why?)

> I had discovered socialist literature at that
> time. Then I spent 5 years reading socialist
> literature observing the treatment of minority
> groups in America: Communists, negroes, and
> the workers especially. Watching the treatment of
> workers in New York and observing the fact that
> they are exploited. I had read about it in socialist
> literature and I saw that the description given in
> this literature was quite correct. I saw I would

become either a worker exploited for capitalist profit or an exploiter, or, since there are many in the category, I would be one of the unemployed. My decision was unemotional, and not set off by any fight with my wife since I have no wife. (Perhaps either I or Embassy officials had told him that most defectors had personal problems at home). At 15 I was looking for something that would give me the key to my environment. My mother had been a worker all her life. All her life she had to produce profit for capitalists. She is a good example of what happens to workers in the United States.

I asked him what her work was and he refused to say. Trying to ascertain what he meant by his last remark I asked whether his mother was old beyond her years or worn out, and his reply was "that is the usual end of people in the United States, isn't it?" He added:

It's the end of everyone in every society. The question is why they end up that way, for whom and under what system they work; surely it is the duty of everyone to work.

(Here he expanded on the idea that it is better to end up worn and tired working in the Soviet Union for the benefit of all of society than to end up the same way in the United States working for one private employer. He prefaced his remarks with "I don't claim to be an intellectual genius.") Then he went on in his philosophy:

I believe that sooner or later communism will replace capitalism. Capitalism is a defensive ideology, whereas communism is aggressive.

Communism is an ideology which implants itself
in every system and which grows."

In the next sentence he raised his voice:

I cannot live in the United States. I shall
remain here, if necessary, as a resident alien.

I asked him what was this socialist literature he had read. He
said rather wearily, "Marx and Engels." Which works by Marx
and Engels? "The standard works." I specifically asked if he had
read anything by Engels and he could not name any. Then he said
that he had read works by American Communists. So I asked
him to name what works he had read and he again refused to say
which works. (I have the impression, in retrospect, that he had
made a point of not naming any one who might have inspired
him, either in person or by their books, to defect, but that he had
at least had advice from somewhere. He seemed almost to hint
at this.) Then I asked him whether he had ever seen anything of
the American socialists or thought of trying to reform American
society through them? His reply was:

The American socialists are to be shunned by
anyone who is interested in progressive ideology.
It is a dormant, flag-waving organization.

Nor had he had any contact with the American communists, he
remarked. He said emphatically: "I never say a Communist in my
life. Only through reading Communist literature and observing
American reality did I conclude that Communism was best for
me personally."

Then the conversation turned to reasons for his hatred of the
United States. These reasons were:

(1) <u>Segregation.</u> I was brought up like any Southern boy to hate negroes. Then (2) socialist literature opened my eyes to the <u>economic reasons</u> for hating negroes. It is so that wages can be kept low. (3) My experience in Japan and the Philippines, where Americans are categorically hated for their <u>militarist imperialism</u>. You'd expect to see it in Japan. But if you've ever seen the Naval Base at Subic Bay in the Philippines you'd know what I mean.

He said he had sympathized with Communist elements there and with their hatred of Americans.

Americans look upon all foreign peoples as something to be exploited for profit. The only Filipinos who are well off are those who cooperate with the Americans.

He said he had been part of an Indonesian invasion force in March 1958 where there had been a

Communist inspired social turnover. We sat off the coast loaded with ammunition and that was enough for me. Also in the Suez Crisis in 1956 we were told we might have to go in.

So I asked him if this was how he felt about the Marines, why had he joined in the first place? He said, "I went into the Marines because we were poor and I didn't want to be a burden on my family." I asked him his impressions of living standards in the Soviet Union and whether his first-hand observations has in any way affected his convictions about socialism? And his reply was, "They don't have as many water heaters and meat pies here but they will in 20 years, through an economic system which is leaving the United States far behind. Any material shortcomings I might see cannot influence me to return." The I must have asked him whether it was Soviet social theory or Soviet successes, such as Sputnik and rapid industrialization, that had attracted him. He replied, "It is the social system, not successes that attracted me." "At the same time," he added, "the Soviet Union could undoubtedly surpass the United States in terms of economic successes." During the course of the interview I had been struck by the fact that he seemed to spend his days sitting alone in his hotel room. He told me he had not wandered around the city very much, and the only expedition he had made by himself had been to Detsky Mir, a children's department store two blocks away, where he said he had bought an ice cream cone or tea. He was impressed b the size of the crowds there, and seemed proud that he had been able to manage even so small an excursion. In other words, I got the impression throughout the interview that he felt rather helpless in Moscow, had seen very little of the city and in fact was markedly uninterested in learning about everyday life, conditions of people in the country he had striven so long to get to.)

I asked him what has struck him most in the Soviet Union and what he had seen there. He had been struck by "the love of art for art's sake" in the Soviet Union. As for what he had seen, he said he has seen the usual tourist attractions, had been to people's home, and seen the whole city of Moscow. But he declined to name anything specific and my impression was he had seen very little, so I asked him his overall impression of Moscow.

> Moscow is an impressive city because the energy put out by the Government is all used toward peaceful and cultural purposes. People here are so well-off and happy and have a lot of faith in the future of their country. Material poverty is not to be seen here.

Gary W. O'Brien

I, knowing many Russians who would have given anything to live in the United States, asked him the reaction of any Russians he had met when he told them his decision to defect. He said:

> The Russians sympathize and understand.
> But they ask me why and are very curious. But
> they understand when I speak of the idealistical
> [sic] reasons they have brought me here whereas
> an American would not understand.

He stressed that these Russians that he had met were extremely interested in the material situation of workers in the United States. (I suspected a little that he had wanted to be treated as something rather special and so I asked him if the Russians he had met paid him any special attention or made a big fuss over him. His answer was "No. They don't treat me as any celebrity.")

These are my observations in the course of the interview.

He had repeatedly referred to the Soviet Government as 'my government'. He said that because of his annoyance with the American Embassy he would not set foot in the Embassy again. I must have suggested at some point in the interview that he was defeating his own purpose, that by refusing to set foot in the Embassy out of pique, he was unable to take the oath renouncing citizenship. He justified his refusal to set foot in the Embassy by saying:

> I have already axed [sic] them to prepare the
> papers. I am sure that if I did enter the Embassy
> they would just give me the same run-around as
> before."

(It was in fact his refusal to go back to the Embassy to take the oath that, so far as I know, made it possible for him later to return

332

to the United States. I doubt that he was consciously aware that he was leaving himself this loophole but he may have had some semi-conscious awareness of it.) He stressed that it would be an honor to acquire Soviet citizenship. I must have asked him why in his view the Embassy would be trying to give him what he called the run-around. He called it "a prestige and labor-saving device." Again I asked him the difference between exploitation of the wage earner in the Soviet Union and the United States since both countries needed capital for industrial investment and he had already agreed that industrialization was a good thing. He replied that people in the Soviet Union, as in the United States, get a wage. But the profit they produce is used to benefit all the people, and not just a single employer. They have an economic system that is not based on credit or speculation.

My own note to myself in the stage of the interview which was toward the end that he has a very primitive understanding of economics. Referring to his defection, he said "my reasons are very strong and good to me". He said he had given his passport to the American Embassy along with both verbal and written statements. He said he did not recommend defection for everybody. He said it meant "coming into a new country, always being the outsider, always adjusting, but I know that I will never have to return to the United States. I believe I am doing right." He said he had been a Marine, had to get out before his three years were over, had been discharged September 11 because of dependency, that his mother was ill, that her situation was the climax of that of the working person in the United States, that her health was poor and that she was living in Fort Worth with his brother. He said that she had been trying to phone him in his room at the Metropole Hotel, begging him not to defect, but that he just let the telephone ring.

Appendix Four - Lecture at Spring Hill College, Mobile, Alabama July 27, 1963 (excerpt from FBI Report) (CE 2649 25 H 924-928)

...Mr. Robert J. Fitzpatrick, S.J., Scholastic, Jesuit House of Studies, Spring Hill College, Mobile, Alabama, advised he recalled Lee Harvey Oswald very well. Fitzpatrick said he was studying the Russian language and learned Eugene Murret, another Jesuit Scholastic, was a cousin of Oswald and that Oswald spent three years in Russia. He said that arrangements were then made to have Oswald speak to a group of the Jesuit Scholastics at the seminary there. He explained that the seminary had invited various speakers to address the Jesuit Scholastics previously and this was in connection with the same series of lectures. He recalled previous speakers had included a Protestant Minister and a Jewish Rabbi. He said it was believed Oswald would have some information which would be extremely interesting to them.

Fitzpatrick recalled Oswald, Oswald's wife, who was named Marina, and their two year only daughter named June, came to Mobile, Alabama, on Saturday, July 27, 1963. He said the Oswalds were accompanied by the parents of Eugene Murret. He also said they were accompanied also by Murret's brother and sister and their respective spouses and several children. Fitzpatrick said he did not attend Oswald's talk, but stayed with the Murrets and Oswald's wife. He further informed that Mrs. Murret was very anxious to talk with Mrs. Oswald without Lee Oswald being present. He explained Mrs. Murret told him she never had the opportunity to communicate at any great length with Mrs. Oswald inasmuch as Oswald had to translate for her. He said that as a result of this, he and Mrs. Murret and Mrs. Oswald walked throughout the seminary grounds for approximately an hour.

Fitzpatrick stated that apparently Marina Oswald could not speak English except for a few words such as yes and no. He said, however, she appeared to be a very fine woman in his opinion. He said that Mrs. Oswald told him she had been raised in the Russian Orthodox faith until she was approximately ten years of age, when her relations died. He said Mrs. Oswald had about the equivalent of what could be considered a high school education in the United States.

Mrs. Oswald stated she was not a communist and loved Russia and the Russian people. He explained that Mrs. Oswald's love for Russia was not the same type as that he had heard expressed by Nazis for the German fatherland. He further informed Mrs. Oswald stated there were many inconveniences in Russia; however, people had not difficulty making a living there. He recalled Mrs. Oswald stated she had no living relatives in Russia and said she met Oswald at a factory dance in Minsk and that they were subsequently married.

Fitzpatrick said Mrs.Oswald told him she liked the United States very much and there appeared to be no conflict with this and her love for Russia. He said she stated she had no opportunity to learn English inasmuch as Oswald kept her completely away from other people. He said Mrs. Oswald appeared to be very happy with Oswald; however, Oswald was definitely the head of the family. He further informed Mrs. Oswald indicated her husband did a great deal of reading, but that it appeared scattered and apparently had no direction or planning.

Fitzpatrick stated Mrs. Oswald only mentioned residing in the city of New Orleans, Louisiana; however, in talking to her he received the impression the Oswalds had lived in other cities of the United States. He stated Mrs. Oswald said her husband was presently out of work and they were having a difficult time financially. He said she told him Oswald is away from home a great deal and she did not know any of his associates or any of his activities. He further recalled that Mrs. Oswald stated she and her husband had a difficult time getting out of Russia, but she did not explain this remark further.

He said Mrs. Oswald was very neatly dressed, but here clothes did not appear to be expensive. He said Oswald, although not shabbily attired, did not appear to know how to wear clothes properly.

Fitzpatrick also recalled that Mrs. Murret had him ask Mrs. Oswald if she would care to go to Mass with her the following morning, which was Sunday. He said Mrs. Oswald stated she would like to do this very much, but could not because of her husband. He further added that on at least two occasions in his talk with Mrs. Oswald she said a Russian work which indicated Oswald was 'without God.'

Fitzpatrick also recalled Mrs. Oswald indicated that neither she nor her husband had been to Mobile previously.

Fitzpatrick said he later talked with Oswald for about 20 minutes after his speech at the Jesuit Seminary. He said this talk with Oswald was in the presence of Mrs. Oswald and the Murret family and a great deal of it was in the Russian language. He said Oswald appeared to be a very tense and high-strung person. He said Oswald never smiled and did not appear to be at all friendly. He recalled Oswald spoke fairly good Russian; however, it definitely was not as smooth or correct grammatically as Mrs. Oswald's.

He further stated Oswald did not mention politics to him and evaded several questions he asked Oswald as to how he managed to leave Russia with his wife.

Fitzpatrick also stated that he asked Mrs. Oswald is he would care to correspond with him in Russian and she told him she would be very happy to do so. He said Mrs. Oswald told him she would answer his letters to him. He said he wrote Mrs. Oswald a letter in Russian, which he mailed about August 8, 1963 and addressed it to 4907 Magazine Street, New Orleans, Louisiana. He advised he placed his return address on his letter; however, he has never received an answer from Mrs. Oswald and his letter was never returned to him. Fitzpatrick said that he learned later from Eugene Murret that the Oswalds had moved form New Orleans about the time he mailed his letter.

He said he last saw Oswald about noon, Sunday July 28, 1963, when the Oswalds and the Murret family had stopped by to say goodbye to Eugene Murret before returning to New Orleans. On this occasion he did not have any conversation with either Oswald or the Murret family, but merely waved at them as they drove away from Spring Hill College.

Fitzpatrick said that as soon as he heard Oswald had been arrested as a suspect in the assassination of President John F. Kennedy, he immediately contacted several of the Jesuit Scholastics who had attended Oswald's speech. He said he obtained the impressions of these individuals of Oswald and some of the remarks Oswald made during his talk. Fitzpatrick said he immediately typed up a summary of these impressions and then recontacted the same individuals to determine if this summary was correct. Fitzpatrick said he then made several additions and deletions and subsequently typed up a five page summary of Oswald's speech and several questions which were asked him by those in attendance.

Fitzpatrick made available the following five page summary mentioned above:

"On Saturday, July 27, 1963, a relative of Lee Oswald, a member of the community of the Jesuit House of Studies, asked Mr. Oswald if he would address the scholastics on his experiences in Russia. The request was not unusual, for the scholastics try from time to time to have either prominent persons or others who have something interesting to relate speak to the scholastics on their experiences. Because Mr. Oswald was an American who had gone to live in Russia and who had returned, obviously for a reason, it was thought that he might be able to communicate the nature of the Russian people themselves better than any official reports might. Those who went to listen to him expected to hear a man who had been disillusioned with Soviet communism and had chosen America to it. What they heard was only partially this.

The major points of Mr. Oswald's address and details from it are given below, probably never in verbatim form, but always true to his intent, at least as he was heard by a number of people.

He worked in a factory in Minsk. When he applied for permission to live in the Soviet Union, the Russian authorities had assigned him to a fairly well advanced area, the Minsk area. He said that this was a common practice; showing foreigners those places of which Russians can be proudest.

The factory life impressed him with the care it provided for the workers. Dances, social gatherings, sports were all benefits for the factory workers. Mr. Oswald belonged to a factory-sponsored hunting club. He and a group of workers would go into the farm regions around Minsk for hunting trips. They would spend the night in the outlaying villages, and thus he came to know Russian peasant life too. In general, the peasants were very poor, often close to starvation. When the hunting party was returning to Minsk, it would often leave what it had shot with the village people because of their lack of food. He spoke of having even left the food he had brought with him from town. In connection with the hunting party, he mentioned that they had only shotguns, for pistols and rifles are prohibited by Russian law.

Some details of village life: in each hut there was a radio speaker, even in huts where there was no running water or electricity. The speaker was attached to a cord that ran back to a common receiver. Thus, the inhabitants of the hut could never change stations or turn off the radio. They had to listen to everything that came through it, day or night. In connection with radios, he said that there was a very large radio-jamming tower that was larger than anything else in Minsk.

More about the factories: factory meetings were held which all had to attend. Everyone attended willingly and in a good frame of mind. Things came up for discussion and voting, but no one ever voted no. The meetings were, in a sense, formalities. If anyone did not attend, he would lose his job.

Mr. Oswald said that he had met his wife at a factory social.

The workers, he said, were not against him because he was an American. When the U-2 incident was announced over the factory radio system, the workers were very angry with the United States, but not with him, even though he was an American.

He made the point: that he disliked capitalism because its foundation was the exploitation of the poor. He implied, but did not state directly, that he was disappointed in Russia because the full principles of Marxism were not lived up to and the gap between Marxist theory and the Russian practice disillusioned him with Russian communism. He said, "Capitalism doesn't work, communism doesn't work. In the middle is socialism, and that doesn't work either."

After his talk a question and answer period followed. Some questions and answers:

Q: How did you come to be interested in Marxism? To go to Russia?

A: He had studied Marxism, became convinced of it and wanted to see if it had worked for the Russian people.

Q: What does atheism do to morality? How can you have morality without God?

A: No matter whether people believe in God or not, they will do what they want to do. The Russian people don't need God for morality; they are naturally very moral, honest, faithful in marriage.

Q: What is the sexual morality in comparison with the United States?

A: It is better in Russia than in the United States. Its foundation there is the good of the state.

Q: What impressed you most about Russia? What did you like the most?

A: The care the state provides for everyone. If a man gets sick, no matter what his status is, how poor he is, the state will take care of him.

Q: What impresses you most about the United States?

A: The material prosperity. In Russia, it is very hard to buy even a suit or a pair of shoes, and even when you can get them, they are very expensive.

Q: What do the Russian people think of Khrushchev? Do they like him better than Stalin?

A: They like Khrushchev much better. He is a working man, a peasant. An example of the kind of things he does: Once at a party broadcast over the radio, he had a little too much to drink and he began to swear over the radio. That's the kind of thing he does.

Q: What about religion among the young people in Russia?

A: Religion is dead among the youth of Russia.

Q: Why did you return to the United States? (The question was not asked in exactly this way, but this is its content.)

A: When he saw that Russia was lacking, he wanted to come back to the United States, which is so much better off materially. (He still held the ideals of the Soviets, was still a Marxist, but did not like the widespread lack of material goods that the Russians had to endure.)

More talk points that were contained in the main part of the talk:

He lived in Russia from 1959 to 1962. He only implied that the practice in Russia differed from the theory, never stated it directly. The policy of Russia was important:

1) After death of Stalin, a peace reaction.

2) Then an anti-Stalin reaction.

3) A peace movement, leading up to the Paris conference.

4) The U-2 incident and its aftermath.

At the factory he had trouble at first meeting the men. They did not accept him at first. He joined a hinting club. He belonged to two or three discussion groups. He praised the Soviets for rebuilding so much and for concentrating on heavy industry. He said at one point that if the Negroes in the United States knew that it was so good in Russia, they'd want to go there.

Another question:

Q: Why don't the Russians see that they are being indoctrinated and that they are being denied the truth by those jamming stations?

A: They are convinced that such contact would harm them and would be dangerous. They are convinced the state is doing them a favor by denying them access to Western radio broadcasts.

Appendix Five - The Radio Transcripts

5.1 Latin Listening Post, August 17, 1963, WDSU, New Orleans, La. (Stuckey Exhibit No. 2, 21 H 621-632)

STUCKEY: This is the first of a series of Latin Listening Post interviews of persons more or less directly concerned with the conflict between the United States and Cuba. In subsequent programs, I will present talks with people connected with the Cuban refugee organizations, people who are connected with President Batista, and United States citizens with direct stakes in the outcome of the Cuban situation. Tonight we have with us a representative of probably the most controversial organization connected with Cuba in this country. The organization is the Fair Play for Cuba Committee . The person, Lee Oswald, secretary of the New Orleans Chapter of the Fair Play for Cuba Committee. This organization has long been on the Justice Department's black list and is a group generally considered to be the leading pro-Castro body in the nation. As a reporter of Latin American affairs in this city for several years now, your columnist has kept a lookout for local representatives of this pro-Castro group. None appeared in public up until this week when young Lee Oswald was arrested and convicted for disturbing the peace. He was arrested passing out pro-Castro literature to a crowd which included several violently anti-Castro Cuban refugees. When we finally tracked Mr. Oswald down today and asked him to participate in Latin Listening Post, he told us frankly that he would because it may help his organization attract more members in this area. With that in mind, and knowing that Mr. Oswald must have had to demonstrate a great skill in dialectics before he was entrusted with his present post, we now proceed on the course of random questioning of Mr. Oswald. Mr. Oswald, if I may, how long has the Fair Play for Cuba Committee had an organization in New Orleans?

OSWALD: We have had members in this area for several months now. Up until about two months ago, however, we have not (sic) organized our members into any sort of active group, until as your say, we had decided to feel out the public, what they think of our organization, our aims and for that purpose we have been as you said, distributing literature on the street for the purpose of trying to attract new members and feel out the public.

STUCKEY: Do you have any other activities other than distributing literature at the present time?

OSWALD: Well, I assume you mean do I have any organizational duties myself?

STUCKEY: Yes.

OSWALD: Yes, as secretary I am responsible for the keeping of the records and the protection of the members' names so that undue publicity or attention will not be drawn to them, as they do not desire it. My duties are as the duties of a secretary of any organization. However, our organization has a president, a secretary and a treasurer. The duties of those people would be more or less self-evident than those that are my duties. I do not however belong to any other organizations at all.

STUCKEY: Are you at liberty to reveal the membership of your organization?

OSWALD: No, I am not.

STUCKEY: For what reason?

OSWALD: Well, as secretary, I believe it is standard operating procedure that our organization, consisting of a political minority, protect the names and addresses of its members and I have every, uh, that is my duty and that is my reason to do that.

STUCKEY: Mr. Oswald, there are many commentators in the journalistic field in this country that equate the Fair Play for Cuba Committee with the American Communist Party. What is your feeling about this and are you a member of the American Communist Party?

OSWALD: Well, the Fair Play for Cuba Committee with its headquarters at 799 Broadway in New York has been investigated by the Senate sub-committees who are occupied with this sort of thing. They have investigated our organization from the viewpoint of taxes, subversion, allegiance and in general, where and how and why we exist. They have found absolutely nothing to connect us with the Communist Party of the United States. In regards to your question about whether I myself am a Communist, as I said I do not belong to any other organization.

STUCKEY: I notice from your pamphlets, one bears the title of "Hands Off Cuba." I am curious as to whether this applies to the Soviet Union as well as the United States.

OSWALD: This organization is not occupied at all with the problem of the Soviet Union or the problem of International Communism. Hands Off Cuba is the main slogan of this committee. It means, it follows our first principle, which has to do with non-intervention, in other words keeping your hands off a foreign state which is supported by the constitution, and so forth and so on. We have our own non-intervention laws, that is what Hands Off Cuba means. As I say we are not occupied at all with the problem of the Soviet Union.

STUCKEY: Does your group believe that the Castro regime in Cuba is not actually a front for a Soviet colony in the Western Hemisphere?

OSWALD: Very definitely. Castro is an independent leader of an independent country. He has ties with the eastern bloc, however, I think it is rather obvious as to why and whom they are because of the fact that we certainly don't have any trade with them. We are discouraging trade with that country, with our allies and so forth, so of course he has to turn to Russia. That does not mean, however, that he is dependent upon Russia. He receives trade from many countries, including Great Britain to a certain extent, France, certain other powers in the Western Hemisphere. He is even trading with several of the more independent African states, so that you cannot point at Castro and say that he is a Russian puppet. He is not. He is an independent person. An independent leader in his country and I believe that was pointed out very well during the October crisis when Castro very definitely said that although Premier Khrushchev had urged him to have on-site inspection at his rocket bases in Cuba, that Fidel Castro refused.

STUCKEY: Do you feel that the Fair Play for Cuba Committee would maintain its present line as far as supporting Premier Castro if the Soviet Union broke relations with the Castro regime in Cuba?

OSWALD: We do not support the man. We do not support the individual. We support the idea of an independent revolution in the Western Hemisphere, free from American intervention. We do not support, as I say, the individual. If the Cuban people destroy Castro, or if he is otherwise proven to have betrayed his own revolution, that will not have any bearing upon this committee. We are a committee who do believe that Castro has not so far betrayed his country.

STUCKEY: Do you believe that the Castro regime is a Communist regime?

OSWALD: They have said, well, they have said that they are a Marxist country. On the other hand, so is Ghana, so is several other countries in Africa. Every country which emerges from a sort of feudal state as Cuba did, experiments, usually in socialism, in Marxism. For that matter, Great Britain has socialized medicine. You cannot say that Castro is a Communist at this time, because he has not developed his country, his system this far. He has not had the chance to become a Communist. He is an experimentor, a person who is trying to find the best way for his country. If he chose a socialist or a Marxist or a Communist way of life, that is something upon which only the Cuban people can pass. We do not have the right to pass on that. We can have our opinions, naturally, but we cannot exploit that system and say it is a bad one, it is a threat to our existence and then go and try to destroy it. That would be against our principles of Democracy.

STUCKEY: As a representative of the Fair Play for Cuba Committee, do you feel that Capitalism in any form, or at least Capitalism in any form, has any place in the future of Cuba?

OSWALD: Well, so far the situation has developed where they, Cuba, is irrevocably lost as far as Capitalism goes and there will never be a Capitalist regime again in Cuba. Cuba may go the way of Czechoslovakia, Yugoslavia or it may go the way to the other extreme. It may go the way of China. In other words, a dogmatic Communist system. That depends on how we handle the matter here in the United States.

STUCKEY: Does the Fair Play for Cuba Committee have any particular position in the Cuban, or rather the Chinese and Russian conflict? Has it taken sides as opposed to China's position or as opposed to Russia's position?

OSWALD: Well, no, we do not believe in international situations of that sort. As the name implies, Fair Play for Cuba Committee, we are occupied only with the one narrow point of Cuba, the problem of Cuba and what it is to us. We are not occupied at all with the problems of the --------Russians or the Yugoslavian-Russian problems whatsoever.

STUCKEY: I have here with me tonight various pieces of literature that Mr. Oswald has been distributing on street corners here in the last week. I'd like to read to you some of the titles. The first is a yellow handbill entitled "Hands Off Cuba. Join the Fair Play for Cuba Committee in New Orleans, Charter Member Branch." There is another pamphlet by the name of "The Revolution Must Be a School of Unfettered Thought –Fidel Castro." There is still another pamphlet entitled "Fidel Castro Denounces Bureaucracy and Sectarianism." And a fourth pamphlet entitled "Ideology and Revolution" by Jean Paul Sartre. I am curious about a fifth pamphlet I have, Mr. Oswald. This, to me, was the most interesting. It is entitled "The Crime Against Cuba" by Corliss Lamont. The theme of this pamphlet is that the fact that the United States committed a grave injustice when it backed the Bay of Pigs invasion in 1961. Now, it has probably a complete ideology for the National Liberation Movement type of philosophy that we hear of in the new countries. Picking among the paragraphs, I see one here that I'd like to hear Mr. Oswald's comment on, and I'd like to quote "It is well to recall that the national emergency proclaimed by President Truman in 1950 during the Korea Was is still in effect in the United States and has been utilized constantly for the curtailment of civil liberty?" What is your comment about the veracity of this statement?

OSWALD: Well, of course, that is the last paragraph of a very long page. That has to do with the fact that propaganda in the United States is slanted and has shown Cuba and Castro to be in a very bad light. Now, they have mentioned, the United States government, has mentioned that Castro has declared an emergency in Cuba. He has not held elections for instance because of the fact that there is an emergency situation in Cuba. Now, the Castro government is declaring that is doing just what this points out. It is doing what we did in 1950 and you recall what happened in that we were going to be in a very, very dangerous situation. We adopted and emergency law which restricted newspapers, broadcasters, radio and TV from giving any opinions, any comments which we not already checked out by certain administrative bureaus of the United States government. That was under our emergency. It is because of us and our attitude and because of the attitude of certain other people, certain other countries in Latin America, certain other countries. This is the parallel, the parallel which this is talking about. An emergency at that time and an emergency in their country at this time.

STUCKEY: Mr. Oswald, this is very interesting to me to find out about the restriction on newspapers in 1950 because I was in the newspaper business at that time and I do not recall seeing any such government bureau established in my office to tell us what to print. Exactly what do you have reference to?

OSWALD: Well, I have reference to the obvious fact that during war time, haphazard guesses and information are not given by anyone. In regards to military strategical comments, such as comments or leaks about new fronts or movements and so forth, news was controlled at that time to that extent, as it is always controlled during a war or a national emergency, always.

STUCKEY: Do you feel that news is controlled in the United States today regarding Cuba?

Gary W. O'Brien

OSWALD: It is self control, yes, imposed by most newspapers. Of course, I don't know whether I am being fair, but of course I would have to point to the Times Picayune-States Item syndicated, since it is the only newspaper we have in New Orleans and a very restricted paper it is. The Fair Play for Cuba Committee has often approached this paper with information or comments and this paper has consistently refused, because of the fact that it is sympathetic to the anti-Castro regime. It has systematically refused to print any objective matter, giving the other man's viewpoint about Cuba.

STUCKEY: Would you care to list the dates and the persons who you talked to at the paper that refused to print your material.

OSWALD: I do not know the name of the reporter. I did speak to the city editor. I spoke to him one week ago and I spoke to him yesterday, Friday, which was immediately after our demonstration in front of the International Trade Mart which was filmed by WDSU-TV shown last night on the news. At that time 2 p.m. I went to the Times Picayune, informed them of our demonstration, which was very well covered by WDSU-TV and they told me at that time that due to the fact that they were not sympathetic to this organization or to the aims and ideals of this organization that they would not print any information that I gave them. They did say that if I would care to write a letter to the editor that might put that in the letter to the editor column.

STUCKEY: Mr. Oswald, does it make any difference to you if any of the activities of the local branch of the Fair Play for Cuba Committee benefit the Communist Party or the goals of international Communism?

OSWALD: Well, that is what I believe you would term a loaded question. However, I will attempt to answer it. It is inconsistent with my ideals to support Communism, my personal ideals. It is inconsistent with the ideals of the Fair Play for Cuba Committee to support ideals of international Communism. We are not occupied with that problem. We are occupied with the problem of Cuba. We do not believe under any circumstances that in supporting our ideals about Cuba, our pro-Castro ideals, we do not believe that that is inconsistent with believing in democracy. Quite the contrary, we believe that it is a necessity in supporting democracy to support Fidel Castro and his right to make his country any way he wants to. Not so much the right to destroy us of our rights about defense. In other words, we do not feel that we are supporting international Communism or Communism in supporting Fidel Castro.

STUCKEY: What other political leaders in Latin America do you feel fulfill the Fair Play for Cuba Committee's requirements for a Democratic political leader?

OSWALD: Well, you know, there's a funny story about Latin America. It goes something like this. Coffee, bananas, sugar and a few other products. In other words, that refers to the so-called banana countries which like Cuba up to this time had a one-crop agriculture, a one-crop economy and where did those crops go? They went to the United States. Now the attitude for those countries who are controlled by the United States, whose economy depends almost 100 per cent upon how much money the United States pours into them, those countries can not be expected to give an independent viewpoint on Cuba or Castro. The few countries which abstained at certain international inter-American meetings during the last year, are those countries which are big enough to support themselves. Those countries being Brazil, Argentina and perhaps on some occasions the democratic republic of Costa Rica, which is by the way, the only democratic republic in all of Central America.

STUCKEY: What is your definition of democracy?

OSWALD My definition, well, the definition of democracy, that's a very good one. That's a very controversial viewpoint. You know, it used to be very clear, but now it's not. You know, when our forefathers drew up the constitution, they considered that democracy was creating an atmosphere of freedom of discussion, of argument, of finding the truth. The rights, well, the classic right of having life, liberty and the pursuit of happiness. In Latin America, they have none of those rights, none of them at all. And that is my definition of democracy, the right to be in a minority, and not to be oppressed. The right to see yourself without government restrictions such countries as Cuba and we are restricted from going to Cuba.

STUCKEY: Mr. Oswald, when was the last time you were in Latin America?

OSWALD: I have been only to Mexico in my life, sir. I am not fully acquainted with Latin America personally, but then I am not the president of this organization either, I am only a volunteer, a secretary to this local chapter. I do not claim to be an expert on Latin America, but then very few people do. Certainly, it is obvious to me, having been educated here in New Orleans and having been instilled with the ideals of democracy and objectiveness, that Cuba and the right of Cubans to self-determination is more or less self evident, and one does not have to travel through Central and South America. One does not have to travel through these countries to see the poverty in Chile or Peru or the suppression of democratic liberties by the Somoa brothers in Nicaragua in order to draw one's conclusions about Cuba.

STUCKERY: Does the Fair Play for Cuba Committee have any opinion about the suppression of democratic liberties in Hungary in 1956 or the poverty in any of the eastern bloc countries today?

OSWALD: Officially no, but we of course have our own opinions about such situations. We consider that Russian imperialism is a very bad thing. It was a bad thing in Hungary. We certainly do not support dictatorships or the suppression of any people anywhere, but as I say and as I must stress, we are preoccupied only with the problem of Cuba, officially.

STUCKEY: Mr. Oswald, you have the title of secretary of the New Orleans chapter of the Fair Play for Cuba Committee, however, you have just said that you have never been to Latin America except for a few ventures into Mexico. In that case, just exactly how do you get your information concerning Latin American affairs or Latin American conditions?

OSWALD: Well, as I say, we are preoccupied with the problem of Cuba. There are correspondents that correspond with the headquarters in New York, directly from Cuba, that is where we get the information about Cuba. Now, in regards to Latin and Central America, you do not have your own correspondents there. The AP and UP cover it very well and they certainly give a very clear picture of the situation in certain countries, Nicaragua, and so forth, as I mentioned, which have very undemocratic regimes, dictatorships, and as I say these things are well known by everyone and they are accepted as truth. For instance, who will be able to find any official or any person who knows about Latin America, who will say that Nicaragua does not have a dictatorship?

STUCKEY: Very interesting that you should mention dictatorships in Nicaragua, because we, naturally familiar with the place, have heard about these dictatorships for many, many years, but it is curious to me who no Nicaraguans fled to the United States last year, whereas we had possibly 50,000 to 60,000 Cubans fleeing from Cuba to the United States. What is the Fair Play for Cuba Committee's official reply to this?

OSWALD: Well, a good question. Nicaraguan situation is considerably different from Castro's Cuba. People are inclined not to flee their countries unless some new system, new factor, enters their live. I must say that very surely no new factors have entered into Nicaragua for about 300 years, in fact the people live exactly as they have always lived in Nicaragua. I am referring to the overwhelming majority of the people in Nicaragua which is a feudal dictatorship with 90 per cent of the people engaged in agriculture. These peasants are uneducated. They have one of the lowest living standards in all of the western hemisphere and so because of the fact that no new factor, no liberating factor, has entered into their lives, they remain in Nicaragua. Now the people who have fled Cuba, that is an interesting situation. Needless to say, there are classes of criminals; there are classes of people who are wanted in Cuba for crimes against humanity and most of those people who are in New Orleans and have set themselves up in stores with blood money and who engage in day to day trade with New Orleanians. Those are the people who would certainly not want to go back to Cuba and who would certainly want to flee Cuba. There are other classes. These are peasants who do not like the collectivization in Cuban agriculture. There are others who have one reason or the other in their legitimate reasons, reasons of opinion, for fleeing Cuba. Most of these people flee by legal means. They are allowed to leave after requesting the Cuban government for exit visas. Some of these people for some reasons or another do not like to apply for these visas or they feel that they cannot get them; they flee, they flee Cuba in boats, they flee any way they can go and I think that the opinion and the attitude of the Cuban government to this is good riddance.

STUCKEY: Mr. Oswald, this is very interesting because as a reporter in this field for some time I have been interviewing refugees now for about three years and I'd say that the last Batista man, officially, that I talked to left Cuba about two and a half years ago and the rest of them I've talked to have been taxicab drivers, laborers, can cutters, and that sort of thing. I thought this revolution was supposed to benefit these people. What is the Fair Play for Cuba Committee's position on this?

OSWALD: Well, as I say there are different classes. A minority of these people are as I say people who were Batista criminals and so forth. However, it may not be true that the people fleeing nowadays are completely cleansed of Batista elements, certainly some of these Batistaites have been hiding or have been engaged in counter-revolutionary activities ever since the Bay of Pigs invasion and even before that, just after the revolution. In other words, they have remained underground. Undoubtedly, the overwhelming majority of people during the last year, for instance, who have fled Cuba have been non-Batistaites, rather peasant class. You say the revolution is supposed to benefit these people. You know, it's very funny about revolutions. Revolutions require work, revolutions require sacrifice, revolutions and our own included, require a certain amount of sacrifice. Sacrificing one's own personal ideas about countries, citizenship, work, indicates people who have fled Cuba have not been able to adapt themselves to these new factors which have entered these peoples lives. Those people are the uneducated. These people are the people who do not remain in Cuba to be educated by young people, who are afraid of the alphabet, who are afraid of these new things which are occurring, who are afraid that they would lose something by collectivization. They were afraid that they would lose something by seeing their sugar crops taken away and in place of sugar crops, some other vegetable, some other product, planted, because Cuba has always been a one-product country, more or less. These are the people who have not been able to adapt.

STUCKEY: Mr. Oswald, you say their sugar crops. Most of the Cubans I have talked to that have had anything to do with agriculture in the last year and a half have not owned one single acre of ground, they were cane cutters.

OSWALD: That is correct and they are the ones that are fleeing the Castro regime. That is correct, sir. That is very, very true and these people worked for the United Fruit Company or American companies engaged in sugar refining, oil refining in Cuba. They worked a few months every year during the cane cutting or sugar refining season. They never owned anything, and they feel now that that little bit of right, the right to work for five months a year has been taken away from them. They feel that now they have to work all year round to plant new crops, to make a new economy and so feel that they have been robbed, they feel that they have been robbed of the right to do as they please because of the fact that the government now depends upon its people to build its economy to industrialize itself, so they figure they have been robbed. What they do not realize is that they have been robbed of the right to be exploited, robbed of the right to be cheated, robbed of the right of New Orleans companies to take away what was rightfully theirs. Of course, they have to share now. Everybody gets an equal portion. This is collectivization and this is very hard on some people, on people preferring the dog-eat-dog economy.

STUCKEY: What do you refer to as the dog-eat-dog economy? Is that Capitalism in your definition?

OSWALD: No, that is an economy where the people do not depend one each other, they have no feelings of nationality, they have no feelings of culture, they have no feelings of any ties whatsoever on a high level. It is every man for himself. That is what I refer to by dog-eat-dog.

STUCKEY: Are you familiar with the existence of a black market in Soviet Russia or in Red China, where the majority of the populace gets their food, their truck crops and vegetables and such from this market. Do you know of such a market?

OSWALD: Well, I know about the fact that there is a market in the Soviet Union only for western apparel, and certain other items. There is no black market in the Soviet Union for food, none whatever. By black market, I assume that you mean a situation where food is either stolen or grown in one area, and taken to another area and sold covertly, under cover. No such system exists in Russia.

STUCKEY: Mr. Oswald, I am curious about your personal background. If you could tell something about where you came from, your education and your career to date, it would be interesting.

OSWALD: I would be very happy to. I was born in New Orleans. For a short length of time during my childhood, I lived in Texas and New York. During my junior high school days, I attended Beauregard Junior High School. I attended that school for two years then I went to Warren Easton High School and I attended that school for over a year. Then my family and I moved to Texas where we have many relatives and I continued my schooling there. I entered the United States Marine Corps in 1956. I spent three years in the United States Marine Corps, working my way up through the ranks to the position of buck sergeant and I served honorably, having been discharged. Then I went back to work in Texas have recently arrived in New Orleans with my family, with my wife and child.

STUCKEY: What particular event in your life made you decide that the Fair Play for Cuba Committee had the correct answers about Cuban-United States relations.

Gary W. O'Brien

OSWALD: Well, of course, I have only begun to notice Cuba since the Cuban revolution, that is true of everyone, I think. I became acquainted with it about the same time as everyone else, in 1960. In the beginning of 1960, I always felt that the Cubans were being pushed into the Soviet bloc by American policy. I still feel that way. Our policy, if it had been handled differently and many others much more informed than I have said the same thing, if that situation had been handled differently, we would not have the big problem of Castro's Cuba now, the big international political problem. Although I feel that it is a just and right development in Cuba still we could be on much friendlier relations with them and had the government of the United States, its government agencies, particularly certain covert, under-cover agencies like the now defunct CIA.

STUCKEY: Now defunct.

OSWALD: Well, its leadership is now defunct. Allen Dulles is now defunct. I believe that without all that meddling, with a little bit different humanitarian handling of the situation, Cuba would not be the problem it is today.

STUCKEY: Is there any particular action of the United States government do you feel pushed Castro into Soviet arms.

OSWALD: Well, as I say, Castro's Cuba, even after the revolution was still a one-crop economy, basing its economy on sugar. When we slashed the Cuban sugar quota, of course, we cut their throats. They had to turn to some other country. They had to turn to some other hemisphere in which to sell this one product. They did so, and they have sold it to Russia and because of that, Russian sugar is now down quite a bit, whereas ours is going up and up and up and I believe that was the big factor, the cutting of the sugar quota.

STUCKEY: Do you think that the United States government, under President Eisenhower, ever wanted to help the Castro regime. Ever offered or shown any help to it.

OSWALD: True to our democratic policies, certain policies were adopted, very late, but adopted, but the government helped Fidel Castro while he was still in the mountains, that is very true. We cut off aid to Batista just before the revolution, just before it. That was too late. We had already done more harm than we could have done before. We were just rats leaving a sinking ship, you see. That was not the thing to do. We have, however, as I say, helped him. We have now cut off all that help.

STUCKEY: There is one point of view which I have heard to the effect that Castro turned left because he could not get any aid for industrialization in Cuba from the United States. Doe the Fair Play for Cuba Committee believe that?

OSWALD: Not entirely, no. We feel that was a factor, certainly. But the current of history is now running to that extreme, in other words, countries emerging from imperialist domination are definitely adopting socialistic solutions, Marxist even on occasion what will be in the future, Communist regimes and Communist inclinations. You see, this is something which is apparently a world trend.

STUCKEY: Does the Fair Play for Cuba Committee believe that this trend should also be copied in the United States?

OSWALD: No, the Fair Play for Cuba Committee is occupied only with the Cuban problem. I do not think they feel that way, no.

STUCKEY: Tonight we have been talking with Lee Oswald, secretary of the Fair Play for Cuba Committee in New Orleans.

Gary W. O'Brien

5.2 Conversation Carte Blanche, August 19, 1963, WDSU New Orleans, La. (Stuckey Exhibit No. 3, 21 H 633-641)

ANNOUNCER: It's time for Conversation Carte Blanche. Here is Bill Slater.

BILL SLATER: Good evening, for the next few minutes Bill Stuckey and I, Bill whose program you've probably heard on Saturday night, "Latin Listening Post" Bill and I are going to be talking to three gentlemen the subject mainly revolving around Cuba. Our guests tonight are Lee Harvey Oswald, Secretary of the New Orleans Chapter of the Fair Play for Cuba Committee, a New York headquartered organization which is generally recognized as the principal voice of the Castro government in this country. Our second guest is Ed Butler who is Executive Vice-President of the Information Council of the Americas (INCA) which is headquartered in New Orleans and specializes in distributing anti-communist educational materials throughout Latin America, and our third guest is Carlos Bringuier, Cuban refugee and New Orleans Delegate of the Revolutionary Student Directorate one of the more active of the anti-Castro refugee organizations. Bill, if at this time you will briefly background the situation as you know it, Bill

BILL STUCKEY: First, for those who don't know too much about the Fair Play for Cuba Committee this is an organization that specializes primarily in distributing literature, based in New York. For the several years it has been in New York it has operated principally out of the east and out of the West Coast and a few college campuses, recently however attempts have been made to organize a chapter here in New Orleans. The only member of the group who has revealed himself publicly so far is 23 year old Lee Harvey Oswald who is the secretary of the local chapter of the Fair Play for Cuba Committee. He first came to public notice a few days ago when he was arrested and convicted for disturbing the peace. The ruckus in which he as involved started when Carlos Bringuier, who is with us tonight, discovered him distributing pro-Castro matieral on a downtown street. Now Mr. Oswald and Bringuier are with us tonight to give us opposing views on the Fair Play for Cuba Committee and its objectives. I believe that I was probably the first New Orleans reporter to interview Mr. Oswald on his activities here since he first came into public view. Last Saturday in addition to having him on my show we had very long and rambling question and answer session over various points of dogma and line of the Fair Play for Cuba Committee and now I'll give you a very brief digest of some of the principal propaganda lines. I use the word propaganda, rather I should say informational lines of the Fair Play for Cuba Committee.

Number one the principal thing that they insist is that Castro's government today is completely free and independent, that it is in no way controlled by the Soviet Union. Another cardinal point of the Fair Play for Cuba Committee's propaganda is that Premier Castro is forced to seek aid from the Russians only because the U.S. government refused to offer him financial aid.

Following another line I asked Mr. Oswald if he had ever, or was a member of the American Communist Party and he said that the only organization to which he belonged was the Fair Play for Cuba Committee. Mr. Oswald also gave me this run down on his personal background. He said that he was a native of New Orleans, had attended Beauregard Junior High School and Warren Eastern High School. Had entered the U.S. Marine Corps, in 1956 and was honorably discharged in 1959. He said during our previous interview that he had lived in Ft. Worth, Texas before coming here to establish a Fair Play for Cuba chapter several weeks ago. However, there were a few items apparently that I suspect that Mr. Oswald left out in his original interview which was principally where he lived after, between 1959 and 1962. We, er, Mr. Butler brought some newspaper clippings to my attention and I also found some too through an independent source, Washington Newspaper clippings to the effect that Mr. Oswald had attempted to renounce his American citizenship in 1959 and become a Soviet citizen. There was another clipping dated 1962 saying that Mr. Oswald had returned from the Soviet Union with his wife and child after having lived there for three years. Mr. Oswald are these correct?

OSWALD: That is correct. Correct, yea.

BILL STUCKEY: You did live in Russia for three years?

OSWALD : That is correct and I think that those, the fact that I did live for a time in the Soviet Union gives me excellent qualifications to repudiate charges that Cuba and the Fair Play for Cuba Committee is communist controlled.

BILL SLATER: Mr. Bringuier, perhaps you would like to dispute that point.

BRINGUIER: I'd like to know exactly the name of the organization that you represent here in the city, because I have some confusion, is Fair Play for Cuba Committee or Fair Play for Russia Committee?

OSWALD: Well that is very provocative request and I don't think requires an answer.

BRINGUIER : Well, I will tell you why because the communists take over Cuba, Cuba was at the head of the Latin American countries and I can show you that in Cuba in 1958 every 37 persons had an automobile and in Russia was 200 persons, in Cuba was 6 persons for one radio and in Russia was 20 persons for one radio, in Cuba was 1 TV set for 18 persons and in Russia was 85 persons for 1 television set, and in Cuba was 1 telephone for every 39 persons and in Russia was 1 telephone for every 580 persons. Cuba was selling the sugar in the American market and the U.S. was paying to Cuba that price in dollars. Right now Cuba is selling sugar to Russia. Russia is paying to Cuba 80% in machinery, and 20% in dollars. I think that Cuba right now is a colony of Russia and the people of Cuba who is living in Cuba every day who is escaping form Cuba every day they disagree with you that you are representing the people of Cuba. Maybe you will represent the er, the colony of Russia here in this moment but not the people of Cuba. You cannot take that responsibility.

OSWALD: In order to give a clear and concise and short answer to each of those, well let's say that the facts and figures from, oh a country like Pakistan or Burma would even reflect some light upon Cuba in relation to how many TV sets and how many radio and all that. This I don't think is the subject to be discussed tonight. The Fair Play for Cuba Committee, and as the name implies, is concerned primarily with Cuban-American relations.

SLATER: How many people do you have in your Committee here in New Orleans?

OSWALD: I cannot reveal that as Secretary of the Fair Play for Cuba Committee.

BUTLER: Is it a secret society?

OSWALD: No Mr. Butler, it is not. However, it is standard operating procedure for a political organization consisting of a political minority, to safeguard the names and the number of its members.

BUTLER: Well the Republicans are in the minority, I don't see them hiding their membership.

OSWALD: The Republicans are not a well, -- The Republicans are an established political party representing a great many people. They represent no radical point of view. They do no have a very violent and sometimes emotional opposition, as we do.

BUTLER: Oh, I see. Well, would you say then the Fair Play for Cuba Committee is not a communist front organization?

OSWALD: The Senate Subcommittee, who have occupied themselves with investigating the Fair Play for Cuba Committee have found that there is nothing to connect the two committees. We have been investigated from several points of view. That is, points of view of taxes, allegiance, subversion and so forth. The findings have been as I say, absolutely zero.

BUTLER: Well, I have the Senate Hearings before me and I think what I have in front of me refutes precisely every statement that you have just made. For instance, who is the Honorary Chairman of the Fair Play for Cuba Committee?

OSWALD: The Honorary Chairman of this Committee, -- the name of that person I certainly don't know.

BUTLER: Well, let me tell you, in case you don't know about your own organization.

OSWALD: No. I don't know about it.

BUTLER: His name is Waldo Frank and I'm quoting form "New Masses" Sept. 1932. The title of this article, 'How I Came to Communism – A Symposium' by Waldo Frank – 'Where I Stand and How I Got There'. Now let me ask you a second question. What is the Secretary for the Fair Play for Cuba Committee? the national secretary?

OSWALD: Well, we have a National Director who is Mr. V.T. Lee, who was recently returned from Cuba and, because of the fact that the U.S. government has imposed restrictions on travel to Cuba, he is now under indictment for his traveling to Cuba. This, however, is very convenient for rightist organizations to drag out this or that literature purporting to show a fact which has not been established in law. I say that the Fair Play for Cuba Committee has definitely been investigated. That is very true, but I will also say that the total result of that investigation was zero. That is, the Fair Play for Cuba Committee is not now on the Attorney General's Subversive List. Any other material you may have is superfluous.

BUTLER: Oh it is.

SLATER: Mr. Oswald, if I may break in now a moment I believe it was mentioned that you at one time asked to renounce your American citizenship and become a Soviet citizen, is that correct.

OSWALD: Well, I don't think that has particular import to this discussion. We are discussing Cuban-American relations.

SLATER: Well, I think it has a bearing to this extent Mr. Oswald you say apparently that Cuba is not dominated by Russia and yet you apparently, by your own past actions have shown that you have an affinity for Russia and perhaps communism, although I don't know that you admit that you either are a communist or have been, could you straighten out that part. Are you or have you been a communist?

OSWALD: Well, I answered that prior to this program, on another radio program.

STUCKEY: Are you a Marxist?

OSWALD: Yes, I am a Marxist.

BUTLER: What's the difference?

OSWALD: The difference is primarily the difference between a country like Guinea, Ghana, Yugoslavia, China or Russia. Very, very great differences. Differences which we appreciate by giving aid, let's say, to Yugoslavia in the sum of a hundred million or so dollars a year.

BUTLER: That's extraneous, what's the difference?

OSWALD: The difference is as I have said, a very great difference. Many parties, many countries are based on Marxism. Many countries such as Great Britain display very socialistic aspects or characteristics. I might point to socialized medicine in Britain.

BUTLER: I was speaking of –

SLATER: Gentlemen I'll have to interrupt, we'll be back in a moment to continue this kind of lively discussion after this message.

COMMERCIAL

SLATER: Tonight Bill Stuckey and I are talking to three guests, Lee Harvey Oswald, who is the local secretary of the a group called Fair Play for Cuba Committee, and with Ed Butler the Executive Vice-President of the Information Council of the Americas (INCA) and Carlos Bringuier a Cuban refugee and obviously anti-Castro. Mr. Oswald, as you might have imagined is on the hot seat tonight, I believe you Bill Stuckey have a question.

STUCKEY: Mr. Oswald I believe you said in a reply to a question of Mr. Butler's that any questions about your background were extraneous to the discussion tonight. I disagree because of the fact that you're refusing to reveal any of the other members of your organization, so you are the face of the Fair Play for Cuba Committee in New Orleans. Therefore anybody who might be interested in this organization ought to know more about you. For this reason I'm curious to know just how you supported yourself during the three years that you lived in the Soviet Union. Did you have a government subsidy?

OSWALD: Well, as I er, well – I will answer that question directly then as you will not rest until you get your answer. I worked in Russia. I was not under the protection of the – that is to say I was not under protection of the American government, but as I was at all times considered an American citizen I did not lose my American citizenship.

SLATER: Did you say that you wanted to at one time though? What happened?

OSWALD: Well it's a long drawn out situation in which permission to live in the Soviet Union being granted to a foreign resident is rarely given. This calls for a certain amount of technicality, technical papers and so forth. At no time, as I say, did I renounce my citizenship or attempt to renounce my citizenship, and at no time was I out of contact with the American embassy.

SLATER: Excuse me, may I interrupt just one second? Either one of these two statements is wrong. The Washington Evening Star of October 31, 1959, page I reported that Lee Harvey Oswald a former Marine, 4936 Connally St., Ft. Wroth, Texas had turned in his passport at the American Embassy in Moscow on that same date and it says that he had applied for Soviet citizenship. Now it seems tome that you've renounced your American citizenship if you've turned in your passport.

OSWALD: Well, the obvious answer to that is that I am back in the United States. A person who renounces his citizenship becomes legally disqualified for return to the U.S.

BUTLER: Right. And 'Soviet authorities – this is right from the Washington Post and Times Herald of November 16, 1959 – Soviet authorities had refused to grant it although they informed him he could live in Russia as a resident alien.' What did you do in the two weeks from Oct. 31, to Nov. 16th, 1959?

OSWALD: As I have already stated, of course, this whole conversation, and we don't have too much time left, is getting away from the Cuban-American problem. However, I am quite willing to discuss myself for the remainder of this program. As I stated it is very difficult for a resident alien, for a foreigner to get permission to reside in the Soviet Union. During those two weeks and during the dates you mentioned I was of course with the knowledge of the American Embassy, getting this permission.

BUTLER: Were you ever at a building at 11 Kuznyetskoya St. in Moscow?

OSWALD: Kuznyetskoya. Kuznyetskoya is – well that would probably be the Foreign Ministry I assume. No I was never in that place, although I know Moscow having lived there.

SLATER: Excuse me. Let me interrupt here. I think Mr. Oswald is right to this extent. We shouldn't get to lose sight of the organization of which he is the head in New Orleans the Fair Play for Cuba.

OSWALD: The Fair Play for Cuba Committee.

SLATER: As a practical matter knowing as I 'm sure you do the sentiment in America against Cuba, we of course severed diplomatic relations sometime ago. I would say Castro is about as unpopular as anybody in the world in this country. As a practical matter what do you hope to gain for your work? How do you hope to bring about what you call "Fair Play for Cuba", knowing the sentiment?

OSWALD: The principals or thought of the FPCC consist of restoration of diplomatic trade and tourist relations with Cuba. That is one of our main points. We are for that. I disagree that this situation regarding American-Cuban relations is very unpopular. We are in a minority surely. We are not particularly interested in what Cuban exiles or rightist members have to say. We are primarily interested in the attitude of the U.S. government toward Cuba. And in that way we are striving to get the United States to adopt measures which would be more friendly toward the Cuban people and the new Cuban regime in that country. We are not all communist controlled regardless of the fact that we have been investigated, regardless of the fact that I had the experience of living in Russia, regardless of the fact that we have been investigated, regardless of those facts, the FPCC is an independent organization not affiliated with any other organization. Our aims and our ideals are very clear and in the best keeping with American traditions of democracy.

BRINGUIER: Do you agree with Fidel Castro when in his last speech of July 26th of this year he qualified President John F. Kennedy of the United States as a ruffian and at thief.

Do you agree with Mr. Castro?

OSWALD: I would not agree with that particular wording. However, I and the Fair Play for Cuba Committee do think that the United States Government through certain agencies, mainly the State Department and the C.I.A. has made monumental mistakes in its relations with Cuba. Mistakes which are pushing

Cuba into the sphere of activity of let's say a very dogmatic communist country such as China is.

SLATER: Mr. Oswald would you agree that when Castro first took power – would you agree that the United States was very friendly with Castro, that the people of this country had nothing but admiration for him, that they were very glad to see Batista thrown out.

OSWALD: I would say that the activities of the United States government in regards to Batista were a manifestation of not so much support for Fidel Castro but rather a withdrawal of support from Batista. In other words we stopped armaments to Batista. What we should have done was to take those armaments and drop them into the Sierra Maestra where Fidel Castro could have used them. As for public sentiment at the time, there were rumblings of official comment and so forth from government officials, er, against Fidel Castro.

BUTLER: You've never been to Cuba, of course, but why are the people of Cuba starving today?

OSWALD: Well any country emerging from a semi-colonial state and embarking upon reforms which require a diversification of agriculture you are going to have shortages. After all 80% of imports into the United States form Cuba were two products, tobacco and sugar. Nowadays, while Cuba is reducing its production as far as sugar cane goes it is striving to grow unlimited, and unheard of for Cuba, quantities of certain vegetables such as sweet potatoes, lima beans, cotton and so forth, so that they can become agriculturally independent...

SLATER: Gentlemen, I'm going to have to interrupt you. Our time is almost up. We've had three guests on Conversation Carte Blanche, Bill Stuckey and I have been talking to Lee Harvey

Oswald, Secretary of the New Orleans Chapter of the Fair Play for Cuba Committee, Ed Butler, Executive Vice-President of the Information Council of the Americas (INCA), and Carlos Bringuier, Cuban refugee. Thank you very much.

NOTES

(Endnotes)

1   11 H 31, 1 H 370. The quotation on page iii is from Aline
     Mosby's interview of Oswald in Moscow in 1959. See
     Appendix 3.1.

2   1 H 225

3   CE 1339, 22 H 559

4   CE 2236, 25 H 135

5   CE 2239, 25 H 139

6   8 H 276-278

7   8 H 292

8   8 H 347

9   McMillan, Priscilla Johnson. *Marina and Lee.* New York:
     Harper and Row, 1977, pp. 147, 160. Marina Oswald
     when testifying before the House Select Committee on
     Assassinations said that while in the Soviet Union Lee
     "read a lot," mostly novels. See Volume II, September 13,
     1978, House Select Committee on Assassinations Report,
     Investigation of President John F. Kennedy.

10   1 H 5

11   9 H 150

12   9 H 93

13   See CE 1117, 22 H 82-84. For a list of books belonging to Lee found in the home of Ruth Paine and taken by Robert Oswald on December 8, 1963, see CE 2466, 25 H 639.

14   1 H 5

15   10 H 59

16   See CE 3134, 26 H 812-817

17   Bugliosi, Vincent. *Reclaiming History: The Assassination of President John F. Kennedy.* New York: W.W. Norton and Company, 2007, p. 936. Bugliosi is referring to the state of Oswald's mind immediately before the assassination. Elsewhere he writes "Oswald was a voracious reader of serious literature who had intellectual proclivities, and most who came in contact with him felt he was bright and spoke very well, but he was dyslexic." See *ibid.*, p. 515.

18   Moss, Armand. *Disinformation, Misinformation and the "Conspiracy" to Kill JFK Exposed.* Hamden, Conn.: Archon Books, 1987, p. 64.

19   9 H 150 (Testimony of Paul Roderick Gregory)

20   9 H 236 (Testimony of George de Mohrenschildt)

21   9 H 95 (Testimony of Gary E. Taylor)

22   11 H 175

23   *Oswald's Ghost: A Robert Stone Film.* PBS Home Video, 2008.

24   2 H 392 (Testimony of Michael R. Paine)

25   de Mohrenschildt, George *I am a Patsy! I am a Patsy!* Appendix to Hearings Before the Select Committee on Assassinations of the U.S. House of Representatives, Ninety-Fifth Congress, Second Session, Volume X11, p. 186.

26   9 H 328

27   2 H 422

28 Kihss, Peter. "Accused Assassin Belied Tenets of Marxism, Experts Here Agree." Reprinted in *The Militant*, December 9, 1963.

29 *The Warren Commission Report: Report of the President's Commission on the Assassination of President John F. Kennedy.* New York: St. Martin's Press, p. 423.

30 Manchester, William. *The Death of a President.* New York: Harper & Row, 1967, p. 145.

31 Davison, Jean. *Oswald's Game.* New York: W.W. Norton, 1983, pp. 293-294.

32 Posner, Gerald. *Case Closed: Lee Harvey Oswald and the Assassination of JFK.* New York: Random House, 1993, p. 5.

33 Loken, John. *Oswald's Trigger Films: The Manchurian Candidate, We Were Strangers, Suddenly.* Ann Arbor, Mich.: Falcon Books, 2000.

34 Holloway, Diane. *The Mind of Oswald: Accused Assassin of John F. Kennedy.* Victoria, B.C.: Trafford Publishing, 2000, pp. 226-227.

35 Bugliosi, *op. cit.*, pp. 943, 945.

36 *The HSCA Final Assassinations Report,* Introduction by Rex Bradford. Ipswich, Ma.: Mary Ferrell Foundation Press, 2007, pp. 61-63.

37 Newman, Albert H. *The Assassination of John F. Kennedy: The Reasons Why.* New York: Clarkson Potter, 1970.

38 Clarke, James W. *American Assassins: The Darker Side of Politics.* Princeton, N.J.: Princeton University Press, 1990.

39 Holland, Max. "The Key to the Warren Report." *American Heritage*, Vol. 46, no. 7, November, 1995.

40 Eddowes, Michael. *The Oswald File.* New York: Clarkson N. Potter, 1977.

41 Epstein, Edward Jay. *Legend: The Secret World of Lee Harvey Oswald.* New York: Reader's Digest Press, 1978.

42 Pacepa, Ion Mihai. *Programmed to Kill: Lee Harvey Oswald, the Soviet KGB, and the Kennedy Assassination.* Ivan R. Dee, 2007.

43 Wrone, David R. *The Zapruder Film: Reframing JFK's Assassination.* Lawrence: University Press of Kansas, 2003, p. 146.

44 Mailer, Norman. *Oswald's Tale: An American Mystery.* New York: Random House, 1995, p. 506.

45 See for example Weberman, Alan J. and Michael Canfield. *Coup d'Etat in America: The CIA and the Assassination of John F. Kennedy,* revised edition. San Francisco: Quick American Archives, 1992; McKnight, Gerald D. *Breach of Trust: How the Warren Commission Failed the Nation and Why.* Lawrence: University Press of Kansas, 2005; Mellen, Joan. *A Farewell to Justice: Jim Garrison, JFK's Assassination, and the Case That Should Have Changed History.* Washington DC: Potomac Books, 2005; Kurtz, Michael L. *The JFK Assassination Debates: Lone Gunman Versus Conspiracy.* Lawrence: University Press of Kansas, 2006.

46 Newman, John. *Oswald and the CIA.* New York: Carroll & Graf, 1995, pp. 317, 427.

47 Garrison, Jim. *On the Trail of the Assassins.* New York: Time Warner, Warner Books, 1988.

48 See *Final Report of the Assassination Records Review Board,* September, 1998.

49 Erikson, Erik. *Young Man Luther: A Study in Psychoanalysis and History.* New York: W.W. Norton and Co., 1958.

50 Stannard, David E. *Shrinking History: On Freud and the Failure of Psychohistory.* New York and Oxford: Oxford University Press, 1980, p. ix.

51   *Ibid.*, p. x

52   Quoted in George M. Kren and Leon H. Rappoport (eds.), *Varieties of Psychohistory.* New York: Springer Publishing Company, p. 4.

53   Stannard, *op.cit.*, pp. 147-151

54   *Ibid.*, p. 156

55   8 H 219–220

56   Sullivan, Walter. "Doctors Question Oswald's Sanity— Leaving Clues for Pursuit a Psychopathic Trait." *New York Times*, November 25, 1963.

57   FBI Investigation of President Kennedy, November 22, 1963, Summary Report, December 9, 1963, CD 1, p. 42.

58   8 H 219 (Testimony of Renatus Hartogs)

59   United Press International and American Heritage Magazine. *Four Days: The Historical Record of the Death of President Kennedy.* American Heritage Publishing, 1964, p. 65.

60   FBI Investigation of President Kennedy, Supplemental Report, January 13, 1964, CD 107.

61   CD 1, p. 42a

62   *Ibid.*, p. 47

63   *Ibid.*, pp. 44, 47

64   CD 107, p. 26

65   *Ibid.*, p. 26

66   *Ibid.*, p. 26

67   CD 1, p. 61

68   CD 107, pp. 18–19

69   Memorandum from William T. Coleman, Jr. and W. David Slawson to J. Lee Rankin (JFK Collection, HSCA (RG 233). p. 33

70   *Ibid.*, pp. 88-89

71   Epstein, Edward Jay. *The Assassination Chronicles: Inquest, Counterplot and Legend.* New York: Carroll & Graf, 1992, p. 42.

72   Goldberg, Alfred. *A History of the United States Air Force 1907—1957.* Princeton: D. Van Nostrand Co., 1957.

73   Epstein, *The Assassination Chronicles*, p. 42

74   See Bugliosi, *op. cit.*, p. 342

75   Epstein, *The Assassination Chronicles*, p. 48

76   Hartogs Exhibit No. 1, 20 H 89-90

77   Hartogs, Renatus, and Lucy Freeman., *The Two Assassins.* New York: Thomas Y. Crowell, 1965, pp. 252—75.

78   *Ibid.*, pp. 260, 262

79   See 8 H 214-224

80   8 H 226

81   Warren Report, p. 375. The Commission corrected the record by noting "Contrary to reports that appeared after the assassination, the psychiatric examination did not indicate that Lee Oswald was a potential assassin, potentially dangerous, that 'his outlook on life had strongly paranoid overtones' or that he should be institutionalized." *Ibid.*, p. 379. However, the Commission then went on to describe Oswald in terms that implied he was dangerous and had paranoid overtones.

82   Warren Report, p. 423

83   *Ibid.*, p. 382

84   *Ibid.*, p. 423

85   Johnson McMillan, *op. cit.*, p. 76

86   *Ibid.*, p. 457

87   See Holloway, *op. cit.*, p. 153

88 See affidavit of David Christie Murray, Jr., 8 H 319

89 Bugliosi, *op. cit.*, p. 600

90 See Appendix 1.1

91 10 H 198

92 Warren Report, p. 390

93 *Ibid.*, p. 390

94 *Ibid.*, p. 390

95 *Ibid.*, p. 407

96 *Ibid.*, p. 407

97 *Ibid.*, p. 407

98 *Ibid.*, p. 376

99 *Ibid.*, p. 376

100 *Ibid.*, p. 414

101 Almond, Gabriel A. and Sidney Verba. *The Civic Culture: Political Attitudes and Democracy in Five Nations.* Princeton, New Jersey: Princeton University Press, 1963.

102 *Ibid.*, p. 326

103 *Ibid.*, pp. 323-324

104 Woods, Jeff. *Black Struggle Red Scare: Segregation and Anti-Communism in the South.* Baton Rouge: Louisiana State University Press, 2004, p. 2.

105 See Appendices 3.1 and 3.2

106 See Appendix 2.30

107 CE 25 (Appendix 1.3)

108 La Fontaine, Ray and Mary. *Oswald Talked: The New Evidence in the JFK Assassination.* Gretna: Pelican Publishing, 1996, p. 172.

109 8 H 104-105 (Testimony of Lillian Murret)

110 Stafford, Jean. *A Mother In History.* New York: Pharos Books, 1992, pp. 24—25.

111 1 H 271

112 Siegel Exhibit No. 1. 21 H 487

113 11 H 118

114 8 H 165 (Testimony of Marilyn Dorothea Murret)

115 de Mohrenschildt, *I am a Patsy! I am a Patsy!*, p. 148.

116 2 H 401 (Testimony of Michael R. Paine)

117 11 H 87

118 10 H 56

119 CE 2064, 24 H 490 (FBI report concerning memorandum furnished by Postal Inspector H.D. Holmes)

120 2 H 422

121 11 H 402

122 de Mohrenschildt, *I am a Patsy! I am a Patsy!*, p. 184.

123 2 H 401 (Testimony of Michael R. Paine)

124 See Appendix 3.1

125 See Appendix 4

126 Woods, *op. cit.*, p. 182

127 *Ibid.*, p. 43

128 Heale, M. J. *McCarthy's Americans: Red Scare Politics in State and Nation, 1935—1965.* Athens: The University of Georgia Press, 1998, p. 247.

129 Carleton, Don E. *Red Scare! Rightwing Hysteria, Fifties Fanaticism, and Their Legacy in Texas.* Austin: Texas Monthly Press, 1985, p. 259.

130 *Ibid.*, pp. 259-260

131 See Appendix 2.52. For possible date of event, see Albert H. Newman, *op. cit.*, p. 327.

132 CE 1409, 22 H 796

133 See Fried, Albert. *McCarthyism, The Great American Red Scare: a Documentary History.* Oxford: Oxford University Press, 1997; Reeves, Thomas C. *The Life and Times of Joe McCarthy.* New York: Stein and Day, 1982; and Caute, David. *The Great Fear: The Anti-Communist Purge under Truman and Eisenhower.* New York: Simon & Schuster, 1978.

134 See Appendix 1.5

135 See Appendix 5.1

136 Rogers, Kim Lacy. *Righteous Lives: Narratives of the New Orleans Civil Rights Movement.* New York: New York University Press, 1993, pp. 17–18.

137 See Vickers, George R. *The Formation of the New Left: The Early Years.* Lexington, Mass.: Lexington Books, D.C. Heath and Company, 1975, pp. 15, 18.

138 See Judis, John B. "American Marxism: Theory Without Tradition", *The World and I On-Line*, June, 1987.

139 Mattson, Kevin. *Intellectuals in Action: The Origins of the New Left and Radical Liberalism, 1945—1970.* University Park, Penn.: The Penn State University Press, 2002, p. 117.

140 John McMillan and Paul Buhle, eds., *The New Left Revisited.* Philadelphia: Temple University Press, 2003, p. 3.

141 CE 228, 16 H 621

142 11 H 118

143 11 H 116

144 Johnson McMillan, *op. cit.*, p. 83

145 See Appendix 3.2

146 Johnson McMillan, *op. cit.*, pp. 105, 123

147 9 H 147

148 9 H 150

149 Stafford, *op. cit.*, p. 103

150 See Appendix 2.1

151 Marx, Karl and Frederick Engels. *Selected Works* (New York: International Publishers, 1969, pp. 31—63.

152 Marx, Karl, edited by Frederick Engels. *Capital, Volume 1: A Critical Analysis of Capitalist Production.* New York: International Publishers, 1967.

153 Lichtheim, George. *Marxism: An Historical and Critical Study.* London: Routledge and Kegan Paul, 1961, p. 177.

154 Marx, *Capital, Volume 1*, p. 35

155 London, Jack. "The Iron Heel" in *Jack London.* London: Octopus Books, 1986, pp. 487—646.

156 CE 228, 16 H 622

157 London, *op. cit.*, p. 584

158 *Ibid.*, p. 600

159 Johnston, Carolyn. *Jack London – An American Radical?* Westport, Conn.: Greenwood Press, 1984, p. 8.

160 *Ibid.*, p. 15

161 *Ibid.*, pp. 37, 183, 185

162 *Ibid.*, p. 71

163 *Ibid.*, p. 131

164 *Ibid.*, p. 31

165 *Ibid.*, p. 115

166 8 H 277

167 Bloom, Alan. "Jean-Jacques Rousseau, 1712-1778," in Leo Strauss and Joseph Cropsey (eds.), *History of Political Philosophy, Second Edition*. Chicago and London: The University of Chicago Press, 1981, p. 543. Oswald may have been exposed to Rousseau in New Orleans. He told Aline Mosby that as a teenager he "always had to dig for my books in the back, dusty shelves of libraries...Books on philosophy, political economy, etc." See Appendix 1.1

168 See Miller, James. *Rousseau: Dreamer of Democracy*. New Haven and London: Yale University Press, 1984, Chapter 2, "The Image of Democracy," pp. 26—48.

169 8 H 277

170 l'Anson Fausset, Hugh. *Walt Whitman: Poet of Democracy*. New York: Russell and Russell, 1942, p. 95.

171 Chase, Richard. *Walt Whitman*. Minneapolis: University of Minnesota Press, 1961, p. 38.

172 Whitman, Walt. *Leaves of Grass*. Prospero Books, p. 1.

173 London, Jack. *Love of Life and Other Stories*. London: Elek, 1946.

174 8 H 254

175 Orwell, George. *Animal Farm: A Fairy Story*. London: Penguin Books, 1987. *Animal Farm* was first published in 1945.

176 11 H 86. Orwell, George. *Nineteen Eighty-Four: A Novel*. London: Penguin Books, 1954. *Nineteen Eighty-Four* was first published in 1949.

177 Ingle, Stephen. *George Orwell: A Political Life*. Manchester, U.K; New York: Manchester University Press, 1993, p. ix.

178 Kubal, David L. *Outside The Whale: George Orwell's Art and Politics*. Notre Dame and London: University of Notre Dame Press, 1972, p. 4.

179 Bugliosi, *op. cit.*, p. 518

180 *Ibid.*, p. 519

181 Warren Report, p. 377

182 CE 2220, 25 H 119

183 1 H 228

184 CE 1339, 22 H 559

185 Warren Report, p. 379

186 Carro Exhbit No. 1, 19 H 313

187 Bugliosi, *op. cit.*, p. 531

188 1 H 227-228

189 Brown, Claude. *Manchild in the Promised Land.* New York: The New American Library, 1965, pp. 62—63.

190 See *Juvenile Detention in New York: Then and Now* (a display at John Jay College of Criminal Justice by the city Department of Juvenile Justice marking its 20th Anniversary)

191 Jean Davison also saw a link between Oswald's confinement at Youth House and his attraction to the Rosenberg pamphlet. She wrote: "What made the Rosenberg pamphlet memorable to him, surely, was that he saw *himself* in it — the 'innocent victim' of a New York court. He held in his hand a message that said to him: Here are allies you can identify with. Here are people who feel as you do about the legal system." *op. cit.*, pp. 55-56. I argue that the link was not just to the court system but to the entire governmental system and reinforced his already negative attitude toward the State.

192 Radosh, Ronald and Joyce Milton. *The Rosenberg File: A Search for the Truth.* New York: Holt, Rinehart and Winston, 1983, p. 340.

193 See *Ibid.* and Schneir, Walter and Miriam Schneir. "Cryptic Answers," *The Nation*, 248(14/21, August 1995.

194 Johnson McMillan, *op. cit.*, p. 358 Oswald is seen holding his notebook in CE 1412-3 (Warren Report, p. 409) shown on the cover of this book

195 See Stovall Exhibit B, 21 H 598; 7 H 231 (Testimony of Guy F. Rose)

196 Warren Report, p. 397. One of the commissioners and later president of the United States, Gerald R. Ford, co-authored a book with John Stiles on Oswald and echoed the same views. Ford and Stiles wrote that Lee's writings "are typical examples of Oswald's chronic state of mind; no system is very good; no leaders are worthy; neither Russian communism nor American democracy operates in the real interest of the people...[W]ith his lack of mental training he is utterly incapable of understanding why these things happen and what can be done about them." See Ford, Gerald R. and John R. Stiles. *Portrait of the Assassin*. New York: Simon & Shuster, 1965, pp. 88—89.

197 1 H 100

198 1 H 109

199 1 H 108

200 8 H 334

201 See Bugliosi, *op. cit.*, p. 640

202 1 H 109

203 1 H 109

204 8 H 339-340. There was also confusion during the testimony of Gary Taylor. After Taylor said he had seen a copy of Oswald's notes on Russia, Jenner asked him to identify a document that he described as "a draft of various stages of his life, including time in Russia, in the Marines, the period in New Orleans and what not." Jenner was obviously showing him CE 93, not the narrative on Russia. Taylor replied: "These are not the same pages of which I was speaking." 9 H 92

205 Warren Report, pp. 395-399

206 *A Century of Struggle: Socialist Party USA, 1901-200.1* New York: Socialist Party USA, n.d.

207 de Mohrenschildt, *I am a Patsy! I am a Patsy!*, p. 83.

208 11 H 173

209 See Appendix 3.2

210 Such a hypothesis is only tentative for as we know, a few days after his return to America, Oswald wrote to the Marine Corps requesting to re-enlist. Political activity might still have been secondary to his family's well-being. See Appendix 2.46.

211 8 H 335

212 Johnson McMillan, *op. cit.*, p. 144

213 9 H 262

214 Johnson McMillan, *op. cit.*, p. 142

215 8 H 334

216 8 H 333. Oswald had to smuggle the manuscript out in order to protect his family and those who had assisted him in preparing it. According to Bates, Lee told her if the notes were published "he would have to change names and things like that. He had actual Russian names of people he talked to and in order to protect people, he'd have to change the names." 8 H 336

217 Johnson McMillan, *op. cit.*, p. 145

218 Bates testified that Oswald told her there was a man in Fort Worth, an engineer, who was interested in having his notes put into book form. See 8 H 336.

219 Oswald, Robert L., with Myrick Land and Barbara Land. *Lee: A Portrait of Lee Harvey Oswald by his Brother.* New York: Coward McCann, 1967, p. 119.

220 9 H 92

221 9 H 262-263. Robert and Gary Taylor asked if they could read the manuscript while de Mohrenschildt said Oswald gave it to him to read. Michael Paine testified that Oswald never told him he had written about Russia or anything else. Paine said "if I had thought he had written about something, I would certainly have been eager to have read it." See 11 H 402.

222 See *The Concise Oxford Dictionary of Politics* (Oxford; New York: Oxford University Press, 1996)

223 CE 92 recounts the personal history of different people Lee had talked to. He claimed to have met one worker named Orisses who served with the famed guerilla fighters who fought the Nazis in World War II deep in the pine forests. The story of these guerillas was made into a 2008 Hollywood movie based on Nechama Tec's book *Defiance: The Bielski Partisans* (Oxford: Oxford University Press, 1993).

224 Mailer, *op. cit.*, p. 114. CE 92 shows that Oswald, although not admitted to university and assigned by the Soviets to be a factory worker, was determined to pursue his studies on his own.

225 Johnson McMillan, *op. cit.*, p. 192

226 1 H 100

227 Albert H. Newman, *op. cit.*, p. 222

228 Johnson McMillan, *op. cit.*, p. 196

229 Warren Commission, p. 423

230 Engels, Frederick. *Anti-Duhring (Herr Eugen Duhring's Revolution in Science.* Peking: Foreign Language Press, 1976, p. 408.

231 Vickers, *op. cit.*, p. 17. Mattson in *op. cit.*, p. 187, called the Port Huron Statement "perhaps the most sophisticated (if not the most significant) document in New Left history."

232 Johnson McMillan, *op. cit.*, pp. 338-339

233 See Bugliosi, *op. cit.*, pp. 682-683; Johnson McMillan, *op. cit.*, pp. 335-338

234 CE 1386, 22 H 711

235 11 H 93

236 de Mohrenschildt, *I am a Patsy! I am a Patsy!*, p. 83

237 2 H 400

238 Johnson McMillan, *op. cit.*, p. 338

239 *Ibid.*, p. 605

240 Lee (Vincent T.) Exhibit No. 3, 20 H 514-516

241 1 H 16

242 See CE 823, 17 H 718-732; CE 824, 17 H 733-740

243 Bugliosi, *op. cit.*, p. 572

244 Epstein, *The Assassination Chronicles*, p. 395

245 Potts Exhbit A-1, 21 H 141. The full text of the *Address Book* with annotations can be found in Holloway, *op. cit.*, pp. 291-308

246 See Epstein, Edward Jay. "Epitaph for Jim Garrison: Romancing the Assassination." *The New Yorker*, November 30, 1992.

247 Scott, Peter Dale. *Deep Politics and the Death of JFK.* Berkeley: University of California Press, 1993, p. 47.

248 *The HSCA Final Assassinations Report*, p. 190

249 CE 1386, 22 H 710-711

250 8 H 18-19

251 CE 1962, 23 H 797-798. A search of the congressional papers of Senator Thurmond held at Clemson University, S.C. by the author revealed there was no record of any such letters from Lee Harvey Oswald to the senator.

252 8 H 240-241

253 11 H 87

254 8 H 292-293

255 5 H 265

256 Warren Report, p. 691

257 Johnson McMillan, *op. cit.*, p. 157

258 9 H 145

259 9 H 148

260 11 H 128-129 (Testimony of Mrs. Donald Gibson)

261 9 H 79, 82

262 9 H 48

263 Epstein, *The Assassination Chronicles*, pp. 483–84.

264 Johnson McMillan, *op. cit.*, p. 232

265 *Ibid.*, p. 234

266 Following de Mohrenschildt's suicide, the HSCA found among his personal possessions a copy of one of the Backyard Photographs with an inscription on the back: "To my dear friend George, from Lee." It was dated April 1963 and signed Lee Harvey Oswald. See *The HSCA Final Assassination Report*, p. 56.

267 1 H 101 (Testimony of Marina Oswald)

268 See Warren Report, p. 407

269 See 10 H 76-77 (Testimony of Philip Geraci III); 10 H 82-85 (Testimony of Vance Blalock); 10 H 35-37 (Testimony of Carlos Bringuier)

270 10 H 37-38

271 10 H 55-56

272 4 H 436

273 CE 3119, 26 H 771

274 11 H 171–75

275 *The HSCA Final Assassinations Report*, pp. 142—43.

276 HSCA Final Assassinations Report – Hearings and Appendix Volumes – Volume X, VII, Junta Revolucionaria Cubana (JURE); Lamar Waldron with Thom Hartman, *Ultimate Sacrifice: John and Robert Kennedy, the Plan for a Coup in Cuba, and the Murder of JFK* (New York: Carroll & Graf, 2005), pp. 160-164; Jerome A. Kroth, *Conspiracy in Camelot: The Complete History of the Assassination of John Fitzgerald Kennedy* (New York: Algora Publishing, 2003), p. 135

277 11 H 341–42

278 11 H 370–72

279 Oleg M. Nechiporenko, *Passport to Assassination: The Never-Before-Told Story of Lee Harvey Oswald by the KGB Colonel Who Knew Him* (New York: Carol Publishing, 1993), p. 77

280 2 H 408

281 2 H 409

282 CE 2064, 24 H 490

283 See Appendix 1.3

284 Lenin, Vladimir. *Imperialism: The Highest Stage of Capitalism.* Broadway, Australia: Resistance Books, 1999.

285 Albert H. Newman, *op. cit.*, p. 33

286 4 H 453. When asked about her comment, Paine said: "Oh, I doubt seriously I said Trotskyite Communist. I would think Leninist Communist, but I am not certain. Reference

to Trotsky surprises me. I have come since the assassination to wonder if he had Trotskyite views...I may have said that. I don't recall...It is possible. I am surprised, however, by the word at that point." (3 H 104) In hearsay testimony, Marina's business manager, James Herbert Martin, told the Commission that Isaac Levine, reportedly a representative of Time-Life, Inc., told Martin that Marina "told him that her husband was a Trotskyite." (1 H 496)

287 See Dobbs Exhibit, No. 6, 19 H 570

288 Warren Report, p. 413

289 Albert H. Newman, *op. cit.*, p. 19

290 Davison, *op. cit.*, pp. 22-23

291 *The Militant*, January 21, 1963

292 *Ibid.*, September 16, 1963

293 *Four Canadians Who Saw Cuba* was a pamphlet published by the Canadian Fair Play for Cuba Committee. See *ibid.*, April 22, 1963.

294 *Ibid.*, August 19, 1963

295 *Ibid.*, December 24, 1962

296 de Mohrenschildt, *I am a Patsy! I am a Patsy!*, pp. 89, 133, 146–7, 309

297 9 H 465

298 See Tinder, Glenn. *Political Thinking: The Perennial Questions.* New York: Harper Collins College Publishers, 6th edition, 1995, pp. 23—59.

299 8 H 269-270

300 5 H 290

301 Bugliosi, *op. cit.*, p. 153

302 4 H 225

303 "That Was The President," from Phil Ochs, *I ain't marching anymore*. Electra Records, 1965.

304 Hixson, Walter L. "Nuclear Weapons and Cold War Diplomacy" in John M. Carroll and George C. Herring, eds., *Modern American Diplomacy*, revised and enlarged edition. Wilmington, Delaware: Scholarly Resources Inc., 1996, p. 194.

305 Such a hypothesis runs counter to Michael Paine's view. In 1979 Paine told HSCA investigators that Oswald believed "the only way injustices in this society could be corrected was through a violent revolution." See HSCA Record 180-10096-10400, June 6, 1978, p. 1, and Bugliosi, *op. cit.*, p. 937

306 Johnson McMillan, *op. cit.*, p. 495

307 *Ibid.*, p. 497

308 3 H 102

309 Johnson McMillan, *op. cit.*, p. 498

310 Bugliosi, *op. cit.*, pp. 124-125

311 Hosty, James P. Jr. with Thomas Hosty. *Assignment: Oswald*. New York: Arcade Publishing, 1996, p. 21.

312 *The HSCA Final Assassinations Report*, p. 196

313 Stephens, Julie. *Anti-Disciplinary Protest: Sixties Radicalism and Postmodernism*. Cambridge: Cambridge University Press, 1998, p. 1.

314 *Ibid.*, pp. 4, 26, 29

315 Sale, J. Kirk. "Ted Gold: Education for Violence." *The Nation*, April 13, 1970, re-printed in *Weatherman*. Berkeley: Ramparts Press, 1970, p. 482. See also Varon, Jeremy. *Bringing the War Home: The Weather Underground, the Red Army Faction, and Revolutionary Violence in the Sixties and Seventies*. Berkeley: University of California Press, 2004.

316 Starobin, Joseph R. *American Communism in Crisis, 1943—1957.* Cambridge: Harvard University Press, 1972, p. xiv.

317 *Ibid.,* p. xv

318 Warren Report, p. 423

319 See Bishop, Jim. *The Day Kennedy Was Shot.* New York: Funk & Wagnalls, 1968, passim.; Bugliosi, *op. cit.,* chapter "Four Days In November"; CE 2064, 24 H 491

320 Mailer, *op. cit.,* p. 782; *Oswald's Ghost*

321 Warren Report, p. 165

322 Kantor, Seth. *The Ruby Cover-Up.* New York: Zebra Books, Kensington Publishing, 1978, p. 428.

323 Blakey, G. Robert and Richard Billings. *Fatal Hour: The Assassination of President Kennedy by Organized Crime.* New York: Berkley Books, 1992, p. 3.

324 15 H 259-260

325 Bugliosi, *op. cit.,* p. 1266

326 15 H 331

327 Benson, Michael. *Who's Who in the JFK Assassination: An A-To-Z Encyclopedia.* New York: Carol Publishing, A Citadel Press Book, 1993, p. 67.

328 Mailer, *op. cit.,* Appendix, p. ii